# Word Processing Skills

## Related titles in the series

Accounting
Advertising
Auditing
Book-keeping
Business and Commercial Law
Business and Enterprise
    Studies
Business French
Business German
Business Italian
Commerce
Cost and Management
    Accounting
Economics
Elements of Banking

Financial Management
Information Technology
Law
Management Theory and
    Practice
Marketing
Office Practice
Personnel Management
Psychiatry
Social Services
Spreadsheet Skills
Statistics for Business
Teeline Shorthand
Typing
Word Processing Skills

# Word Processing Skills

## Using WordPerfect for DOS (Version 5.1)

Roger Carter and Ann Gautier
*Information Technology Unit*
*The Buckinghamshire College*

**MADE SIMPLE**
**B O O K S**

Made Simple
An imprint of Butterworth-Heinemann Ltd
Linacre House, Jordan Hill, Oxford OX2 8DP

**Ɐ** A member of the Reed Elsevier group

OXFORD   LONDON   BOSTON
MUNICH   NEW DELHI   SINGAPORE   SYDNEY
TOKYO   TORONTO   WELLINGTON

First published 1994

© Roger Carter and Ann Gautier 1994

**British Library Cataloguing in Publication Data**
Carter, Roger
  Wordprocessing Skills: Using WordPerfect
  for DOS (Version 5.1). – (Made Simple Books)
  I. Title  II. Gautier, Ann  III. Series
  652.5

ISBN 0 7506 1566 4

Printed and bound in Great Britain by
Hartnolls Limited, Bodmin, Cornwall

# Contents

# Preface

Despite much competition, WordPerfect remains the world's most used word processing package. Wherever there's an office, whether in industry, education, or government, the chances are that someone in it will be using WordPerfect. One reason for WordPerfect's continuing popularity has to be its sheer power. It offers more features, desktop publishing capabilities, and office automation aids, than most other word processors.

Most users only scratch the surface of its capabilities. The aim of this book is to show you how to get the best out of WordPerfect, reaching beyond the keystrokes to the real skills needed to produce good looking documents in an efficient way. We focus on the creative task of applying WordPerfect to real business problems. But we don't assume any prior experience of WordPerfect, and you will find a full Keystroke Guide at the end of the book.

You will find plenty of business examples in this book to help you develop your word processing skills. Our hope is that in working through it you will not only become something of a word processing expert but you will also enjoy the process of getting there.

Many of these examples are based on the Skern Lodge Outdoor Centre, Bideford, North Devon. We wish to thank Skern Lodge for permission to use its name and material.

*Roger Carter and Ann Gautier*
*Information Technology Unit*
*The Buckinghamshire College*

# About this book

## 0.1 Learning software skills

Computers consist of hardware (the keyboard, disk drives, printers and so on), and software (spreadsheet programs, word processing programs, drawing programs, etc.). Learning to use the hardware is easy. It doesn't take long to master the mechanics of inserting floppy disks into disk drives, or using the keyboard. But learning to use the software is often difficult and time consuming.

Software manufacturers will protest that their products are quick and easy to learn. What they mean is that learning the *mechanics* of their software − which keys to press to perform particular operations − is child's play. But this is not the crucial issue. The crucial issue is *learning how to apply the software creatively in real-life situations to achieve effective results in an efficient way*. It doesn't take long to grasp the basics of a word processing or spreadsheet program to produce a boring looking document. It takes considerably more skill and creativity to use that software to produce, quickly and efficiently, an eye-catching and well-designed document that makes the most of the computer's and printer's capabilities.

And that's the difference between the 'skills' books in the Made Simple series and most other software manuals and books. These 'skills' books focus on the creative task of applying the software to real-life problems. The easy mechanical bit − which keys to press − is soon picked up, either from the onscreen 'help' system provided with most software packages or from the Keystroke Guide at the end of the books.

## 0.2 Before you begin

This book doesn't describe how to use floppy disks, or the printer, or how to find your way around the keyboard; nor does it deal with basic operations like formatting disks or switching between one disk drive and another. So before beginning you need to know how to use the computer hardware. If you don't know this, then before proceeding further you need to spend an hour or so with your machine. Get a colleague to help you, or refer to the handbook that came with your computer.

We also assume that the software described in this book is already installed on your computer. If it isn't, you need to install it. Your software manual will tell you how.

We don't, however, assume that you have any prior experience of the software. So besides teaching you how to apply the software to real business problems, we provide a Keystroke Guide at the end of the book. (However, if you have some knowledge of the software already, this will stand you in good stead, as it will cut down on the time you spend dipping into this guide.)

## 0.3 How this book is organized

Each chapter in the main 'skills' part of this book adopts the following pattern:

- First comes the list of objectives. These describe what you will achieve by working through the chapter.
- Next comes the list of software routines that you will use as you work through the chapter. These might include, for example, inserting graphics in your document, and printing it. Alongside this list of routines you will find references to the Keystroke Guide; look these up when you want to find out how to carry out the routines.
- In many chapters a description of the example that you will be working on comes next, together with teaching material on the principles involved, an explanation of why a computer is used rather than manual methods and the benefits that the computer provides. The purpose is to develop your ability to use the software creatively to solve actual problems.
- Later in the chapter there will normally be further exercises that you might like to try if you wish to explore the capabilities of the software further.

## 0.4 How to use this book

We suggest that you approach each chapter in the following way:

1 Read the objectives carefully to determine what you will be achieving. They will give you a sense of direction and motivation.
2 Read through the teaching material and the description of the example that normally comes next, in order to grasp the principles involved. You don't have to do this in front of your computer, of course.
3 Now go to your computer and attempt the exercises that are built around the example, putting into practice these principles. Early chapters include detailed guidance on the steps to follow, but later chapters are somewhat less prescriptive, relying instead on your own developing skills to solve problems. To find out which keys to press to carry out a particular routine, use the Keystroke Guide at the end of the book; the list of routines at the start of the chapter will direct you to the relevant sections. You will find some keystroke tuition in the chapters themselves, in particular the early chapters. If you feel the need for further practice, try the further exercises that appear in the chapter.

Apart from the opening chapter, you can work through the chapters in any order. However, easier examples that teach the more basic principles appear towards the beginning of the book, and if you are new to the software you should attempt these early on. Chapter 1 introduces you to the software and includes basic keystroke routines, so this should be worked through first.

## 0.5 The accompanying disk

Supplied with this book is a floppy disk containing files that you will need to use with many of the exercises. There are two sets of files, consisting of text and graphic files. The first set is for users with printers which have built-in fonts, the second for users with printers with no fonts. You will probably find it helpful to copy these files into the directory used by WordPerfect on your computer's hard disk. To do this, insert the floppy disk in the drive, and from the DOS prompt type:

```
COPY A:*.* C:\WP51
```

if your printer has built-in fonts. Otherwise, type:

```
COPY A:\NOFONTS\*.* C:\WP51
```

(This assumes that WordPerfect has been installed in the directory C:\WP51. If it is in a different directory, you will need to substitute that directory's name in this command.)


## 0.6   About WordPerfect

Word processing is the most popular computer application, and this is reflected in the fact that there are more word processing programs than any other type of software. However, way out in front is WordPerfect, the world's most widely used word processor. It is available on almost every type of computer, and each release enjoys increasing popularity. This book deals with the DOS version of WordPerfect (which runs on any PC), the current release being version 5.1.

This book, although written for version 5.1, can also be used with earlier versions. (The main differences are: earlier versions do not offer the pop-up menu alternative to the function key method of activity commands; they do not support the mouse; and some graphics facilities may be lacking.) WordPerfect for Windows is not covered in this book.

One reason for WordPerfect's success must be the fact that it has, for a number of years, offered unrivalled power and a multitude of advanced features. Other word processing programs now offer equivalent power and features, but WordPerfect has established itself as the standard. Wherever there's an office, whether in industry, education or government, the chances are that someone in it will be using WordPerfect.

A second reason for WordPerfect's success is the fact that, despite its advanced features, it is relatively easy to use. This is particularly the case with later versions, which provide an alternative user-friendly menu route to its various commands, together with support for the mouse. Both of these will benefit new and occasional users (though touch-typists who make constant use of the program will find it faster to stick with the original method of using special keys such as function keys to activate commands.)

A powerful computer program like WordPerfect is necessarily complex. Users sometimes think that because they have learned which keys to press to carry out its main routines they have mastered the application. This is not the case, as is testified by the many poorly laid out and inefficiently produced documents generated by computers. Used skilfully, a program such as WordPerfect can improve productivity greatly and generate good looking documents every time. The aim of this book is to go beyond the keystrokes to the real skills that you need to get the best out of your computer and WordPerfect.

# 1
# Editing a prospectus

## 1.1  What you will achieve in this chapter

This chapter covers the basics of word processing with Word-Perfect. When you have completed it, you should be able to:

- Use WordPerfect's menu system and Help system.
- Retrieve a document from disk into WordPerfect.
- Move around the document, inserting and deleting text.
- Print your edited document.
- Save your edited document to disk.
- Retrieve a second document and move between it and the first document.
- Exit a document.

The particular skills you will learn are how to edit a document accurately and quickly.

If you have made some use of WordPerfect, and feel that you already know how to carry out all these tasks, you can probably skim through this chapter. However, make sure you carry out the exercises, as you will be using the documents that you produce in later chapters.

## 1.2  Routines you will use in this chapter

As you work through this chapter, you will be getting to grips with the routines listed below. The description given in this chapter should enable you to work out how to use them. If you experience difficulties, either use WordPerfect's onscreen Help system (described on page 6), or refer to the Keystroke Guide at the end of this book. The Keystroke Guide section number for each routine is given below in brackets.

- Use WordPerfect's Help system (22).
- Use WordPerfect's Cancel key (4).
- Use WordPerfect's Repeat key (46).
- Retrieve a document from disk (48).
- Move around a document (35).
- Delete text, and undelete it if you change your mind (10).
- Switch between two documents (60).
- Print a document (45).
- Save a document to disk (51).
- Exit a document (12).
- List the WordPerfect documents stored on your disk, and carry out housekeeping tasks on those files such as deleting, moving, or renaming them (29).
- Use the mouse to navigate the menu system and edit documents (33).

## 1.3 What's the use of word processing?

Computers are used for many things, from weather forecasting to designing buildings. But the thing that they are used for most of all is word processing. Not many of us forecast the weather (at least, not for a living), and not many of us design buildings. But all of us write letters, many of us write reports and other longer documents, and a few of the more demented among us spend endless hours writing books. Word processing greatly eases this task, and produces a much better looking result when you've finished.

As a rough guide, word processing doubles your writing productivity. That means twice as many letters, reports, books, etc. in the same time. Or, if that doesn't sound too exciting, the same number in half the time. The reason is that you can make changes to your document quickly and easily on the screen, avoiding the need to retype everything totally.

And with a powerful word processing program like WordPerfect, coupled to a high-quality printer, you can print your work in a variety of typefaces, include in it drawings and pictures, to produce a truly professional end-product.

Later in this book you will learn how to achieve that really good looking finish. In this chapter you will be learning how quick and easy it is to edit a document in WordPerfect.

## 1.4 A first look at WordPerfect

When you run WordPerfect, you see its editing screen (Figure 1.1). To begin with, this screen is empty apart from the *cursor* and the *status line*. Once you start typing a document, or if you retrieve an existing document from disk, it will be displayed here.

- The *cursor* is a small line, the width of a typed character, which blinks on and off. It indicates your position within the text of the document, i.e. where the next character that you type will appear.
- The *status line* shows:
  - the document number (normally '1', but '2' if you are working on a second document — see later in this chapter);
  - your page number within the document (i.e. the page where the cursor is located);
  - your line position (Ln), measured in inches from the top of the page;
  - your horizontal position (Pos) within the line, measured in inches from the left of the page;
  - other relevant status information; for example, when you retrieve a document from disk, its name will appear on this line.

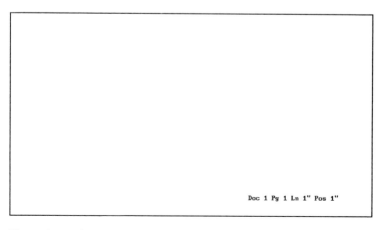

Doc 1 Pg 1 Ln 1" Pos 1"

**Figure 1.1** The WordPerfect editing screen

In the case of the new, empty document shown in Figure 1.1, the cursor is positioned at the top left of the screen, and the status line indicates that you are on page 1, line 1″, and horizontal position 1″. You will gather from this that WordPerfect is providing a 1″ margin at the top of the page and a 1″ margin at the left (though as you will learn later it's easy to change these).

Note that 'Pos' will flash if the Num Lock key is on, and it will be displayed in capitals if Caps Lock is on.

You may wonder why you need all this status information. One reason is that there is a lot more to using a computer than using a typewriter, and it is useful to be warned that Caps Lock is on, or to be reminded of the name of the file you're using. A second reason is that you can't tell by looking at the document on the screen what page you're on or the size of any margins, and so the measurements in the status line are essential if you need to position some text or a picture very precisely.

## 1.5   Commands in WordPerfect

Word processors such as WordPerfect provide you with a whole armoury of commands, to carry out tasks such as retrieving files, saving files, printing files and a host of others. In WordPerfect there are three alternative ways of accessing these commands:

1   *By pressing function keys*, perhaps in combination with the Shift, Alt, and Ctrl keys. For example, to exit WordPerfect you press F7; to print the document that you're currently working on, press Shift-F7 (i.e. hold down Shift and press F7). This is the fastest way of using WordPerfect's commands, provided you know which key to press. To help you with this, a keyboard template is provided with the package which you can place around the function keys. This lists the functions available on each key. The function names are printed on it in different colours:
   - *Black* indicates that you press the function key by itself;
   - *Green* indicates to press Shift and the key;
   - *Red* indicates to press Ctrl and the key;
   - *Blue* indicates to press Alt and the key.

2   *By pressing Alt-=* (i.e. hold down Alt and tap the = key) to display a *menu bar* at the top of the screen. This is shown in Figure 1.2, and lists the main categories of commands. Each of these leads to a drop-down menu, as illustrated in Figure

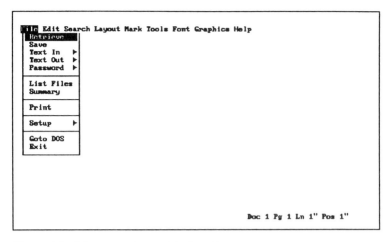

**Figure 1.2**  The menu bar, with the File menu open

1.2. Press the arrow keys to move the highlight from option to option, and Enter to choose the highlighted option. This method of choosing commands is slightly slower than the function key method, but is very suitable for beginners as it makes it easy to pick out commands.

3  *By pressing the right button of the mouse* to display the menu bar, and pointing and clicking left to choose menu options. Using the mouse is a neat way of navigating the menu system and editing documents, and is described in Section 33 of the Keystroke Guide.

   If you know which function key to press, then the first method is the quickest way to access a WordPerfect command. Using the mouse or pressing Alt-= for the menu bar, though convenient if you don't know which key to press, is slower. So in this book we will mainly describe the function key method.

## 1.6  Navigating menus

Menus, listing alternative choices, appear in many places in WordPerfect's command system. For example, when you press Shift-F7 to print, the Print menu shown in Figure 1.4 on page 12 appears. It's important that you know how to navigate these menus:

- To choose a menu option, either press the emboldened letter of the option, or the number of the option. If you use the mouse, point to the option and click left. Then, when you wish to exit the menu, press F7. (F7 is WordPerfect's 'exit' key.) If you use the mouse, pressing the right button will exit a menu and return you to the editing screen.
- To cancel a menu, press F1. (F1 is WordPerfect's 'cancel' key.) However, if you wish to exit the menu bar shown in Figure 1.2, you must press F7.

## 1.7   WordPerfect's Help system

WordPerfect provides a comprehensive onscreen Help system, available at the touch of its 'Help' key, F3. Normally when you press this, the screen shown in Figure 1.3 appears. This describes the two alternative (but complementary) routes into the menu system:

1   You can at this point press the first letter of the feature that you wish to find out about, e.g. 'P' for printing, 'R' for retrieving documents from disk, 'S' for saving documents, etc. A list of features appears, with the keystrokes alongside.

2   Alternatively, you can press the function key that you want help with, e.g. press Shift-F7 for help on printing. This will

```
Help              Licence Number:  WP9991234567       WP 5.1    06/09/90


     Press any letter to get an alphabetical list of features.

          The list will include the features that start with that letter,
          along with the name of the key where the feature can be found.
          You can then press that key to get a description of how the
          feature works.

     Press any function key to get information about the use of the key.

          Some keys may enable you to choose from a menu to get information
          about various options.  Press HELP again to display the template.




Selection: 0                              (Press ENTER to exit Help)
```

**Figure 1.3**   The opening Help screen

take you to a menu of choices — type the number or highlighted letter of the one you want, and a screen of Help text appears.

You can also press F3 a second time, and a template displaying the function keys' uses appears on the screen.

If you press F3 while at a menu or while using a command, you don't get the opening Help screen. Instead, WordPerfect takes you straight to the Help topic dealing with your current action. (A computer help system of this sort is said to be *context-sensitive*.)

To return from the Help system to what you were doing in WordPerfect, press the spacebar or the Enter key. ('Help' is the one place that you can't get out of by pressing F1 or F7, the reason being that pressing these keys takes you to their Help screens.)

## 1.8 Introduction to the exercise

Many of the examples in this book are drawn from Skern Lodge Outdoor Centre near Bideford in North Devon. It runs a range of activity courses, mostly for teenagers. In this exercise you have to edit part of a course prospectus that's to be sent to potential customers. This will involve deleting bits of text and inserting some new text. Other editing tasks such as moving and copying text are covered in a later chapter.

Your starting point is the draft of part of the prospectus, which is on the disk that came with this book. So have this disk handy. Note that a document that's stored on disk is often referred to as a *file*.

In the days before computers, this exercise would have been really long winded and boring. The draft document would have existed only as *hard copy*, i.e. on paper. Editing would have involved retyping the whole lot, not just the bits you wanted to change. And if you made a typing error, out would come the eraser or the Tipp-Ex. Then if you decided later that you wanted wider margins, or double spacing, or the page to break at another point in the text, you would have to type it all again. And next year, with its further minor changes, would require the whole document to be retyped yet again. (Of course, this isn't a real problem in the case of a very small document such as the one you will be editing in this exercise. But most documents are much longer than this.)

Another big advantage of computers is the added security that they provide. With a properly organized system, it's very difficult to lose material. In the days of paper-only documents, you would have only one or two copies perhaps; with computers, you will normally have backups stored on disk in secure locations in separate sites, as well as hard copy on paper. When people lose computer-generated material, it's because they failed to observe proper security procedures.

As you gathered from the list of objectives at the start of this chapter, this example will give you practice not just in editing, but in retrieving, printing and saving files.

It will also show you how you can have two documents present in WordPerfect at the same time, and how you can switch between them. This has many uses. With it you can:

- Make notes in one document while working on another.
- Refer to outline in one document while composing a letter or report.
- Copy or move material from one document to another.
- Have the same document present twice in WordPerfect, so that you can refer to one page while working on another.

As a further subsidiary exercise, you will be using WordPerfect's file housekeeping facility, which allows you to manage files stored on disk. You access this via the File menu on the menu bar (under 'List Files'), or by pressing the F5 List key. It includes facilities for deleting, renaming, moving, copying, viewing and printing stored files.

If you are new to WordPerfect, explore some of its Help system to find out about the various routines you will be using in the exercise. They are as follows:

- Retrieve files, on the Shift-F10 key.
- Save files (F10).
- Print documents (Shift-F7). (Note the *View Document* facility that's available on the Print menu, to display on the screen what the document will look like when printed.)
- Switch between two documents (Shift-F3).
- List files (F5).
- Exit WordPerfect (F7).
- The Cancel key (F1).
- The Repeat key (Esc).

How to use the Help system to find out about routines such as this is outlined in the previous section, and explained in more detail in Section 21 of the Keystroke Guide at the end of this book.

## 1.9 How to edit

Word processing is so popular because you can edit documents such as the Skern Lodge prospectus quickly and easily. Editing (i.e. deleting, copying, moving or otherwise manipulating existing material) generally involves three steps:

1 Move the cursor to the start of the material to be edited.
2 Select the material.
3 Carry out the editing operation.

Sometimes steps 2 and 3 are combined, as when you are performing a simple editing task such as deleting a single character or a single word.

### Moving around
With practice, you will become adept at these tasks. You will be able to decide instantly which is the best way to move to the next edit, whether by pressing the arrow keys (to move a line or character at a time), Ctrl and the arrow keys (to move a word left or right, or a paragraph up or down), or other keys for larger jumps than this. The various possibilities are listed in Section 35 of the Keystroke Guide. In the case of a long document you might also use WordPerfect's search facility to jump instantly to a particular word — this is described in Chapter 5. The mouse also provides a quick way of moving around, and is worth trying out — see Section 33 of the Keystroke Guide.

### Deleting
There are various ways too of deleting material. The Delete key deletes the character at the cursor: hold down Delete to delete several characters. The Backspace key works similarly, deleting characters to the left of the cursor. To delete words rather than

characters, press Ctrl with these keys. Other possibilities are
listed in Section 10 of the Keystroke Guide.

   The mouse is a valuable aid, as it allows you to select quickly a
block of text by 'dragging' over it (i.e. by moving over it while
holding down the left button). You then press Delete (then Y to
confirm) to delete the selected block.


## Repeat

Another facility that WordPerfect provides for speeding up editing
is its Repeat key, Esc. Press this to repeat your previous action a
given number of times. The default number is 8: so if you press
Esc once, then the down arrow once, you will move down 8 lines.
In a similar way you could delete 8 words quickly. To change the
default to some other number, press Esc, then the number, then
Enter. To change it for the current operation only, press Esc,
then the number, then carry out the operation. For more on the
use of Esc, refer to WordPerfect's Help system (i.e. press F3,
then press Esc).


## Cancelling

If you delete some text then change your mind, use WordPerfect's
Cancel key (F1) to cancel the deletion. What happens is that
WordPerfect stores the last three deletions in the computer's
memory. So you can restore up to this number; earlier deletions
are lost. Note that WordPerfect restores the deleted text *at the
current cursor position*. For more on the use of this key, refer to
WordPerfect's Help system or to Section 4 of the Keystroke
Guide.


## Inserting new text

Besides editing existing text, you will also want to insert new text
into documents such as the Skern Lodge prospectus. This involves
two steps:

1   Move the cursor to the point at which you wish to insert the
    new text.
2   Type the new text.

There's slightly more to this, though. WordPerfect, in common with all word processors, offers you two typing modes, *Insert* and *Typeover*. Normally, you will want to work in insert mode (which is in any case the default mode), as then anything you type pushes existing text along (to the right). In typeover mode, on the other hand, anything you type goes on top of and erases existing text. To switch between the two modes press the Insert key. The word 'Typeover' will be displayed on the status line when you are in that mode, to warn you that anything you type will overwrite existing material.

### Rewriting the screen

When you make changes to some text, WordPerfect does not instantly reformat the screen display. You can do this yourself by pressing the down arrow key, but it's quicker to use the Screen Rewrite command (Ctrl-F3, then 3). You will be trying this out in the exercise.

### Editing exercises

In the exercise below you should make a point of trying out all the possibilities described in this section, in order to discover which is the quickest in a particular situation. If necessary, repeat the exercise to make sure that you master the various editing techniques.

Other kinds of editing that you will be carrying out in later exercises include text enhancements, such as emboldening, underlining and the use of various fonts. You cannot see on the ordinary WordPerfect (text) screen exactly how these will turn out on paper. However, WordPerfect provides a *View Document* facility, switching to a graphics screen mode to display more or less exactly what will appear when you print. View Document is available from the Print menu (obtained by pressing Shift-F7).

## 1.10   The exercise: Skern Lodge prospectus

1   Begin by making a backup of the disk that came with this book, and storing it in a secure location away from your computer. The best thing to do is to write-protect the original disk, then copy it to a blank disk using the DOS *diskcopy* command, and use the copy for this and subsequent exercises.

```
Print

    1 - Full Document
    2 - Page
    3 - Document on Disk
    4 - Control Printer
    5 - Multiple Pages
    6 - View Document
    7 - Initialise Printer


Options

    S - Select Printer                          Apple LaserWriter Plu
    B - Binding Offset                          0"
    N - Number of Copies                        1
    U - Multiple Copies Generated by            WordPerfect
    G - Graphics Quality                        Medium
    T - Text Quality                            High




Selection: 0
```

**Figure 1.4**   The Print menu

Alternatively, you could copy all the files on the floppy disk into the WordPerfect directory on your hard disk, and use them from there. Either use the DOS *copy* command for this, or use the file copy feature provided by WordPerfect's List Files facility (see Section 29 of the Keystroke Guide).

2   Run WordPerfect. If you wish to use the floppy disk prepared at step 1 for this exercise (rather than copy the exercise files to your hard disk), then insert the floppy disk into your disk drive (Drive A), and change WordPerfect's default drive to Drive A. To do this, press F5, then =, then type 'A:', then press Enter twice to display the files on the disk. Retrieve the file called PROSP1.EX. The text of this file will appear on your screen.

3   Before making any changes to this file, save it under the name PROSP2.EX. This means that if you mess up the file on disk during this exercise, you can always start again. (So besides the copy of the disk, you now have a further copy of this file. However, it's better to err in this direction than fail to make any copies at all.)

4   If you have not already done so, explore WordPerfect's Help system, looking up the various features listed at the end of the section 'Introduction to the exercise' on page 7.

5   Now try moving around the document using the arrow keys and other keys described in this chapter and in Section 35 of the Keystroke Guide, and by using the mouse. If the cursor

is located towards the end of a line, observe how it behaves when you move up and down the document. Why do you think it sometimes jumps sidewise as it moves from line to line?

Also try accessing the menu bar (by pressing the right mouse button, or Alt-=).

6  Edit the document as shown in Figure 1.5. Refer if necessary to the section above ('How to edit'). A couple of hints:
   – To join up two paragraphs, position the cursor at the start of the second paragraph and press Backspace until the two become one.
   – To force a new paragraph, position the cursor where the new paragraph should begin and press Enter twice.

While editing, don't forget to try the Screen Rewrite command (Ctrl-F3, 3), and try the effect of undeleting some of your changes (F1). Don't correct misspellings at this point – you will be applying WordPerfect's spell checker to these later.

7  Add in the following new paragraph at the end of the prospectus:

   ARRIVALS

   Guests are requested to arrive after 1 pm for courses starting at lunchtime, and after 5 pm for courses starting in the evening.

8  After editing, save the document, replacing the old version on the disk.

9  Before this draft prospectus was written, a list of topics to be included in it had been produced in WordPerfect and saved on disk under the name TOPICS.EX. Since you have added an extra topic to your prospectus, this should be added to the TOPICS document. (Note that you will be using TOPICS in a later sorting exercise.) You can retrieve this file without exiting your PROSP2.EX document. The procedure is:
   – switch to the second screen (when you do so, 'Doc 2' will be displayed in the status line);
   – use the List Files key (F5) to display the list of files in the default directory;
   – select TOPICS.EX from this list, and retrieve it;
   – now add the new heading – ARRIVALS – to the end of this document.

THE SERVICE
~~All staff~~
Everyone at Skern Lodge ha~~s~~ *ve* a real commitment to offer value
for money and personal service. ◥

Our policy is to ensure that everyone staying recieves
individual attention.

MANAGEABLE GROUPS          *you will be*          *one of our*

On arrival at Skern Lodge ~~your group is~~ greeted by~~a~~ Course
Director~~s~~ who looks after you throughout your stay.  Your group
is divided into smaller working groups of eight paying guests.

SAFETY FIRST
*Skern Lodge*
¿Instructional staff are qualified teachers and/or instructors    //New
with qualifications in a range of specialist activities. // Our    *para.*
selection process for staff is risorous and standards of
expertise are high.

OUR TRANSPORT                              *by staff*

We have our own mini-buses which are used⁄for transporting
groups between activities where neccessary.

JUNIOR SCHOOLS
           *junior school*
Our special⁄package gives you an exciting programme at an
economical price. Activities are complemented by one or two
visits to local attractions, and there never seems to be a
minute to spare.

SENIOR SCHOOLS
               *senior*
We have been organising⁄school activity courses at Skern Lodge
*ten*  for over ~~10~~ years and each course is separately planned. We do
not have a standard programe - your course is tailor-made for
your school.

SPECIALIST GROUPS

Some recent courses at Skern Lodge include:

*   Management training

*   Field studies courses

*   Self-catering for canoe clubs and surfers

      *Single line spacing*

**Figure 1.5**   Edits to be made in the Skern Lodge prospectus

10   Exit from TOPICS.EX by pressing the Exit key and saving
     the document under its current name, replacing the previous
     version.

11   Exit Doc 2. You are now back in Doc 1 and the PROSP2.EX
     file.

12   Make a hard copy of your revised prospectus. Before printing,
     though, choose View Document (via the Print menu), to see
     how it will look. Figure 1.6 shows this.

13   After printing, exit WordPerfect.

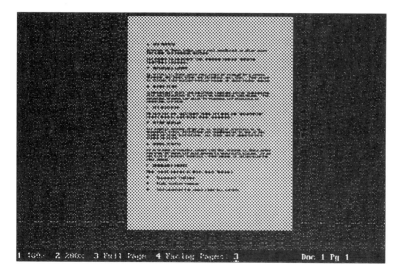

**Figure 1.6** The prospectus on the View Document screen

## 1.11 Exercises using the Repeat and List Files facilities

If you do these exercises, don't save your changes when you exit the file.

1 Run WordPerfect, retrieve the file PROSP2.EX, and practise using Esc to move quickly around the document:

   a Press Esc. Note that 'Repeat value = 8' appears on the screen.

   b Press the down arrow, and note what happens.

   c Repeat a and b to move down the document.

   d Practise using Esc with the up, left and right arrow keys.

2 Use Esc to repeat a character:

   a Position the cursor immediately below any of the headings in the document, at the left of the screen.

   b Press Esc then type '64'.

   c Type the Underline key (__). The underscore will be repeated 64 times across the screen.

3 With PROSP2.EX still retrieved on the screen, use List Files (F5) to locate the PROSP2.EX file and view it (by selecting

the option 'Look'). Note the difference between the stored version (no underscore) and the screen version. Why is this? Press F7 twice, then:

a  Press the List Files key then Enter.
b  Choose Name Search then enter TOPICS.EX to locate the file of this name. Note how much quicker this is than arrowing through the list of files.
c  Choose Look to view this file.
d  Press the Exit key (F7) twice to return to the editing screen.

4  Use List Files to make a copy of TOPICS.EX, and then delete this copy. To do this, repeat 3a and 3b above, then:

c  Choose Copy. The prompt 'Copy this file to:' appears.
d  Enter TOPICS2.EX as copied filename. TOPICS2.EX is added to the list of files.
e  Now delete TOPICS2.EX by highlighting it, then pressing Del, then Y to confirm the deletion.

5  Use WordPerfect's Help system to look up information about the List menu options. To do this press F5 (for List), then F3 for context-sensitive help. Read the general information on List that appears. Next:

```
  04-92  10:29a        Directory C:\WP51\*.*
Document size:        0   Free: 2,744,320 Used: 6,756,694      Files:    100

.    CURRENT    <DIR>                    ..    PARENT    <DIR>
 TEXT       .     <DIR>  07-02-92 10:03a   8514A    .VRS    4,066   14-11-89 11:26a
ALTA    .WPM      104  10-04-91 00:50a   ALTB     .WPM      141  10-04-91 00:53a
ALTH    .WPM       86  21-03-91 02:27p   ALTI     .WPM       88  19-06-91 02:00p
ALTN    .WPM      105  04-12-90 03:02p   ALTRMAT  .WPK      919  27-02-90 00:41a
ALTS    .WPM       91  19-06-91 01:42p   APLASPLU .PRS   40,265   01-05-90 11:05a
ATI     .VRS    6,041  14-11-89 11:26a   BALLOONS .WPG    2,006   14-11-89 11:26a
BKGRND-1.WPG   11,391  14-11-89 11:26a   BUTTRFLY .WPG    5,278   14-11-89 11:26a
CHARACTR.DOC   42,251  14-11-89 11:18a   CHARMAP  .TST   42,131   14-11-89 11:26a
CHARS   .       3,527  25-01-91 12:00p   CODES    .WPM    7,335   14-11-89 11:18a
CONVERT .EXE  105,281  14-11-89 11:18a   CURSOR   .COM    1,452   14-11-89 11:18a
EGA512  .FRS    3,584  14-11-89 11:26a   EGAITAL  .FRS    3,584   14-11-89 11:26a
EGASMC  .FRS    3,584  14-11-89 11:26a   EGAUND   .FRS    3,584   14-11-89 11:26a
EHANDLER.PS     2,797  06-11-89 04:30p   ENDFOOT  .WPM    3,623   14-11-89 11:18a
ENHANCED.WPK    3,355  27-02-90 00:51a   EPFX80   .PRS    5,655   10-06-91 11:28a
EQUATION.WPK    2,978  27-02-90 00:51a   FIXBIOS  .COM       58   14-11-89 11:18a
FOOTEND .WPM    3,561  14-11-89 11:18a   GENUIS   .VRS   12,367   14-11-89 11:18a
GO      .BAT      253  02-08-91 09:11a   GOC      .BAT      486   12-07-91 00:38a
GRAB    .COM   15,618  14-11-89 11:18a ▼ GRAPHCNV .EXE  136,064   14-11-89 11:18a

1 Retrieve; 2 Delete; 3 Move/Rename; 4 Print; 5 Short/Long Display;
6 Look; 7 Other Directory; 8 Copy; 9 Find; N Name Search: 6
```

**Figure 1.7**  List files

a   Press 5 for help on Short/Long Display and Look.
b   Press Enter to exit Help, then F7 to exit List.

6   You can use the Cancel key (F1) to move text, by first deleting the text, then moving to the new location, and then cancelling the deletion. Try this out for yourself.
7   The View Document menu offers four choices of view. Try selecting each one in turn to see how they differ.

# 2
# Creating a brochure

## 2.1 What you will achieve in this chapter

In this chapter you will learn how to create a document in WordPerfect with various formatting effects. When you have completed it, you should be able to:

- Create a new document in WordPerfect.
- View and edit the control codes that WordPerfect inserts in a document.
- Change the layout of a document, including margins, justification, line spacing and page breaks.
- Change the page size and orientation.
- Change WordPerfect's default settings for the above.
- Indent paragraphs.
- Format a document in columns.

The skills you will learn will help you lay out documents attractively on the page, so improving their effectiveness. Further presentation skills will be developed in Chapters 3 and 10, where we deal with character enhancements (underlining, emboldening, etc.), fonts, graphics and other desktop publishing topics.

## 2.2 Routines you will use in this chapter

As you work through this chapter, you will be getting to grips with the following routines. The 'Keystroke Guide' section number for each routine is given below in brackets.

- Reveal the control codes WordPerfect inserts in a document (49).

- Change the margins in a document (40).
- Change the justification (26).
- Change the line space (28).
- Change the tab settings (62).
- Change the page size and orientation (42).
- Force a new page (39).
- Change the default settings that WordPerfect applies to documents (53).
- Indent paragraphs (23).
- Format text in columns (36 and 43).

## 2.3   The brochure

Figure 2.1 shows the brochure that you will be working on in this chapter and in Chapters 3 and 10. Like all the documents in this book, it is for the Skern Lodge Outdoor Centre described on page 7.

Creating the high-tech 'desktop publishing' effects shown in Figure 2.1 must await Chapter 10. Nevertheless, in this chapter you will get half-way there, producing an attractively laid-out document which makes proper use of margins, line spacing, tabs and other presentation techniques that hark back to the days of the typewriter.

What's the point of using a computer rather than a typewriter to produce a good looking document? There are in fact many advantages, but the main ones are:

- *Automation*. Traditional layout techniques such as those discussed in this chapter can be applied much more efficiently using software such as WordPerfect. For example, having developed a layout for a document such as this brochure, you can save that layout style on disk, then reuse it with other documents.
- *Flexibility*. With a computer, text entry and page layout are quite separate operations, and you can carry out the latter after the former. This means that having typed your document, you can experiment freely with the layout till it looks just right. (Using a typewriter, you can only alter the layout by retyping the whole thing.)
- *Desktop publishing*. A computer allows you to use a variety of fonts, and to incorporate graphics and other desktop

outdoor centres

# SKERN LODGE
## OUTDOOR CENTRE

### MANAGEMENT TRAINING - THE PRACTICE OF TEAMWORK

Skern Lodge has achieved a wide reputation in teamwork and personal development training for industrial and commercial organisations for over 12 years.   In presenting a PRACTICAL TEAMWORKING course we are providing an opportunity to explore in a practical way how to bring about individual and team development.  The focus is on the skills and individual needs to be a helpful influence in a working team.  We look at the way members of a team can interact to achieve high quality results.

### Outdoor Training

This form of training can be very enjoyable and rewarding.   The benefits, however, can be difficult to translate into the workplace and therefore we focus heavily on applying the learning to daily work. This is the constant message of PRACTICE TEAMWORKING.

Real issues are dealt with using a mixture of indoor and outdoor exercises which provide points for discussion and practical learning to take back to the workplace.

### Results

As a result of a Skern course your team will have a clearer understanding of how certain behaviour patterns affect others.

We guarantee the following:

*       The team will have a better feeling for each other

*       Individuals will have a clearer vision and greater confidence for the future

*       All members will have improved their ability to listen and identify each other's strengths and skills.

At Skern the team will laugh a lot and share emotions that will develop a powerful synergy.

**Figure 2.1**   The brochure

publishing effects in your document. The end result can match that produced by commercial print houses, provided you have a suitable printer attached to your computer.

Being able to produce printed output like this brochure not only enhances your own image and value to the business but it also makes your job much more fun.

## 2.4  Layout principles

Unfortunately, many documents produced on a computer look awful. This isn't normally the fault of the computer, the software or the printer. It's the fault of the person who created the document. Common errors are an inappropriate mix of fonts, overuse of various effects such as emboldening and underlining, poor arrangement of material on the page and failure to make proper use of margins and other areas of white space to enhance the document's appeal.

Character enhancements (such as emboldening, and the use of fonts), graphics and other effects are discussed in later chapters; here we are concerned with the layout of the document on the page. As with anything to do with design and artistry, there are few hard-and-fast rules, and it's important that you seek the advice and constructive criticism of others. Points you have to bear in mind include: the size of the margins; whether or not to justify the text (i.e. get the computer to insert extra spaces so that it lines up at the right margin); and whether to organize the text in columns.

Here are some generally observed rules:

- Match the line spacing to the size of type. If the space between the bottom of the characters on one line and the top of the characters on the next is less than the height of the characters, then the page will look cramped. (In applying this rule, ignore characters such as 'f' or 'g' which extend above or below the rest.)
- Don't cram too much on the page. Space, such as margins, can be used to enhance the layout and show the contents to best advantage.
- Make sure the bottom margin is equal to or wider than the top margin.
- Avoid long lines − the eye finds it easier to scan short lines. If the average line length exceeds 12 words, think about wider margins, or split the page into columns. But don't put more than three columns on an A4 portrait page.

- If you have narrow columns, you may find it best to avoid justifying the text. Otherwise too much space will be inserted between words, giving the effect of 'rivers' of white flowing down the page. Splitting words at the end of lines (hyphenation) obviously reduces this effect, and you can get WordPerfect to do this automatically.
- If the document is to be bound, allow a wider left margin than right. WordPerfect can take care of this by automatically inserting a 'gutter' margin for you.

## 2.5  WordPerfect's codes

What we are discussing in this chapter is not so much the creation and editing of text, but its appearance or *formatting*. You can see the characters that make up the text on WordPerfect's editing screen, but not formatting information that records things like margin sizes, fonts and the like. WordPerfect stores this information as codes, inserted in your document along with the text. If you want to see these codes, you must open the *Reveal Codes* screen:

- Press the Reveal Codes key, Alt-F3 (or F11, if you have an extended keyboard).

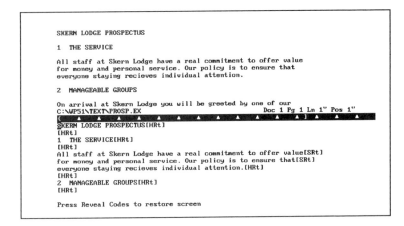

**Figure 2.2**  The Reveal Codes screen

The editing screen will be cut in half, the Codes screen appearing below it as shown in Figure 2.2. The status line, and a bar below that showing the tab positions, separate the two screens.

As you can see, the Codes screen shows all the characters that make up the text together with various codes that control the formatting. These codes are displayed within square brackets. Whenever you perform a formatting operation, such as setting a margin, WordPerfect records what you've done by inserting the corresponding codes in your document, at the current cursor position.

Codes are also used to record line endings, 'carriage' returns, and tabs:

- The end of a line is marked by the *soft* return code [SRt].
- A carriage return (i.e. the Enter key pressed at the end of a paragraph) by the *hard* return code [HRt].
- A tab by the code labelled [Tab].

Of course, you can see the effects of these return and tab codes on the ordinary editing screen, so you don't normally need the Codes screen to tell you where they are. But this is not the case with most formatting codes, such as those controlling margin sizes or line spacing. If you want to check and if necessary edit these, you need to switch on the Codes screen.

When working at the Codes screen, any operation that you perform, such as entering or deleting text, or moving the cursor, shows simultaneously on the editing screen. The various editing and cursor movement keys behave in the usual way, as does the Cancel key.

It's important to note that when experimenting with different formats, such as different margin settings, WordPerfect does not delete from your document the codes for previous settings that you tried. As a result you may build up at the start of your document a whole series of, e.g. margin codes, only the one that appears last having any effect on the subsequent text. It's good practice to delete the unwanted codes, as their presence in the document may cause confusion later.

## 2.6   Formatting in WordPerfect

As we've said, when you carry out a formatting command, Word-

Perfect records what you've done by inserting formatting codes in your text at the current cursor position. That means that the formatting takes effect *from the point in your text at which you applied it*. For example, if you select double-line spacing when the cursor is located half-way down page 3, then double-line spacing will begin at that point. Earlier text will have the default single-line spacing.

So how would you apply an effect such as double-line spacing to just one paragraph? And, conversely, how would you ensure that a formatting effect like this is applied to the whole document?

To apply a formatting effect such as double-line spacing to one paragraph:

- Position the cursor at the start of the paragraph and choose the appropriate command. Then position the cursor at the end of the paragraph and apply the command to restore the default format (in this case single-line spacing).

To apply a formatting effect to the whole document:

- Position the cursor at the start of the document, then choose the formatting command.

Here's the general procedure for applying a formatting effect such as page size, margins, line spacing, tab settings and justification:

1 Move the cursor to the point at which you want to apply the effect.
2 Press Shift-F8, WordPerfect's Format key. The Format menu shown in Figure 2.3 appears.
3 Choose the option you require (i.e. press its number or the highlighted letter). A list of settings then appears.
4 To alter a setting, choose it in the usual way (by pressing its number or the highlighted letter), and overtype the current setting.
5 Press Enter, then make the next choice (which may be Enter or F1 to return to the previous screen, or F7 to exit). Each setting that you change will result in a code being inserted in your document.

Any formatting changes you make are stored in and affect the

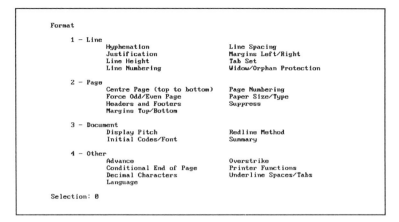

```
Format

     1 - Line
              Hyphenation                       Line Spacing
              Justification                     Margins Left/Right
              Line Height                       Tab Set
              Line Numbering                    Widow/Orphan Protection

     2 - Page
              Centre Page (top to bottom)       Page Numbering
              Force Odd/Even Page               Paper Size/Type
              Headers and Footers               Suppress
              Margins Top/Bottom

     3 - Document
              Display Pitch                     Redline Method
              Initial Codes/Font                Summary

     4 - Other
              Advance                           Overstrike
              Conditional End of Page           Printer Functions
              Decimal Characters                Underline Spaces/Tabs
              Language

     Selection: 0
```

**Figure 2.3** The Format key options

current document only. However, as mentioned already, once you've got a document's layout right, you can store all the formatting settings as a 'style' that can then be applied to other documents. Styles are explained in Chapter 9.

## 2.7 Default formats

WordPerfect has default settings for all these formats. For example, the default left and right margins are 1″, the default tab spacing is .5″, and the default line spacing is single. Note in particular that the default justification is 'full', meaning that extra spacing will be inserted between words so that line endings all line up at the right. These defaults don't appear as codes on the Reveal Codes screen, instead they are automatically applied to all new documents.

It is, of course, a nuisance to be saddled with defaults that you never wish to use. For example, most of your documents might require margins of 1.2″. Fortunately, you don't have to make this change for every document you create, you can instead change the defaults. The procedure for this is explained in Section 53 of the Keystroke Guide.

Note that any changes you make to the defaults will affect new documents only, not existing documents.

## 2.8   The exercise: starting the brochure

It's now time to begin exploring the variety of page layout and other techniques that WordPerfect provides for producing documents like the Skern Lodge brochure. You'll continue this exploration in the further exercise at the end of this chapter, and in the exercises in the next chapter. The important point in all these exercises is to experiment with different settings — margins, line spacing, etc. — not just so that you improve your WordPerfect skills, but so that you get a feel for what works as far as appearance is concerned and what doesn't. The exercises suggest a few things to try, but you should add to these some ideas of your own.

Don't forget that if you do try different settings for, e.g. margins in your document, WordPerfect does not delete the codes for previous settings, it merely overrides their effect with the later codes. It's up to you to tidy things up by deleting unnecessary codes at the Reveal Codes screen. As explained in the last section, you can edit codes using the Del and Backspace keys in the usual way, as well as the F1 Cancel key. For example, to restore a deleted code in a new place, move the cursor and press F1, 1.

In this exercise you'll be typing the text of the brochure into WordPerfect and applying the document layout formats discussed so far in this chapter. You'll also be using the Tab key to indent the first line of paragraphs (this works as on a typewriter), and the Indent key (F4) to indent a complete paragraph. Later in the chapter, you'll be setting out your text in columns.

1   Run WordPerfect, and on the blank opening screen type the text shown in Figure 2.4. Save your document, calling it BROCHUR1.EX.

2   Press the Reveal Codes key (Alt-F3) to open the Codes screen. Observe the two kinds of codes present in your document — what do they signify? (Turn to page 23 if you can't remember.) Try moving the cursor around and note how it changes on the Codes screen when it lands on a code. What happens if you delete a [HRt] code? Or if you try to delete a [SRt] code? Press the Reveal Codes key again to close the Codes screen.

3   Look at the document on the View screen to see how it fits on the page.

4   Change the left and right margins of the document from 1″ to 1.25″, using the Format key and choosing 1 (Line). (The menu shown in Figure 2.5 appears.) Remember first to move

```
SKERN LODGE OUTDOOR CENTRE

MANAGEMENT TRAINING - THE PRACTICE OF TEAMWORK

Skern Lodge has achieved a wide reputation in teamwork and
personal development training for industrial and commercial
organisations for over 12 years. In presenting a PRACTICE
TEAMWORKING course we are providing an opportunity to explore in
a practical way how to bring about individual and team
development. The focus is on the skills and individual needs to
be a helpful influence in a working team. We look at the way
members of a team can interact to achieve high quality results.

Outdoor Training

This form of training can be very enjoyable and rewarding. The
benefits, however, can be difficult to translate into the
workplace and therefore we focus heavily on applying the learning
to daily work. This is the constant message of PRACTICE
TEAMWORKING.

Real issues are dealt with using a mixture of indoor and outdoor
exercises which provide points for discussion and practical
learning to take back to the workplace.

Results

As a result of a Skern course your team will have a clearer
understanding of how certain behaviour patterns affect others.
```

**Figure 2.4**  BROCHURI.EX

to the beginning of the document! Make the required margin entries at this menu. Look at the margin code on the Codes screen, and then check the document's appearance on the View screen.

5  Repeat this for the top and bottom margins, this time pressing the Format key and choosing 2 (Page) for the menu shown in Figure 2.6. Again, look at the Reveal Codes screen to see your margin codes − check that it looks like Figure 2.7.

6  Have you noticed that the right line endings on the editing screen differ from those on the View screen? This is because the default justification is Full, but WordPerfect can't display this on the editing screen. With the cursor at the beginning of the document, change the justification to Left, and view the document on the View screen to see the change. Then at the Codes screen look at the [Just:Left] code.

7  Pressing the Tab key after each *, add the following to the end of the document. When you have finished, look at the [Tab] codes on the Reveal Codes screen.

```
Format: Line

    1 - Hyphenation                        No

    2 - Hyphenation Zone - Left            10%
                           Right           4%

    3 - Justification                      Full

    4 - Line Height                        Auto

    5 - Line Numbering                     No

    6 - Line Spacing                       1

    7 - Margins - Left                     1"
                  Right                    1"

    8 - Tab Set                            Rel; -1", every 0.5"

    9 - Widow/Orphan Protection            No


Selection: 0
```

**Figure 2.5**  Format Line menu

We guarantee the following:

* The team will have a better feeling for each other.
* Individuals will have a clearer vision and greater confidence in the future.
* All members will have improved their ability to listen and identify each other's strengths and skills.

```
Format: Page

    1 - Centre Page (top to bottom)    No

    2 - Force Odd/Even Page

    3 - Headers

    4 - Footers

    5 - Margins - Top                  1"
                  Bottom               1"

    6 - Page Numbering

    7 - Paper Size                     8.27" x 11.69"
        Type                           Standard

    8 - Suppress (this page only)



Selection: 0
```

**Figure 2.6**  Format Page menu

```
SKERN LODGE OUTDOOR CENTRE

MANAGEMENT TRAINING - THE PRACTICE OF TEAMWORK

Skern Lodge has achieved a wide reputation in teamwork and
personal development training for industrial and commercial
organisations for over 12 years. In presenting a PRACTICE
TEAMWORKING course we are providing an opportunity to explore in
a practical way how to bring about individual and team
development. The focus is on the skills and individual needs to
be a helpful influence in a working team. We look at the way
B:\CHAP2\BROCHUR1.DFT                    Doc 1 Pg 1 Ln 1.25" Pos 1.25"
[L/R Mar:1.25",1.25"][T/B Mar:1.25",1.25"]SKERN LODGE OUTDOOR CENTRE[HRt]
[HRt]
MANAGEMENT TRAINING [-] THE PRACTICE OF TEAMWORK[HRt]
[HRt]
Skern Lodge has achieved a wide reputation in teamwork and[SRt]
personal development training for industrial and commercial[SRt]
organisations for over 12 years. In presenting a PRACTICE[SRt]
TEAMWORKING course we are providing an opportunity to explore in[SRt]
a practical way how to bring about individual and team[SRt]
development. The focus is on the skills and individual needs to[SRt]

Press Reveal Codes to restore screen
```

**Figure 2.7** Codes screen showing margin codes

At Skern the team will laugh a lot and share emotions that will develop a powerful synergy.

8 These bulleted paragraphs would look better if the text were fully indented. Try deleting each [Tab] code and use the Indent key instead.
9 Save the file, replacing the previous version of BROCHUR1.EX.

## 2.9 Inserting page breaks

When you have filled the current page with text, WordPerfect automatically 'breaks' the page, i.e. starts a new page. It displays a broken line across the screen, and inserts the [SPg] code in your document. The 'S' in this code stands for 'soft' − it's called a *soft* page break because WordPerfect automatically adjusts its position if you subsequently add or delete some text earlier in the document.

For an example of this, have a look at the two-page document called W&O.EX on the disk that accompanies this book. It is shown in Figure 2.8.

This soft page break contrasts with a *hard* page break, which is one *you* insert in the text when you wish to force a page break at a specific position. To force a page break:

• Place the cursor at the point where you want the break, and press Ctrl-Enter.

```
Snorkling.

Snorkel training takes place in the safety of the Skern Lodge
swimming pool or a large natural rockpool.  The sessions are
designed to teach the basic skills of the sport.

It is recommended that participants should be good swimmers and
free from any respiratory ailments.

Windsurfing.

-----------------------------------------------------------------
Available by special request from June each year.  An RYA
Instructor teaches firstly on a simulator and then on the water.
Junior size sails are used for introducing beginners to the
sport.

Archery.

Providing Archery in our programme gives a good balance against
the more physical activities.  The sport teaches concentration,
full body co-ordination and self-discipline, everyone measuring
his own improvement throughout the session on our full size
targets.
B:\CHAP4\W&0.EX                              Doc 1 Pg 2 Ln 1" Pos 1"
```

**Figure 2.8**   WordPerfect's page break

WordPerfect displays a double broken line across the screen, and inserts the [HPg] code in your document. To remove a hard page break, you need to delete this code (at the Reveal Codes screen).

The same principles apply when your text is organized into columns (these are discussed below). WordPerfect automatically starts a second column when the first is full, inserting the [SPg] code at that point. Pressing Ctrl-Enter will force a hard column break, inserting the [HPg] code in the text.

We discuss page breaks further in Chapter 4.

## 2.10   Columns

In the exercise that follows you'll be laying out your brochure in columns. The kind of column often used in documents like a brochure is called *newspaper columns*. Another type of column is called *parallel columns*, used for things like inventories, where entries appear side by side. A third type is called *tabbed columns* — these are used for tables. WordPerfect provides facilities for all three:

- *Newspaper columns*. With these, your text flows continuously down through the columns, rather as it does down an ordinary page. In fact, you can think of an ordinary page as a single, very wide newspaper column. Column breaks work in the same way as the page breaks described in the last section. You set newspaper columns via WordPerfect's Column key, Alt-F7 (see Section 36 of the Keystroke Guide for details). An example of newspaper columns is shown in Figure 2.9.

- *Parallel columns.* These are used for side-by-side entries. Unlike newspaper columns, the text in a parallel column is allowed to spill over onto a new page, while text in the other column stays put. A variation is *parallel with block protect*, which protects your entries from being split by a page break. If the entry in one column spills over the page break, it and the entries alongside it in the other columns are moved as a block to the next page (leaving a gap in all columns at the foot of the previous page). Again, Alt-F7 is the key to press when you want parallel columns (and again details are in the Keystroke Guide, Section 44). An example of parallel columns is shown in Figure 2.10.

- *Tabbed columns.* These are used for entering text or numbers in a table. Having typed an entry in a column, pressing the Tab key moves the cursor to the next column ready for its entry. Apart from pressing Tab, all you need do to create tabular columns is to enter the type and position of the tab entries before you begin. You do this via the Shift-F8 Format key. You enter the type of tab settings you want (L, C, R, D, or .) at the appropriate positions on the ruler bar that Word-Perfect displays (shown in Figure 2.11):

SKERN LODGE OUTDOOR CENTRE

MANAGEMENT TRAINING – THE PRACTICE OF TEAMWORK

Skern Lodge has achieved a wide reputation in teamwork and personal development training for industrial and commercial organisations for over 12 years. In presenting a PRACTICAL TEAMWORKING course we are providing an opportunity to explore in a practical way how to bring about individual and team development. The focus is on the skills and individual needs to be a helpful influence in a working team. We look at the way members of a team can interact to achieve

B:\CHAP2\BROCHUR1.EX

Real issues are dealt with using a mixture of indoor and outdoor exercises which provide points for discussion and practical learning to take back to the workplace.

Results

As a result of a Skern course your team will have a clearer understanding of how certain behaviour patterns affect others.

We guarantee the following:

*    The team will have a better feeling for each other.

Col 1 Doc 1 Pg 1 Ln 2.08" Pos 1.25'

**Figure 2.9** Newspaper columns

| Q   What qualifications do the staff have? | A All instructors have first aid/life saving certificates. All staff are always reviewed and appraised regularly. |
| Q How long has the Centre been used? | A Skern Lodge has been operating now for ten years. Most staff return year in and year out. All staff follow an induction course. |
| Q What happens in bad weather? | A We always have bad weather alternatives, usually organised by changing the weekly programme. |

**Figure 2.10**   Parallel columns

L   Left tab, i.e. the ordinary tab which lines up the leftmost character of your entry at the tab position.

C   Centre tab, which centres the word on the tab position.

R   Right tab, which lines up the rightmost character at the tab position.

D   Decimal tab, which lines up the decimal points in number entries.

Dot leaders, i.e. a row of dots instead of spaces in front of each tabbed entry. Used by itself, this setting right-tabs the entry, but it can combined with any of the other types of tab.

When entering these, you may want to delete WordPerfect's default tab settings from the ruler line. Section 61 of the Keystroke Guide covers this, and tables are dealt with in detail in Chapter 6.

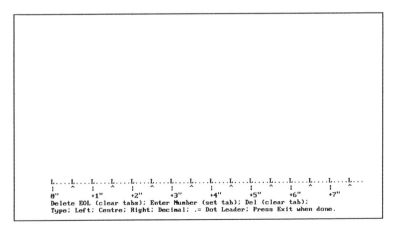

**Figure 2.11**   The ruler bar

## 2.11 The exercise: setting columns in your brochure

In this exercise you will apply newspaper and tabbed columns to the brochure you created earlier in this chapter. (You saved it as BROCHUR1.EX.) Take time out to experiment with the various column formatting possibilities — we've given just a few suggestions here. For newspaper columns, you will be working at the menu shown in Figure 2.12.

1   Change the appearance of BROCHUR1.EX to two newspaper columns by inserting the newspaper column code at the beginning of the second heading 'MANAGEMENT TRAINING...' (i.e. move the cursor to this point, press Alt-F7, Define, On, as explained in Section 36 of the Keystroke Guide. Use the Rewrite command to reformat the text on the screen).

2   View the document, and note that the first column is longer than the second. Achieve a more even balance by inserting a hard column break at the appropriate position in column 1. (To work out where, take the average of the last line positions for each column — cursor to them then look at the Ln reading on the status line.)

3   Now the text is in newspaper columns, it would look better with full justification. Find the [Just:Left] code and delete it to achieve this.

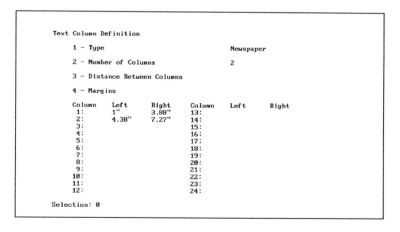

**Figure 2.12**   Text Column Definition menu

4  Turn off the column style at the end of the text (Alt-F7 again), and then type the table shown below (which is in tabulated columns). You must first, of course, enter the required tab settings for columns 2, 3 and 4. You will also need to delete some of WordPerfect's default tab settings.

```
SAMPLE ADULT WEEKEND PROGRAMME
DAY        AM      PM                  EVENING

Friday             Arrive after 5 pm   Skating
Saturday   Abseil  Sail and waterski   Competition
Sunday     Surf    Canoe
                   Depart 5 pm
```

5  Save the file, replacing the previous version. Then exit the file.

## 2.12  Further exercises

Regard Exercise 1 below as compulsory – it asks you to make a change to your PROSP2.EX file that you'll be using later. The other exercises are optional – you should not save any changes that these ask you to make.

1  Retrieve your PROSP2.EX file and change the left margin to 2.5″ and the right margin to 2″. Add to its end the text in Figure 2.10, formatted as parallel columns with block protect. The document is now two pages long, with a [SPg] code. Save the file, replacing the previous version.
2  Change the page orientation to *landscape*, and look at the code in the Reveal Codes screen. Now view the document (at the View Document screen). You will see that the text which isn't in columns is rearranged correctly, but the parallel columns have not been rearranged to fit the new page width. Why is this? Try to correct their format to match the rest of the document in landscape orientation. If you get stuck, there is a solution in the Keystroke Guide, Section 36.
3  Change the line spacing on items 6 to 8 to double. Look at the [LnSpac] code.
4  Delete the line space code at the beginning of item 6 and use the Cancel key to restore it at the beginning of item 5.

5   Use the Help key to look up general information on tab setting, in particular how to set evenly spaced tabs.

6   Retrieve BROCHURE.EX, move the cursor to the end of the text below the tabulated columns and change the tab settings to the default ones. That is, starting at 0″ and repeating every 0.5″, enter 'L'.

7   Still in the BROCHURE.EX file, change the top and bottom margins to some other size. The cursor should be located after the current [T/B Mar] code when you do this. Why? Having made this change, there will be two [T/B Mar] codes in the document, one of which is superfluous. What should you do, and why?

8   If you wished to return your brochure layout to a normal page instead of columns, you would have to delete the [Col Def] code. Try this out.

9   Change WordPerfect's default tab settings (using the Setup key, Shift-F1). Now switch to the (empty) Doc 2 screen and reveal the Codes screen. The tabs displayed along the bar at the centre of the screen should be the new ones you have set. Change the default back to the original settings.

# 3
# Enhancing your brochure

## 3.1 What you will achieve in this chapter

This chapter focuses on the appearance of your documents. When you have completed it, you should be able to:

- Centre text both horizontally and vertically on the page, and align it with the right margin.
- Apply character enhancements, including emboldening, underlining and italics.
- Use different fonts and font sizes to change the appearance and size of your text, including switching the case of existing text between upper and lower case.
- Use different types of hyphenation within words.
- Use hard spaces where appropriate between words.
- Use WordPerfect's 'date' feature to insert the current date in a document.

Note that we only deal with a few easy-to-apply fonts in this chapter. The full range of font style and sizing possibilities are covered in Chapter 10, on desktop publishing.

The skills you will learn will help you improve the appearance and impact of your documents, and to add emphasis where necessary, by applying appropriate textual enhancements. Using the mouse can speed up some of these tasks, and you will practise using this.

## 3.2 Routines you will use in this chapter

As you work through this chapter, you will be getting to grips with the following routines. The Keystroke Guide section number for each routine is given below in brackets:

- Centre a line of text horizontally (6).
- Right-align a line of text (14).
- Use centre justification (26).
- Centre a page of text vertically (5).
- Add enhancements such as emboldening and underlining (3 and 66).
- Make use of a limited range of easily applied fonts to change the size and appearance of text (15).
- Change the case of existing text to upper or lower (2).
- Hyphenate words automatically or manually (22).
- Insert hard spaces between words (19).
- Insert today's date in your text (9).

## 3.3 Enhancement principles

In Chapter 2 you improved the appearance of your brochure by applying a variety of page layout techniques. In this chapter you will be working at improving the appearance of the text of the brochure. The result is shown in Figure 3.1.

One of the great things about using a word processor like WordPerfect instead of a typewriter is that you can separate the task of making your material look good from the task of actually generating the text. It means that, while doing the actual writing, you concentrate entirely on the words, without being side-tracked by the appearance.

As you might imagine, WordPerfect offers you a great deal of scope in the enhancements you can apply to your text. You can, if you wish, desktop publish books using it. The only real limitation is the printer that's connected to your computer. If you have a laser printer, you will probably have a range of different fonts (character styles) available to you, including Helvetica and Times Roman (used in documents such as this book). A cheaper printer may limit you to boring typewriter-like fonts, such as Courier.

Because of the computing power that's on offer, there's a big temptation to use as many facilities as possible, and the result can look a real mess, with many different fonts and font sizes applied in the same document. So it's worth starting off with a few rules:

# SKERN LODGE OUTDOOR CENTRE

MANAGEMENT TRAINING – THE PRACTICE OF TEAMWORK

Skern Lodge has achieved a wide reputation in teamwork and personal development training for industrial and commercial organisations for over 12 years. In presenting a PRACTICAL TEAMWORKING course we are providing an opportunity to explore in a practical way how to bring about individual and team development. The focus is on the skills and individual needs to be a helpful influence in a working team. We look at the way members of a team can interact to achieve high quality results.

*Outdoor Training*

This form of training can be very enjoyable and rewarding. The benefits, however, can be difficult to translate into the workplace and therefore we focus heavily on applying the learning to daily work. This is the constant message of PRACTICE TEAMWORKING.

Real issues are dealt with using a mixture of indoor and outdoor exercises which provide points for discussion and practical learning to take back to the workplace.

*Results*

As a result of a Skern course your team will have a clearer understanding of how certain behaviour patterns affect others.

We guarantee the following:

*   The team will have a better feeling for each other

*   Individuals will have a clearer vision and greater confidence for the future

*   All members will have improved their ability to listen and identify each other's strengths and skills.

At Skern the team will laugh a lot and share emotions that will develop a powerful synergy.

*Course Brochure*

**SAMPLE ADULT WEEKEND PROGRAMME**

| DAY | AM | PM | EVENING |
|---|---|---|---|
| Friday | | Arrive after 5 pm | Skating |
| Saturday | Abseil | Sail and Waterski | Competition |
| Sunday | Surf | Canoe | |
| | | Depart 5 pm | |

**Figure 3.1**  The brochure with textual enhancements added

- Avoid using more than three different fonts and font sizes in the same document. Two is sufficient for most documents. This rule is of particular relevance when you come to explore the full range of font possibilities in Chapter 10. (In this chapter we look at just a few font style and sizing possibilities, i.e. the limited range that are immediately available on the Font key (Ctrl-F8).)
- The spacing between lines should not be less than the height of your characters, otherwise the result will look cramped. (We mentioned this rule in Chapter 2, where we dealt with line spacing.)
- Make sparing use of enhancements such as emboldening and underlining. Obviously headings should be enhanced. In a document such as this book one might italicize new terms, or embolden important points, but there must be clear justification for enhancing other text.
- Text in headings can be lower case, perhaps with initial capitals. Lower case is easier to read than upper case.

You can apply text alignment and enhancement features either while you are typing the document or after you have created the text. In the first exercise in this chapter you will be applying them while typing in a new document (a dinner menu), in the second exercise you will be applying them to an existing document (the brochure). As a general rule, it is more efficient to apply these enhancements as you are typing in the text. Otherwise, you have to 'block' existing text before you can apply an enhancement (page 44).

Before applying character enhancements to the brochure, we'll start by looking at WordPerfect's text alignment features. You will practise these by creating Skern Lodge's dinner menu, shown in Figure 3.2. As you can see, the lines are centred horizontally, and the whole thing is centred vertically on the page.

The file you will create in this exercise can be used for each day's dinner menu. The first three lines don't need changing from day to day (WordPerfect will automatically enter the current date), and some of the dishes may remain on the menu from one day to the next. Even if they do change, the various enhancements will remain and do not have to be reapplied.

```
     Skern Lodge Outdoor Centre


            Dinner Menu
             2 December 1994



               Celery Soup


            * * * * * * * * * * * *


               Roast Lamb
               Grilled Sole
              Roast Potatoes
             Creamed Potatoes
                Broccoli
                  Peas


            * * * * * * * * * * * *


           Apple Pie and Cream


            * * * * * * * * * * * *


           Cheese and Biscuits


            * * * * * * * * * * * *
```

**Figure 3.2**   Skern Lodge dinner menu

## 3.4  **Alignment**

In Chapter 2 you used some of the features available on the Shift-F8 key: this applies things like centring or right alignment to a whole document or a complete block of text within a document. In this chapter you will be using the alignment features on the F6 key: this works on the current line only (being turned off at the first soft or hard return).

- Shift-F6 centres the current line, Alt-F6 aligns it at the right margin. Note that you should press these with the cursor at the start of the line. If you press them elsewhere in the line, they only affect the characters to their right.

To cancel this alignment effect:

- Either use the Reveal Codes screen (Alt-F3) and delete the [Centre] or [Flsh.Rgt] codes, or place the cursor on the first character of the aligned text and press Backspace.

Note that you can apply these features and other enhancement features to a block of lines by using the Alt-F4 Block key. The procedure is described on page 44 below and in Section 2 of the Keystroke Guide.
   To centre text vertically on the page:

- Move the cursor to the start of the current page, and use the Shift-F8 (Format) key to insert the vertical centring code. Note that this code must be in front of any other code (if any) located at the start of the page. The Keystroke Guide, Section 5 gives details.

You must repeat this process for every page you want centred vertically; you can't apply it globally to the entire document.

## 3.5   Orientation

Normally, you will use portrait orientation for your documents. In the case of standard A4 paper, this means that the page is 8.27″ wide by 11.69″ deep. WordPerfect defaults to this size and orientation. Occasionally, though, you may want to print wide documents, i.e. have the printer deal with the paper sideways, so that the document comes out 11.69″ wide by 8.27″ deep. We would want to do this, for example:

- For a very wide table or spreadsheet.
- To achieve a special effect for a menu or programme of events.

To change the orientation, position the cursor at the top of the page you want to affect, then press the Shift-F8 Format key and choose Page Format to go to the Paper Size/Type menu shown in Figure 3.3. If a landscape orientation is listed on this menu, highlight it with the cursor and choose Select.

Exit back to your document, and you will see on the Reveal Codes screen that a [Paper Sz/Type] code has been inserted. This has a forwards effect, meaning that each subsequent page will be in landscape orientation. To switch subsequent pages back to portrait orientation, you will have to insert a portrait orientation code at the top of the appropriate page. (Again, use the Paper Size/Type menu for this.)

If the orientation you require is not listed at the Paper Size/Type menu, you will have to define it by adding a new paper definition. Section 42 of the Keystroke Guide gives full details.

## 3.6   Automatic date entry

You can have WordPerfect enter the date either as ordinary text or as a code. In the former case, it's as though you had looked up today's date and typed it in. In the latter case, the current date (as held in the computer's clock) will always be displayed whenever you view or print the document.

To use this feature, press Shift-F5 (Date/Outline). The menu shown in Figure 3.4 appears. Then:

```
Format: Paper Size/Type
                                              Font  Double
Paper type and Orientation   Paper Size    Prompt Loc    Type  Sided  Labels

Envelope - Wide              9.5" x 4"      Yes  Manual  Land  No
Standard                     8.27" x 11.69" No   Contin. Port  No
Standard - Wide              11.69" x 8.27" No   Contin. Land  No
[ALL OTHERS]                 Width ≤ 8.5"   Yes  Manual        No









1 Select; 2 Add; 3 Copy; 4 Delete; 5 Edit; N Name Search: 1
```

**Figure 3.3**   Paper Size/Type menu

```
1 Date Text; 2 Date Code; 3 Date Format; 4 Outline; 5 Para Num; 6 Define: 0
```

**Figure 3.4**  Data/Outline menu

- Choose Date Text to insert the date as text.
- Choose Date Code to insert the date as a code.
- Choose Date Format to alter the way the date is displayed.

## 3.7  Character enhancements

WordPerfect provides a range of different enhancements which, provided you have a suitable printer, can improve greatly the attractiveness of your text and the emphases you can apply to it. If you wish to apply these while you are typing some text, the procedure is:

1  Switch on the enhancement by pressing the appropriate function key (see below). A pair of enhancement codes is inserted at your current cursor position in the document, the first turning the enhancement on, the second turning it off. This is illustrated in Figure 3.5.
2  Type the text. It will be inserted within the two codes.
3  Switch off the enhancement by pressing the function key

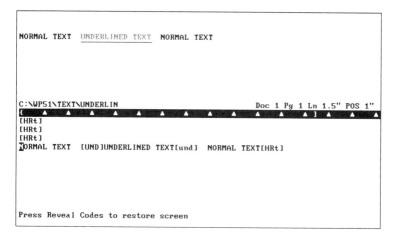

**Figure 3.5**  Text showing the underline codes

again. Alternatively, press the right arrow key once to move the cursor immediately beyond the enhancement-off code.

If you have already typed the text, you must 'block' (i.e. select) the text you wish to enhance and then press the enhancement key. The procedure is:

1  Place the cursor at the start of the text you wish to enhance.
2  Press Alt-F4 (the Block key).
3  Move the cursor to the end of the block.
4  Press the appropriate function key to enhance the block.
5  If you wish to return the cursor to the start of the block, press the Goto key (Ctrl-Home) twice.

You can if you wish block your text backwards, i.e. start at the end of the block at step 1 above and move the cursor to the start at step 3.

If you prefer to use the mouse, the procedure is rather easier:

1  Drag over the text you wish to enhance.
2  Choose the enhancement you wish to apply.

The various enhancements are clustered on the F6 and F8 keys. Common enhancements require only a single keypress, e.g. press F6 for bold, and F8 for underline. Less common enhancements require a sequence of keypresses. You have already used some of those available on Shift-F8 (Format), others are available on Ctrl-F8 (Font). The options available on Ctrl-F8 include:

- Size, i.e. different type sizes (superscript, subscript, fine, small, large, very large, and extra large). The Size menu is shown in Figure 3.6. The superscript/subscript options allow you to type small characters half a line above/below the current line.
- Appearance, i.e. different type styles (bold, underline, double underline, outline, italic, shadow, small capitals, redline, strikeout). The Appearance menu is shown in Figure 3.7.

```
1 Suprscpt: 2 Subscpt: 3 Fine: 4 Small: 5 Large: 6 Ury Large: 7 Ext Large: 8
```

**Figure 3.6**  Size menu

```
1 Bold 2 Undln 3 Dbl Und 4 Italc 5 Outln 6 Shadw 7 Sm Cap 8 Redln 9 Stkout: 0
```

**Figure 3.7**  Appearance menu

Note that bold and underline are more easily obtained by pressing F6 and F8.

## 3.8  Checking out enhancements

Many of the enhancements described above cannot be displayed on the ordinary (character-based) editing screen. So WordPerfect indicates them by using colours or, in the case of black-and-white screens, by shades of grey and inverse video effects. (You can change the choice of colours and effects via the Shift-F1 (Setup) key, as described in Section 53 of the Keystroke Guide.)

If you want to see on the screen how your enhancements will look when printed, use the View Document feature (on the Shift-F7 Print key).

To see the enhancement codes that are inserted in your document, use the Reveal Codes screen (Alt-F3). You can remove enhancements by deleting the codes at this screen.

Finally, your printer may not be able to print certain enhancements. Some printers, for example, cannot cope with italics. To find out what effects your printer does support, retrieve the file PRINTER.TST from the WordPerfect directory on your hard disk and print it out.

## 3.9  The dinner menu exercise

For this exercise you will create the document shown in Figure 3.2. As you type in the text, apply the character enhancements shown in the figure (the details are given below). Also practise centring individual lines and, if you wish, right-aligning them. Afterwards, though, delete the alignment codes at the Reveal Codes screen then use the most efficient method for aligning this document: press the Shift-F8 Format key at the start of the document (as you learned in Chapter 2), and choose Centre Justification. This centres the entire document.

In detail, the steps for carrying out the enhancements are as follows. You will find it helpful to have the Reveal Codes screen switched on during this exercise.

1  The first line — SKERN LODGE OUTDOOR CENTRE — uses the very large size in the size menu on the Font key (Ctrl-F8), so choose this before typing the text. Press the right arrow key to move past the second [vry large] code before inserting several carriage returns. To see how this will print, view the document. Note that this line should be typed in lower case with initial capitals; in the further exercises below you will apply an enhancement that changes this to full capitals.

2  The next line — Dinner Menu — is in extra large italics, i.e. two enhancements have been applied. Both are available on the Font key: extra large on the Size menu, and italics on the Appearance menu. Choose the enhancements; type the text; then press End. Now insert a couple of carriage returns by pressing Enter twice.

3  The date, emboldened, must be inserted here, so press the Bold key (F6), then the Date key (Shift-F5) and select date as a code, then press the Bold key again.

4  Type the rest of the menu, then centre it vertically. To do this, position the cursor right at the start of the document, in this case on the initial code [Just:Centre], then press Shift-F8 to insert the vertical centring code. View the document to see the effect.

5  Save the completed document as MENU.EX.

## 3.10    Further exercises on the dinner menu

In the blocking exercises below, practise using both the mouse method for blocking text and the keystroke method. Which do you find most efficient?

1  Embolden the first line of the above document by blocking it and pressing the Bold key.

2  Change the emboldened date to underlined by deleting one of the [Bold] codes, blocking the text and pressing the Underline key.

3  Change the first line from initial capital letters to upper case by blocking the text, pressing Switch, and selecting Uppercase.

4   Change the orientation of the document from portrait to landscape.
5   Delete the [Centre Pg] code, then restore it after the first line of text. (Recall that pressing F1,1 restores deletions.) View the document to see how this changes its appearance.

There's no need to save the changes you've made to the document.

## 3.11   Hyphens

If you have right-justified your document or laid it out in newspaper columns, there will be large gaps between some words on some lines. In the case of left-justified text, some lines will have large gaps at the right, giving a 'ragged' effect. To ameliorate this untidy appearance, you can hyphenate words at the end of the line. They will then be split at the hyphen, reducing the gaps.

Hyphens will therefore improve the appearance of your document. Be careful not to overdo hyphens, however: several consecutive lines ending in hyphens will look odd. It is, in fact, considered to be bad practice to hyphenate more than two consecutive lines.

You can choose between manual and automatic hyphenation. WordPerfect defaults to manual hyphenation, relying on you to hyphenate where you think necessary. There are three types of manual hyphen you can apply:

- *Hyphen character*. This is what's inserted in the text if you press the hyphen key (to the right of the zero at the top of the keyboard, marked '-'). A [-] code is inserted in the document. This kind of hyphen is always displayed and printed, even if the word is not at the end of a line. (Certain words are, of course, hyphenated, and you may want to use this for them.)
- *Soft hyphen*. You insert this by pressing Ctrl-hyphen. This will only display and print if the word lies at the end of the line and breaks at the hyphen. If subsequent editing moves the word from this position, then the hyphen disappears (although it remains invisibly present in the text). WordPerfect inserts an emboldened hyphen in the codes screen to mark this kind of hyphen.
- *Hard hyphen*. This kind of hyphen acts like an ordinary

character of text − it will not cause the word to split at the
end of a line. To insert this, press Home and then hyphen.
No special code is inserted in this case, it is treated as ordinary
text.

Often, though, you will want WordPerfect to apply automatic
hyphenation to your document. In this case, it will insert soft
hyphens at appropriate positions in words lying at the end of
lines. If you subsequently edit the text, so that different words
appear at the ends of lines, WordPerfect will still hyphenate them
automatically without any further action on your part.

You can turn on hyphenation while you are typing the text.
Alternatively, you can type the text first, then:

1   Go back to the beginning of the document (or wherever you
want hyphenation to start) and turn hyphenation on using the
Shift-F8 (Format) key.
2   Keep pressing the down arrow key to carry out the hyphenation, until you reach the end of the document (or whenever
you want to end the automatic hyphenation). WordPerfect
uses its dictionary and hyphenation code file to carry out the
hyphenation, but for some words it will ask you to decide
where to locate the hyphen. The procedure will be fairly
obvious, but is explained in Section 22 of the Keystroke
Guide.

With automatic hyphenation turned on, WordPerfect will check
line endings whenever you scroll down through your document.
This will slow things down, so you may want to turn off this
process. To do so, delete the [Hyph On] code at the Reveal
Codes screen.

## 3.12   Spacing

WordPerfect breaks lines when there is a space between two
words. This can at times have the unfortunate effect of putting
'Mr' at the end of one line and 'Jones' at the start of the next. In
fact, you want to keep the two words together on the same line,
and to achieve this you must insert a *hard space* between them.
Instead of pressing the spacebar after typing 'Mr', press Home
then the spacebar.

## 3.13 The brochure exercise

In this exercise, you should apply the enhancements shown in Figure 3.1 to your brochure (the detailed steps are described below). Since the text already exists (you saved it under the name BROCHUR1.EX), you will have to block the text in each case before applying the appropriate enhancement. Use either the mouse or the keyboard for blocking, whichever you found most efficient in the earlier exercise.

Save the finished result as BROCHUR2.EX. Do not overwrite your existing file (BROCHUR1.EX) as you will be using this in a later exercise.

In detail, the steps are:

1 Use the Centre key to centre the first line of text.
2 Use the Bold key and the Font key to make the heading bold and extra large.
3 Make the next heading (MANAGEMENT TRAINING – THE PRACTICE OF TEAMWORK) large.
4 Apply italics to each of the subheadings.
5 In the table, embolden the heading and underline the column headings.
6 Use the soft hyphen to hyphenate manually through the document. Since the brochure is fully justified, you will need to view the document (using Shift-F7, Preview) to check the new line endings. Make sure you don't have more than two consecutive lines hyphenated (see 3.11 above). You will need to keep switching between the View and editing screens to check for this and for large spaces between words that could be reduced by hyphenating.

## 3.14 Further exercises

Do not save the changes you make to your document in these exercises.

1 Retrieve the original BROCHUR1.EX file that does not contain the hyphenation you applied above. Turn on automatic hyphenation at the start of the document, then scroll downwards to have WordPerfect hyphenate the text.

2   Test out the hard space by deleting the ordinary space at some line endings and inserting a hard space instead.

3   Select some text using the Block key, then press the Switch key (Shift-F3). Choose Uppercase or Lowercase from the menu that appears, and observe what happens to your text.

4   Block some text then experiment with the appearance options on the Font key.

# 4
# Printing the prospectus

## 4.1  What you will achieve in this chapter

This chapter will show you how to control many different aspects of printing. When you have completed it, you should be able to:

- Control the pagination of documents, by inserting page breaks as required, and removing bad page breaks.
- Insert headers (in the top margin), footers (in the bottom margin), and page numbers.
- Add footnotes and endnotes.
- Advance the cursor to a preset position on the page in order to, e.g. 'fill in the blanks' on a pre-printed form.
- Add additional non-printing commentary to your document, including a document summary.

The skills you will learn will help make your documents look their best when they finally appear in print.

## 4.2  Routines you will use in this chapter

As you work through this chapter, you will be getting to grips with the following routines. The Keystroke Guide section number for each routine is given below in brackets.

- Insert a hard page break (39).
- Apply block protection (2).
- Apply the widow/orphan protection command both to the current document (67) and as a default to all documents (53).
- Use the conditional end-of-page command (39).

- Insert page numbering (41).
- Insert headers and footers (20).
- Suppress headers (20).
- Insert footnotes (16).
- Create a document summary (11).
- Change the default so that document summaries are automatically prompted (53).
- Insert a document comment (7).
- Use the Advance option to advance the cursor at print-time (1).

## 4.3 The prospectus

The female half of this book's authoring team likes to look her best when she turns up for work. She wants to create an impression. As a result, people pay far more attention to her than to the rather dishevelled male component of the team. The same principle applies to a printed document. A valuable message or brilliant style are not enough: if you want it to make an impact it must look good.

As you might expect, WordPerfect provides many features for printing your work to best effect.

Figure 4.1 shows the prospectus as it will look when you print it later in this chapter. Notice the following features:

- *Page numbers*. These should normally be included on all documents which run to two or more pages.
- *Headers*. This is repeated text that prints at the top of every page, such as the chapter headings in this book. *Footers* refers to repeated text that prints at the bottom of every page.

The larger the document, the more necessary it is to provide such features to help the reader find his or her way around. If you are producing specialist documents, such as reference books, you will value further features provided by WordPerfect:

- *Footnotes* – These are additional material or references usually printed at the foot of a page.
- *Endnotes* – A collection of footnotes, normally printed at the end of a document.

## SKERN LODGE PROSPECTUS

**outdoor centres**

### THE SERVICE

All staff at Skern Lodge have a real commitment to offer value for money and personal service. Our policy is to ensure that everyone staying receives individual attention.

### MANAGEABLE GROUPS

On arrival at Skern Lodge you will be greeted by one of our Course Directors who looks after you throughout your stay. Your group is divided into smaller working groups of eight paying guests.

### SAFETY FIRST

Skern Lodge instructional staff are qualified teachers and/or instructors with qualifications in a range of specialist activities.

Our selection process for staff is rigorous and standards of expertise are high.

### OUR TRANSPORT

We have our own mini-buses which are used by staff for transporting groups between activities where necessary.

### JUNIOR SCHOOLS

Our special Junior School package gives you an exciting and challenging programme at an economical price. Activities are complemented by

Skern Lodge Prospectus

one or two visits to local attractions, and there never seems to be a minute to spare.

### SENIOR SCHOOLS

We have been organising senior school activity courses at Skern Lodge for over ten years, and each course is separately planned. We do not have a standard programme - your course is tailor-made for your school.

### SPECIALIST GROUPS

Some recent courses at Skern Lodge include:

* Management training
* Field studies courses
* Self-catering for canoe clubs and surfers

### ARRIVALS

Guests are requested to arrive after 1 pm for courses starting at lunchtime, and after 5 pm for courses starting in the evening.

### GENERAL INFORMATION

Here are the answers to some of your questions.

Q What qualifications do the staff have?

A All instructors have first aid/life saving certificates. All staff are always reviewed and appraised regularly.

Q How long has the Centre been used?

A Skern Lodge has been operating now for ten years. Most staff return year in and year out. All staff follow an induction course.

**Figure 4.1** The printed prospectus

WordPerfect will number these automatically and insert them at print-time in the correct location on the page.

Naturally, WordPerfect allows you to control where page breaks occur in your document. Nothing looks worse than a heading on the bottom of one page with its body text on the next. Almost as bad is a table of numbers that is split by a page break. You can have WordPerfect automatically prevent disasters like this, and you can also insert page breaks manually.

Also, you may wish to use WordPerfect to 'fill in the blanks' on pre-printed forms, or to leave a gap of a certain size in your document in order to paste there a picture. Its *Advance* feature allows you to do this, by giving a command to advance the cursor the required vertical and horizontal distance.

These and other printing facilities are covered in this chapter.

## A word of warning

All of these facilities work by inserting codes in your document. Many of them, such as codes for page numbers, headers and footers, will be located at the top of the document. This means that they will be applied to every page of the document, including the first page. However, if you add any ordinary text in front of them, WordPerfect will not apply them to the first page (but they will apply to subsequent pages).

## 4.4 More on page breaks

Page breaks, introduced in Chapter 2, are covered in depth in this section. You will recall that when your current page is full, WordPerfect inserts automatically a soft page break, so that subsequent text appears on a new page.

In the prospectus that you worked on in Chapter 2, WordPerfect had inserted a soft page break in the Specialist Groups text. The result was not very attractive. However, you can override soft page breaks in a variety of ways, and you will be trying these in the exercise:

• Inserting a *hard page break*. This forces a page break at any point you choose. To do so, place the cursor at that point and press Ctrl-Enter. The [HPg] code will be inserted in the text, and your screen will look like Figure 4.2. To remove this hard page break, find the code on the Reveal Codes screen and delete it.

• Inserting a *conditional end-of-page*. This facility allows you to keep an exact number of lines together on a page, so avoiding, for instance, splitting a heading from body text below it. It works by inserting a conditional end-of-page code in the line immediately above the lines you wish to keep together. So if you wish to keep a heading and the next two lines together, you should apply the command in the line above the heading to keep the next four lines together. The code in this case would be [Cndl EOP:4]. To use this facility press the Shift-F8 Format key and choose Other. The menu in Figure 4.3 appears.

• Inserting a *block protect* code. This facility (also on the Format key) allows you to prevent a table (or any other block of text) from being split in two by a page break. To apply this, first select the block with the Alt-F4 (Block) key. The [Block

```
This is lowering oneself down a rock face on a rope, using a
special friction device and a safety rope.  It gives a tremendous
sense of personal achievement and it's great to hear the support
and encouragement from all your Skern Lodge friends.
Our main cliff is 130 ft high and we have several other coastal
locations for those who are still calling for more!
================================================================================

Raft Racing.

An action-packed river descent using improvised rafts made by the
group out of a special collection of equipment.  It is great fun
for everyone and is always a popular activity at Skern Lodge.

Water-skiing.

Feel the thrill of speeding over the water as we open up the
throttle!  We work closely with the British Water Ski Federation
to teach safely and with a high success rate.  A learning bar is
used before progressing on to the rope.

Snorkling.

C:\WP51\BOOK\W&O.EX                      Doc 1 Pg 2 Ln 1.17" POS 1"
```

**Figure 4.2**   Hard page break

```
Format: Other

     1 - Advance

     2 - Conditional End of Page

     3 - Decimal/Align Character    .
         Thousands Separator        ,

     4 - Language                   UK

     5 - Overstrike

     6 - Printer Functions

     7 - Underline - Spaces         Yes
                     Tabs           No

     8 - Border Options




Selection: 0
```

**Figure 4.3**   Format Other menu

Pro:On] and [Block Pro:Off] codes are inserted at the beginning and end of the protected block.
- Applying *widow/orphan* protection. This facility, also on the Format key, prevents the last line (a *widow*) or the first line

(an *orphan*) from being split from the rest of the paragraph by a page break. (So a widow is the last line printed at the top of a page, an orphan is the first line printed at the bottom of a page.) Both are considered bad formatting style, and to prevent them you should insert a widow/orphan protection code at the start of your document. WordPerfect will then force the last two lines of a paragraph onto the next page to prevent a widow, or the first line of a paragraph onto the next page to prevent an orphan.

Note that you can make WordPerfect default to providing automatic widow/orphan protection for all your (new) documents — use the Shift-F1 (Setup) key for this.

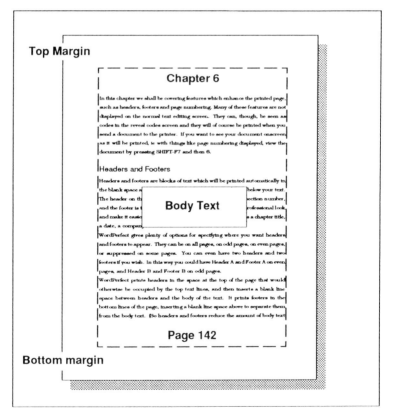

**Figure 4.4**   The position of headers and footers

## 4.5 Headers and footers

Headers and footers are blocks of text which will be printed automatically at the top and bottom of the page. They can include such things as a chapter title, a date and a company name and logo. You will be using this feature to insert the header shown in Figure 4.1 in your prospectus.

WordPerfect gives plenty of options for specifying where you want headers and footers to appear. They can be on all pages, on odd pages, on even pages, and suppressed on some pages. Typically, you may want to suppress them on the first page of the document, and you will be doing this with the prospectus.

You can even have two headers and two footers if you wish — so you could have WordPerfect print Header A and Footer A on even pages, and Header B and Footer B on odd pages. In the exercise, you will be aligning Header A with the right margin on odd pages, and Header B with the left margin on even pages.

Many word processing packages print headers and footers in the top and bottom margins of the page. WordPerfect, however, prints them in the top and bottom space that would otherwise be occupied by the body of the text. So headers and footers reduce the amount of body text that can be printed on a page (two lines for a header, two for a footer — see Figure 4.2).

To create a header or footer, place the cursor at the beginning of your document and press the Format key, then 2 (Page) for the Format Page menu shown in Figure 2.6 on page 28. Then press 3 (Header) or 4 (Footer), then choose 1 for Header/Footer A or 2 for Header/Footer B. WordPerfect stores the header/footer text that you type in with the header/footer code, so you can see it at the Reveal Codes screen. More information is in Section 20 of the Keystroke Guide.

To suppress a header or footer on an individual page, choose 8 (Suppress) at the Format Page menu.

Note that WordPerfect inserts a blank line to separate headers and footers from the body text. If you wish to add further separating lines, press the Enter key after the header text or before the footer text.

To edit a header or footer, repeat the above steps, then choose Edit and make the required changes. To delete a header or footer, switch on the Reveal Codes screen and delete the code.

## 4.6 Page numbering

WordPerfect gives you a range of options in setting page numbers. You can decide:

- The position of the numbers (top or bottom margins, and left or right or centre).
- The start number (normally '1', but it could be another number if you are printing only part of a larger document).
- The numbering style (Arabic or Roman).

Page numbers, like headers and footers, reduce the number of lines of body text per page by two: one line for the number, and one line for the space between the number and the body text. It also inserts page number codes in the document (Section 41 of the Keystroke Guide).

### *Inserting page numbers*

WordPerfect defaults to giving no page numbers. To insert numbering:

1 Place the cursor at the top of the starting page of your document.
2 Press Shift-F8 (Format), then press 2, 6 to arrive at the Format Page Numbering menu shown in Figure 4.5.
3 Press 4 (Page Number Position) to see the Page Numbering Position screen shown in Figure 4.6.
4 Type the number of the position of your choice. You will be returned to the previous menu.

When you exit back to your document you will have to go to the View screen to see the page numbering.

### *Page numbering options*

The various page number options provided by WordPerfect are outlined below and described in detail in Section 41 of the Keystroke Guide.

- *Starting page number.* You can choose a number other than 1 as the starting page number, or you can restart the numbering

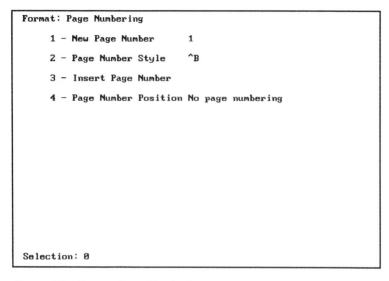

**Figure 4.5** Format Page Numbering menu

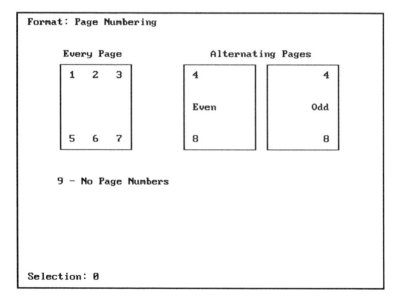

**Figure 4.6** Page Numbering Position menu

at any page within the document. Simply place the cursor at the top of the page where you want the numbering to begin and choose 1 (New Page Number) at the Page Numbering Format menu. Then enter the new number.

- *Suppress the page number*, so that it does not appear on an individual page. The procedure is the same as for suppressing headers and footers.

- *Page number style*. The default numbering style is Arabic. If you want another style, perhaps including some text (for example 'Page'), then choose the Page Number Style option on the Page Numbering Format menu. This option defaults to ^B, which is the page numbering code. Enter the text which you want to add, and press Ctrl-B to reinsert the page numbering code.

## 4.7   Footnotes

You may wish to insert subsidiary material, such as titles of books or articles for further reading, as *footnotes* in your document. WordPerfect's footnote feature allows you to place a numbered marker in the text and then insert the related information at the foot of the same page[1]

We have included an example on this page. As it is the first footnote in this document, it has been given the number 1.

WordPerfect automatically numbers footnotes. It will also renumber them if, later on, you add more footnotes or delete existing ones.

To create a footnote, position the cursor at the point in your document to which the footnote refers and press the Ctrl-F7 (Footnote) key. The procedure from then on is fairly obvious – for details see Section 16 of the Keystroke Guide. The footnote number that WordPerfect inserts in your text will be displayed on the screen with the superscript attribute or colour. (A footnote code will also be inserted at the same point.) To see the footnote, view the document (Shift-F7, 7).

The default footnote style is as follows:

- The footnote text is in single spacing.

[1]   This is a footnote.

- The footnote number in the body text is in superscript, i.e. it prints slightly above the rest of the line of text.
- The footnote number is indeed a number (rather than a letter or character).
- A 2″ horizontal line separates the bottom of the body text from the footnotes.
- The footnote aligns with the left margin.

You can change any of this at the Footnotes Option menu, also on Ctrl-F7. The changes you make take effect from the position in your document of the footnote code, so they do not affect previous footnotes.

## 4.8 Endnotes

*Endnotes* are footnotes which are grouped together at the end of the document (or indeed at any location of your choice within the document). The procedure for creating endnotes is similar to that for footnotes, including starting off by pressing Ctrl-F7. For details see Section 13 of the Keystroke Guide.

Note that WordPerfect inserts a hard page break after endnotes, so that any text added after them will start on a fresh page.

## 4.9 Advance

WordPerfect's *Advance* feature is often used with pre-printed forms, as it allows you to instruct your printer to print text at positions up, down, left or right from the current printing position. So you can get the printer to move from field to field on the form, inserting material from the prepared document at the precisely defined locations on the form − in other words, to 'fill in the blanks'.

### Simple use of Advance

An important use of Advance, and one you will be applying to the brochure, is to leave a gap in your text of a precise size (2″ in fact) to allow a picture to be inserted later. It's a good idea to insert a non-printing comment where the Advance command occurs in your text, to explain its purpose, and you will be learning how to do this in the prospectus exercise (coming up next).

To apply the Advance command, move the cursor to the point in your text where you wish the advance to occur, then:

1  Press Shift-F8 (Format), then 4 (Other), then 1 (Advance).
2  Choose Up, Down, Left, Right, Line, or Position.

These options allow you to advance to:

• A position measured in inches up, down, left, or right from the current cursor position.
• A specified vertical position relative to the top edge of the page.
• A specified horizontal position relative to the left edge of the page.

So if you want to advance to a point 2″ to the right and 1″ down from your current cursor position, first choose Right then enter 2″, then choose Down and enter 1″.

When you carry out this command you will not see any change on the text editing screen. However, the change will be reflected in the cursor position on the status line, and the [Adv] code will be inserted in your document. To see the effect of the command, you have to view the document.

### Creating a masterfile

One of the more complex uses of the Advance feature is to create masterfiles which are then used for printing to pre-printed forms. An example of a pre-printed form – a memo – is shown in Figure 4.7. As you can see, it has empty fields (spaces) where information from the masterfile is to be inserted. For each field on this form you insert, in the masterfile, an Advance command

# MEMORANDUM

To:                                        Date:


From:                                      Ref:

**Figure 4.7**   Example of a pre-printed form

to move to the position of the field together with the text that is to go into the field.

A masterfile is shown in Figure 4.8. In essence, the procedure to create and use a masterfile is as follows:

1 Create and save the masterfile. As explained below, this consists mainly of Advance codes together with non-printing comments explaining what has to go in each field on the pre-printed form.
2 When you wish to use the master, retrieve it then save it under a new name to create the copy you will be using for the current print job. This preserves the master unchanged in readiness for future print jobs.
3 Use this copy to enter the text that you wish to print in the various fields on the pre-printed form. After typing in an entry for a field, you simply press the down arrow key to move to the next Advance command for the next entry.
4 Print to the pre-printed form. The Advance commands will ensure each entry is inserted at the required position on the form.

Each time you wish to create text for printing to the pre-printed form, go through steps 2–4 above.

In order to create a master for something like the memo form

To:

Date:

From:

Ref:

Type memo text below this box

C:\WP51\BOOK\EXS\MASTER.EX                    Doc 1 Pg 1 Ln 1.3" Pos 1.5"

**Figure 4.8** Masterfile showing comments boxes

shown in Figure 4.7, you have first to measure the positions of each field on the form relative to the top and left of the page (since you will be using the Line and Position options of the Advance command). Then create the masterfile, containing the following information for each field on the pre-printed form:

- A comments box containing instructions on what has to go in the field (use Ctrl-F5).
- An Advance to Line command to move the cursor to the field's vertical position on the form (use Shift-F8).
- An Advance to Position command to move the cursor to the field's horizontal position on the form (use Shift-F8).
- A carriage return (press Enter). This allows you to press the down arrow key to move to the next Advance command when you type text into the masterfile.

The codes that have been inserted in the masterfile in Figure 4.8 are shown in Figure 4.9.

## 4.10   The exercise: printing the prospectus

You will be practising the features described in this chapter on your PROSP2.EX file, so begin by retrieving this document. You will be inserting quite a few codes at the start of the document;

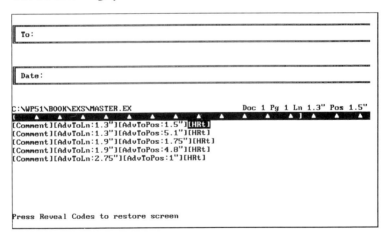

**Figure 4.9**   Masterfile showing codes

make sure that you don't add any ordinary text in front of them, or WordPerfect will not apply them to the first page of the document.

1   You want to insert a small photograph of Skern Lodge in the prospectus after the 'Manageable Groups' paragraph. So at this point in the text, insert the command *advance down 2"*. Then use the Reveal Codes screen to look at the [Adv] code that's been inserted, and view the document to check the effect.

2   Note where the page break occurs between page 1 and page 2: in this part of the exercise you will be adding page numbering, and this is going to affect the amount of text on the page and therefore the page break position. Using the Shift-F8 (Format) key, insert the page numbering at bottom centre and change the style to 'Page ^B'. (^B is the special code which puts the correct number on each page. To enter it press Ctrl-B.) Back at the editing screen, what effect has this had on the position of the page break?

3   The prospectus is going to be printed on both sides of the page, so let's put in two headers: Header A to be right-aligned with the margin on odd pages, and Header B to be left-aligned on even pages. The header text you should enter is 'Skern Lodge Prospectus', and you should apply emboldening and small size print to it (on the Font key). Note how this further reduces the amount of body text on the page, and therefore the position of the page break.

4   You now decide that the whole prospectus should have the heading '*SKERN LODGE PROSPECTUS*', so type this at the top of the document in very large size print and emboldened italics. Make sure that this heading is inserted after all your format codes, otherwise WordPerfect will not apply these codes to the current page.

5   Putting in this heading means that the header is not needed on page 1. So suppress Header A on that page. What has happened to the position of the page break?

6   Once all headers, footers, and page numbering are in place, you can address any problems of bad page breaks. In the prospectus, we have an unacceptable page break occurring within the 'Junior Schools' paragraph. Practise each of the possible options to correct this:

- Insert a hard page break at the beginning of the heading.
- Delete the [HPg] and with the cursor above the heading, insert a conditional end-of-page command keeping the next 7 lines of text together.
- Delete the [Cndl EOP] code, block the whole of the 'Specialist Groups' text, and protect the block using the Format key.

The first option (the hard page break) is the quickest to apply, but it has potential disadvantages. What are they?

Would widow and orphan protection have any effect on this particular page break?

7 Now print your document. Then save it under the same filename. You will be doing more work on it shortly.


## 4.11   Document comments

WordPerfect allows you to insert *comments* − notes and reminders − in your document. These are to help you, the author, and they will not be printed with your document. (However, you can change them to ordinary document text which *will* print.) For example, a comment added to the Advance command in the last exercise would remind you what to put in the space that's left when printing. An example of a comment is shown in Figure 4.10. To add a comment, position the cursor, then press the Ctrl-F5 (Text In/Out) key, and type. The comment will be displayed within a box on the editing screen, and as a [Comment] code on the Reveal Codes screen.

If you find that comments distract you while editing, you can alter WordPerfect's setup configuration so that they don't appear on the editing screen.


## 4.12   Document summary

Another kind of non-printing text which is intended to help you, the author, is the *document summary*. You have probably often been in the situation of wanting to retrieve a document, but can't remember its name. So you've had to scan laboriously through a number of documents on your disk until you hit the right one.

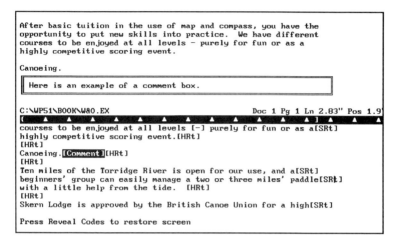

```
After basic tuition in the use of map and compass, you have the
opportunity to put new skills into practice.  We have different
courses to be enjoyed at all levels - purely for fun or as a
highly competitive scoring event.

Canoeing.
┌──────────────────────────────────────────────────────────┐
│ Here is an example of a comment box.                       │
└──────────────────────────────────────────────────────────┘
C:\WP51\BOOK\W8O.EX                       Doc 1 Pg 1 Ln 2.83" Pos 1.9
```

```
courses to be enjoyed at all levels [-] purely for fun or as a[SRt]
highly competitive scoring event.[HRt]
[HRt]
Canoeing.[Comment][HRt]
[HRt]
Ten miles of the Torridge River is open for our use, and a[SRt]
beginners' group can easily manage a two or three miles' paddle[SRt]
with a little help from the tide.  [HRt]
[HRt]
Skern Lodge is approved by the British Canoe Union for a high[SRt]

Press Reveal Codes to restore screen
```

**Figure 4.10**   Example of a comment box in a document

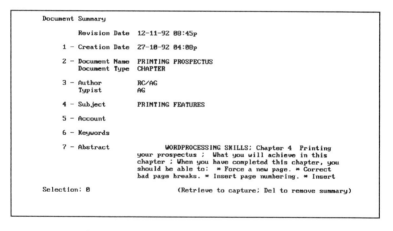

```
Document Summary

         Revision Date  12-11-92 08:45p

    1 - Creation Date  27-10-92 04:00p

    2 - Document Name  PRINTING PROSPECTUS
        Document Type  CHAPTER

    3 - Author         RC/AG
        Typist         AG

    4 - Subject        PRINTING FEATURES

    5 - Account

    6 - Keywords

    7 - Abstract            WORDPROCESSING SKILLS; Chapter 4  Printing
                        your prospectus ;  What you will achieve in this
                        chapter ; When you have completed this chapter, you
                        should be able to:  * Force a new page. * Correct
                        bad page breaks. * Insert page numbering. * Insert

    Selection: 0                    (Retrieve to capture; Del to remove summary)
```

**Figure 4.11**   The document summary for this chapter

The document summary feature provides a neat solution to this problem.

You can create a summary from any point in your document. Press the Shift-F8 (Format) key, then 3 (Document). The menu shown in Figure 4.12 appears. Choose 5 (Summary). WordPerfect displays a list of summary items, such as *creation date*, *document title*, *author*, etc. You can choose any of these and enter the

```
Format: Document

    1 - Display Pitch - Automatic Yes
                       Width      0.1"

    2 - Initial Codes

    3 - Initial Base Font        Courier 10cpi

    4 - Redline Method           Printer Dependent

    5 - Summary




Selection: 0
```

**Figure 4.12**   Format Document menu

appropriate information. Press the F3 (Help) key if you are
unsure what to enter into the various fields. You can enter some
information into the summary automatically. Press Retrieve (Shift-
F10), and the prompt 'Capture Document Summary Fields? No
(Yes)' appears. Type 'Y', and WordPerfect will fill in the following
fields:

- *Author/Typist*. The author and typist entered in the previous
  summary during the current session will be entered. If you
  have previously entered none, nothing will be inserted.
- *Subject*. WordPerfect searches the document for the word
  'Re:', then copies the text from that point up to the next
  carriage return.
- *Abstract*. WordPerfect copies the first 400 characters from the
  document and inserts them in this field.

You can also configure WordPerfect to present you with the
summary menu whenever you save a document for the first time.
To do this, press the Setup key and choose Environment,
Document Management/Summary. Press the Help key at this
point for assistance.

How does the document summary feature help you search for files? In two ways:

- When you use the 'Look' feature in List Files, any file containing a document summary will display that summary first. You can then scroll down to see the rest of the document if you need to.
- When you use the word search feature in List Files, you can restrict the search to the document summary. You can therefore search for a particular author, or a date, or any other entry in your document summaries.

## 4.13 The exercise: adding explanatory text

This exercise continues with the PROSP2.EX that you worked on earlier in this chapter.

1 As a reminder of the purpose of the Advance command that you inserted at the start of the last exercise, insert a comment box at the same point in the text. Your comment should state what's to go in this space. Note that WordPerfect displays the comment on the editing screen, but not on the View screen.

2 Insert a document summary, using the Retrieve key to fill in the Abstract field automatically. Make appropriate entries in other fields, using the Help key if you are not sure what to enter.

3 Save your document again (under the same filename), then use the List Files key to view the summary.

## 4.14 Further exercises

Still using PROSP2.EX, practise the following without saving:

1 Edit the page numbering and the headers by changing them to italics.

2 See what problem occurs if you insert a footer and a page number with the same alignment, e.g. centred. What would you do about this problem?

Now exit from PROSP2.EX and carry out the following exercises:

1　Change the WordPerfect setup to prompt for a document summary on first saving a file.
2　Retrieve (Shift-F10) the TOPICS.EX file which you used in an earlier chapter, move the cursor to the end of the document and retrieve (Shift-F10) a file called W&O.EX at the end of it. This, in effect, creates a new file. Now press the Save (F10) key. WordPerfect should display the Document Summary menu. Press the Retrieve key and type 'Y' to fill in some fields automatically. Then type in the Document Name field the following:

Exercise on document summaries

Fill in as many fields as you wish, then press F7 to exit back to the 'Document to be saved' prompt, and enter SUMMARY.EX as the name of this file.
3　Now press F5 to list the files and choose Long Display from the menu (see Figure 4.13). You will see the filenames listed on the right of the screen, with any document names (from summaries) listed at the left. Notice that Long Display sorts the list by document name rather than filename. Move the highlight bar to the SUMMARY.EX file that you've just

```
25-03-93  00:56p              Directory C:\WP51\BOOK\CHAP4\*.*
Document size:        0  Free: 62,234,624 Used:      77,289    Files:        6
Descriptive Name              Type    Filename      Size     Revision Date

Current Directory                         .          <DIR>
Parent Directory                          ..         <DIR>
Chap1 - Add in ARRIVALS       Ex      TOPICS  .EX    10,975   25-03-93 00:49p
Chap2 - Parallel Cols         Ex      PROSP2  .EX     7,700   25-03-93 00:50p
Chap4 - Document Summary      Ex      SUMMARY .EX    15,665   25-03-93 00:54p
Chap4 - Fig 4.1, font/graphic Fig     FIG4-1  .      29,809   25-03-93 00:51p
Chap4 - Page Breaks           Ex      W&O     .EX     5,800   25-03-93 00:56p
Chap4 - Page Nos, H&Fs        Ex      BROCHUR2.EX     7,252   25-03-93 00:52p

1 Retrieve; 2 Delete; 3 Move/Rename; 4 Print; 5 Short/Long Display;
6 Look; 7 Other Directory; 8 Copy; 9 Find; N Name Search: 6
```

**Figure 4.13**　List, in Long Display

created, and select Look from the menu to see the document summary information. Your screen should look like Figure 4.14. You may wish to try the Name Search feature in the List menu, which now searches for the document name instead of the filename.

Notice that Long Display takes longer than the ordinary short display the list of files. You may find this is a price worth paying for the extra information that it gives you.

4 While still in the SUMMARY.EX file, practise inserting footnotes. Place the cursor at the end of the first heading 'TOPICS TO BE INSERTED IN SKERN REPORT'. Insert a footnote here by pressing Ctrl-F7, Footnote, Create Footnote. At the Footnote screen, type 'This file is used in Chapter 1'. Notice the '1' in your text when you exit back to the document. Check the View Document screen to see how the page now looks. Also have a look at the footnote code in the Reveal Codes screen.

5 Now move the cursor to the end of the next heading ('SKERN LODGE ACTIVITIES'), and repeat the above steps to create the footnote 'This file is used in Chapter 4'. Remember to view the document to check how the footnote looks on the page.

6 If you don't like the way the footnotes are displayed, experiment with changing the footnote options – press Ctrl-F7, Footnote,

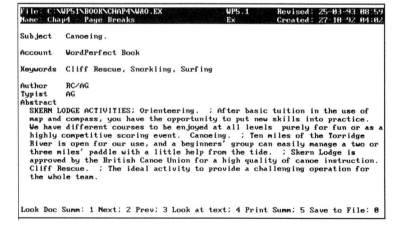

**Figure 4.14** The document summary displayed by Look

Options. Make sure the cursor is on the first footnote code so that the option code will be inserted in front of it; otherwise this code will not be affected by your changes.

Exit SUMMARY.EX, saving the changes. Now retrieve your BROCHUR2.EX file, and carry out the following exercises:

1   Insert a hard page break at the beginning of the heading 'SAMPLE ADULT WEEKEND PROGRAMME', making sure that the cursor is at the start of the relevant codes. This is now a two-page document.
2   Insert page numbering in the bottom centre position, in the following style: Page i.
3   Insert a header — Course Brochure — as follows:

    ● right-aligned on odd pages;
    ● left-aligned on even pages;
    ● small size font, italics, and emboldened.

    You now have a great many format codes at the beginning of the document. If the header codes occur before the [L/R Mar] code, the header text will extend into the default margin space. (You can see if this is happening by viewing the document.) Why is this?
    In this case, delete all the header codes and restore them after the [L/R Mar] code, using the F1 (Cancel) key.
4   Suppress the header on the first page.
5   Print or view the document to see the effects of all this work.
6   Exit and save SUMMARY.EX.

Now retrieve from the course disk the file W&O.EX. This is a two-page document. Observe the position of the page break between pages 1 and 2, then practise the following:

1   Insert widow and orphan protection at the beginning of the document, and observe its effect.
2   Delete the [W/O On] code that you've just inserted and use the conditional end-of-page command to force the 'Windsurfing' heading over to the next page and keep it with the first two lines of the paragraph.
3   Print or view the document to see the effects of your changes.
4   Change your system to default to widow and orphan protection.

## 4.15 Further exercise: the Advance feature

One of the more sophisticated and complex uses of the Advance feature is in setting up masterfiles which are then retrieved and saved under a new name for printing to pre-printed forms.

1 To try this out for yourself you will first have to print some empty forms. Retrieve the file called FORM.EX from the course disk; it contains the memo form shown in Figure 4.7. Print several copies – these will be the pre-printed forms that you will be using in this exercise.

2 Now retrieve another file called MASTER.EX. This is an incomplete masterfile for use with the memo form. You have to finish the job by adding the appropriate commands for the last two fields – 'From' and 'Ref'. The file will be displayed on the screen as a number of comment boxes, with the cursor beneath the first box.

If you look at the Reveal Codes screen, you will see that the codes needed for each field are:

- Comment (obtained by pressing Ctrl-F5).
- Advance to Line (obtained by pressing Shift-F8).
- Advance to Position (obtained by pressing Shift-F8).
- Hard Return (obtained by pressing Enter).

3 Measure the vertical and horizontal positions on the memo form of the last two fields. Then move the cursor to the end of the master document (below the codes for 'Date'), and insert in each field the above codes, with suitable comments and measurements. These codes must be entered in the order listed above.

4 Save and exit the MASTER.EX file.

Now retrieve this master document and use it for creating a memo. First, though, save it as MEMO.EX to protect the master-file from changes.

1 First, enter data in each field. After entering an item, move to the next field by pressing the down arrow key.

2 Now have a look at the View Document screen. You should

see that your data has been entered at different vertical and horizontal positions on the page.

3   Next try printing the memo. You must first load one of the memo forms you printed at the start of this exercise into the printer, then print your new document to it.

# 5
# Correcting the prospectus

## 5.1 What you will achieve in this chapter

WordPerfect provides a wide range of editing tools, and this chapter concentrates on some of the most important. When you have completed it, you should be able to use these tools to:

- Correct your text by checking for typing and spelling errors.
- Improve your text by replacing particular words with synonyms.
- Search for text and/or codes, and optionally delete them or replace them with other text/codes.
- Move, copy, and delete blocks of text.
- Apply commands restrictively to blocks of text.
- Display two documents on the screen simultaneously.

The skills you will learn will help you use WordPerfect in an effective and efficient way to make textual corrections and improvements to your documents.

## 5.2 Routines you will use in this chapter

As you work through this chapter, you will be getting to grips with the following routines. The Keystroke Guide section number for each routine is given below in brackets.

- Use WordPerfect's spell check (56).
- Use the thesaurus (65).
- Use the Search feature to look for text and/or codes (52).
- Use the Replace feature to search for and replace text and/or codes (47).

- Use the Replace feature to search for and remove text and/or codes (47).
- Select a block of text using the Block key and perform on it the operations of saving, printing, searching, and spell checking (2).
- Use the Block key to move, copy, delete, or append a block of text (2).
- Use the Block key to move, copy, delete, or append a tabulated column (2).
- Use the Move key to move, copy, or delete a block of text (34).
- Use the Screen key to split the screen in two in order to display two documents simultaneously (57).

## 5.3   Editing tools

Composing a document is a very creative process. First you have to organize your thoughts; then you have to express your thoughts on paper (or on the computer screen) in words that will hold the reader's attention and impart understanding. Then comes the more routine editing bit: checking for spelling and typing errors; thinking up alternative words to add variety or greater meaning; reorganizing the document by moving whole sections of text from one place to another; and so on.

This is where word processors come into their own. Not only do they eliminate all those crossings out and messy alterations that plague handwritten documents, they provide a range of facilities to automate the editing task. This automation brings two main benefits:

- They improve the productivity of secretaries and other word processor users, so that business costs are reduced.
- They cut out or reduce the boring parts of the job, so that the work is more interesting, and staff learn a greater range of skills.

The productivity improvements can be enormous, up to 200% in certain situations. It does not take much imagination to see how a word processor can increase greatly output in some offices. One example is the solicitor's office, with legal documents largely made up of standard paragraphs. In this case it's merely a matter of storing the paragraphs under suitable names or numbers on disk, and inserting them as required in any documents that have to be produced. In other offices it may require more insight and imagination to make maximum use of the automation possibilities that are inherent in word processors.

This chapter will introduce you to some of the possibilities, and help you apply them to your work. One of the more rewarding aspects of using a word processor is thinking up new ways in which it can make your life easier.

## 5.4 Spell checking

One of the tools provided by a word processor is automatic spell checking, to locate and correct typing or spelling errors. Spell checking makes finding and correcting words so easy that you may find it more efficient to ignore any typing errors that you make while keying in a document. Each time you stop to correct a typo, you have to break into your work sequence, cursor back to the start of the error, delete the offending characters, retype, and then pick up from the point at which you left off. This is very inefficient, and compares badly with letting the word processor locate errors and assist in correcting them.

When you invoke the spell check function, the word processor compares the words in your document with a dictionary of words stored on disk, and stops at each word that it does not find in its dictionary. It then displays a list of similar words from the dictionary. You can then choose a word from those on offer or, if the word you want is not on the list, make a manual correction.

Of course, place names, people's names, and specialized technical words, will not appear in the dictionary, so the word processor will stop at these even though you have typed them correctly. In this case you have the option of adding the word to the dictionary so that the word processor will recognize and pass over it in the future.

WordPerfect's dictionary file is called WP{WP}UK.LEX. The 'UK' part of the name indicates that it is a (UK) English dictionary.

```
Check: 1 Word; 2 Page; 3 Document; 4 New Sup. Dictionary; 5 Look Up; 6 Count: 8
```

**Figure 5.1** The first spell check menu

(If you do any foreign language writing, you can acquire a foreign language dictionary from your WordPerfect dealer.) Any words that you add to the dictionary are stored in a supplementary dictionary file named WP{WP}UK.SUP. WordPerfect creates this file the first time you add a word to the dictionary. If you wish, you can look at and edit this file just like any other WordPerfect document file.

The procedure to apply spell checking in WordPerfect is as follows:

1   Position the cursor on the word or page you wish to check. If you are checking the entire document, it doesn't matter where the cursor is.
2   Press Ctrl-F2 (Spell check). The menu shown in Figure 5.1 appears. As you can see, the first three options allow you to check just the current word, or the current page, or the entire document. The other options are described below.
3   Choose 1, 2, or 3 to carry out the spell check. If WordPerfect does not find a word you have typed in its dictionary, it will search the dictionary for similar words and list them on the screen, together with a second spell check menu. An example of a list with this menu is shown in Figure 5.2. Note that each word in the list is referenced by an identifying letter.
4   Either replace your word with one from this list (by pressing

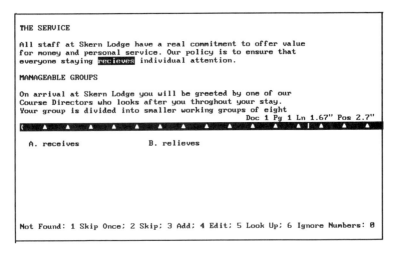

**Figure 5.2**   Second spell check menu with list of alternative words

the identifying letter for your chosen word in the list), or select an option from the menu at the foot of the screen. This allows you to skip the word, add the word to the supplementary dictionary, edit the word manually, plus a couple of other options. For details of this menu, see Section 56 of the Keystroke Guide.

5   When the spell check is finished, WordPerfect displays a word count of the section of your text (the page or the document) that it has spell checked, and returns you to the (first) spell check menu.

## 5.5   Thesaurus

Similar to the spell check tool is the thesaurus. Use this if you are working on a document in which you are repeatedly using the same word, or if you feel a word you have chosen is not the most appropriate. It enables you to vary your style or adopt a more appropriate vocabulary by presenting you with a list of synonyms. It also provides a list of antonyms (words with the opposite meaning). Like the spell check facility, a word you choose from the list automatically replaces your existing word in the document.

To use the thesaurus, move the cursor to the word you wish to replace and then:

1   Press Alt-F1 (Thesaurus). If WordPerfect finds the word in its thesaurus file, it lists alternative words together with a menu, as shown in Figure 5.3. As with the spell check, each word is referenced by an identifying letter. (If WordPerfect cannot find your word in the thesaurus, it displays the message 'Word not found' followed by the prompt 'Word:'. You can enter an alternative word at this prompt if you wish, in which case WordPerfect will repeat its search of the thesaurus.)

2   Select Replace Word if you wish to replace your word by one from the list. Otherwise press Exit (F1 or F7) to exit the thesaurus without replacing.

3   If you have chosen Replace Word, press the identifying letter of word of your choice. If the word you want is in the second column, press the right arrow key first to move the identifying letters to that column.

Note that the list of alternative words shown at the thesaurus

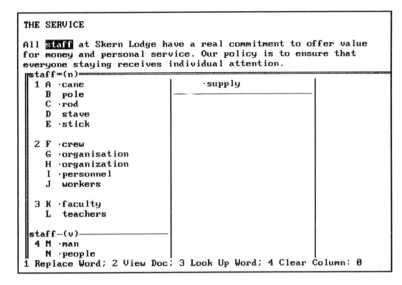

```
THE SERVICE

All ▓staff▓ at Skern Lodge have a real commitment to offer value
for money and personal service. Our policy is to ensure that
everyone staying receives individual attention.
staff=(n)
   1 A ·cane                        ·supply
     B  pole
     C ·rod
     D  stave
     E ·stick

   2 F ·crew
     G ·organisation
     H ·organization
     I ·personnel
     J  workers

   3 K ·faculty
     L  teachers
staff-(v)
   4 M ·man
     N ·people
1 Replace Word; 2 View Doc; 3 Look Up Word; 4 Clear Column: 0
```

**Figure 5.3**   Thesaurus menu

menu is grouped into nouns, verbs, adjectives and antonyms.
The words at the head of each group (called *headwords*) and the
words within each group marked with bullets, can also be looked
up in the thesaurus by pressing the identifying letter.

## 5.6   Searching and replacing

Suppose you have just typed a long document and wish to go
instantly to the point at which you typed 'self-catering'. Or suppose
you have used the words 'Skern Lodge' on a number of occasions
and want to replace them with 'SKERN LODGE'. This kind of
task is no problem for WordPerfect.

Search and replace tools can make a big contribution to your
productivity, if you consciously plan your work with their use in
mind. Here's one example to illustrate what we mean. In writing
this book, we are repeatedly using the word 'WordPerfect'. It
may be a great name for a product, but it's a pain to type. The
solution? Type 'wp' instead, and then have WordPerfect carry
out an automatic replacement at the end. Searching and replacing
can be carried out for any *string* of characters. By 'string' we
mean a collection of consecutive characters such as one or more
words, a part of a word, or even codes such as underlining,
margins and line spacing. (So you can use this facility to replace

automatically one code by another throughout your document.)

The F2 key is used for this task. Press F2 by itself for forward searching, Shift-F2 for backward searching, and Alt-F2 for search and replace.

To search from your current cursor position:

1 Press F2 to search forwards, or Shift-F2 to search backwards.
2 Enter the search string. If you want to search for a whole word rather than a string within a word, put a space before and after the string.
3 Press F2 again to carry out the search. WordPerfect finds the first occurrence of the string and positions the cursor on it.
4 If you wish to repeat the search to find the next occurrence, press F2 again twice (or Shift-F2 twice in the case of a backward search).

To replace one string by another:

1 Press Alt-F2.
2 At the 'w/Confirm? No (Yes)' message that appears on the status line, type 'Y' if you want the opportunity to confirm or reject each individual replacement; or press 'N' (or any other key) if you want to accept the default of no confirmation (i.e. automatic replacement throughout the document).
3 Press the up arrow key if you want to search backwards from the current cursor position (otherwise WordPerfect will search forwards).
4 Type the search string.
5 Press F2.
6 Type the replacement string.
7 Press F2.

Note the following features of search and replace:

● You can restrict your replacements to a block of text by first selecting the block (using the Block key Alt-F4, or by dragging over the block with the mouse), then pressing the Replace key. (See Exercise 5 below. Use of the Block key is covered in detail in the next sections.)
● If you do not enter anything as the replacement string, then WordPerfect will replace the string with nothing, i.e. it will delete it.
● To return to your original cursor position after carrying out a

search or replacement, press Ctrl-Home (the Goto key) twice.

● If you enter lower case letters in your search string, WordPerfect will match (i.e. search for) either lower case or upper case. However, it will match upper case characters only with upper case. For example, if you enter 'The', it will find 'The' or 'THE' but not 'the'.

## 5.7 The exercise: correcting your prospectus

The features described above can be usefully applied to your prospectus file – PROSP2.EX – so retrieve it now. Save the file, replacing the previous version, after you successfully complete each part of the exercise:

1 There are some spelling errors in the prospectus, so use the Ctrl-F2 key to correct the spelling of the whole document. The spell check will highlight the name 'Skern'; since you are repeatedly using this name, you should add it to your secondary dictionary file.

2 After the spell check, list the directory holding the WordPerfect program files (on the F5 key). Search for and look at the file called WP{WP}UK.SUP (this is the secondary dictionary file); you should see the word 'Skern' in it.

3 Use the thesaurus to find an alternative for the word 'staff' in the first paragraph. From the list that appears, look up the word 'personnel'. You should now have two lists of words, with the identifying letters on the second column containing the 'personnel' synonyms. In order to widen the choice of possible alternatives, look up one of these – 'crew'; the identifying letters move over to the third column. Press the down arrow key to scroll down all the words in this list.

  Having surveyed the various possibilities, you decide to replace the word 'staff' with 'personnel'. So use the left arrow key to move the identifying letters to the appropriate column, and choose this word.

4 Use the Replace key (Alt-F2) to change all instances of 'Skern Lodge' to italicized text. The main heading is already in italics, so start the replacement with the cursor below this heading. This will allow you to choose automatic replacement, since the search will proceed forwards from your cursor position

and thus exclude the heading. Your search string is 'Skern Lodge'; your replacement string should look like this: [ITALC]Skern Lodge[italc]. However, don't type these codes, but enter them using the Font key (Ctrl-F8).

5   The bulleted points in 'Specialist Groups' contain tabbed text, i.e. after each bullet there is a [Tab] code. They would look better if indented, so use the Replace key to search for [Tab] and replace with [->Indent]. (Again, don't type these codes but enter them by pressing the appropriate function key.) If the [Tab] code has not been used elsewhere in the file, you can select Replace without confirmation. If [Tab] has been used elsewhere, you should first select the bulleted text with the Block key (Alt-F4).

## 5.8   Block operations

Block operations allow you to carry out major reorganizations of your text, such as moving material from one place to another, or deleting large blocks of text. They also allow you to carry out tasks such as saving standard paragraphs to disk for incorporation in other documents, or applying features such as spell checking to a selected block.

You learned to use WordPerfect's Block feature in Chapter 3, where you selected blocks of text to enhance with, e.g. italics or some other font. In this chapter we are more concerned with using the Block feature to reorganize text. This can involve moving a block from one place to another, copying a block, deleting a block, and so on.

When you manipulate a block by moving or copying it, the block is stored in the computer's memory, and then 'retrieved' or 'pasted' into the new location.

The basic procedure is described in Section 2 of the 'Keystroke Guide', and involves the following steps:

1   Select the block, either by dragging over it with the mouse or pressing the Block key Alt-F4 (or F12) and highlighting it with the arrow keys.

2   Press the function key that carries out the required block operation, or alternatively press the right mouse button to select from a menu of choices. WordPerfect applies the operation to the block, then deselects the block. (To deselect the

block without carrying out an operation on it, simply press the
F1 Cancel key anywhere in the document, or press the left
mouse button.)

3   If you wish to reselect the block for a further block operation,
press Alt-F4 again, then press Ctrl-Home twice.

At step 2 you could apply any of the following operations:

- Save the block to a file — press F10 (Save) and enter a file-
name.
- Print the block — press Shift-F7 (Print).
- Spell check the block — press Ctrl-F2.
- Delete the block — press the Delete key.
- Move, copy, or append the block — press Ctrl-F4 (Move),
and make suitable menu choices (see next section).
- Apply various enhancements, e.g. on the Ctrl-F8 key, as
described in Chapter 3.

We describe some of the more complex block operations in the
next sections. First, a hint on how you can speed up block
marking:

- Having pressed the Block key, simply press the key that
denotes the end of the block. For example, press Enter to
extend the block to the next hard return (i.e. the end of the
current paragraph), or the full stop to extend it to the next
full stop, etc.
- You can also use the F2 Search key to extend the block to a
string of two or three characters lying at the end of the block.
- You can press the Ctrl-F4 Move key (described below) instead
of Alt-F4 to mark quickly an entire sentence, paragraph, or
page for moving, copying, deleting or appending. The first
menu that appears asks which selection (sentence, paragraph
or page) you want.

## 5.9   Moving, copying, deleting, and appending blocks

The operations of deleting or moving a block can be carried out
using the Delete key:

- *Delete* the block — press the Delete key at step 2 above.
- *Move* the block — delete the block, then move to the point in

the document where you want the block moved, and press the F1 Cancel key.

A general set of block operations (delete, move, copy, and append) is available on the Ctrl-F4 Move key. The procedure is:

1  Select the block, then press Ctrl-F4. If the required block is a complete sentence, paragraph or page, then there's no need to select the block before pressing Ctrl-F4.
2  Choose from the menu whether to apply the operation to the whole block of text (by pressing 1) or some other option such as tabular column – normally you will choose 1. Tabular columns are dealt with below.
3  Choose from a further menu whether to move, copy or delete the block, or append it to the end of another file stored on disk.
4  Move the cursor to the point in the document where you want the block moved or copied, or in the case of an append operation type the target document's name. Then press Enter.

Note that you can move or copy a block from one document to another. The procedure is:

1  Retrieve both documents, one in the Doc 1 screen and the second in the Doc 2 screen.
2  Carry out steps 1 to 3 above in the document containing the block to be moved or copied.
3  At step 4, press Shift-F3 (Switch) to switch to the second document window, then move to the required position in that document and press Enter.

You could also move a block between one document and another by pressing the Delete key instead of Ctrl-F4, and using the Restore key (F1,1) at the required position in the second document.

## 5.10  Moving and copying tabulated columns

In Chapter 2, you used WordPerfect's facilities for creating tables using tabs. You can use the Block key to rearrange the columns of this table. It is important to note, though, that this operation will only work if there is just one tab code in front of each line of the column you wish to edit. This means that you can't edit the first column in this way (as it has no tabs preceding it), nor can you edit a column with more than one tab code in front of it.

The procedure involves the following steps:

1   Using the Block key, mark the column to be moved. The block should start at the first character of the column, and end immediately after the last character, as shown in Figure 5.4.
2   Press the Ctrl-F4 Move key and choose Tabular Column. Your screen should look like Figure 5.5.
3   Either choose Move or Copy, then move the cursor to the new location and press Enter; or choose Delete to delete the column; or choose Append to append the column to the end of a file on disk.

## 5.11    Creating a window

We described on page 85 how to move or copy a block of text from one document to another. The procedure involves retrieving both documents, one into the Doc 1 screen, the other into Doc 2. To perform this kind of operation it's helpful to be able to see both documents at the same time on the screen, and WordPerfect's split screen facility (shown in Figure 5.6) allows you to do just this. As you can see, the screen is split into two 'windows'.

There are many uses for this feature. For example:

```
              PROGRAMME FOR PERIOD APRIL-JUNE

  COURSE            DATE          INCOME     NUMBER OF
                                             GUESTS

  Under 10s         2-5 April     2,100        14
  Managers          5-10 May      1,350         9
  Young Adults      20-27 June    2,250        15
```

```
  Block on                          Doc 1 Pg 1 Ln 2.17" Pos 4.7"
```

**Figure 5.4**   First stage of highlighting a column to be moved

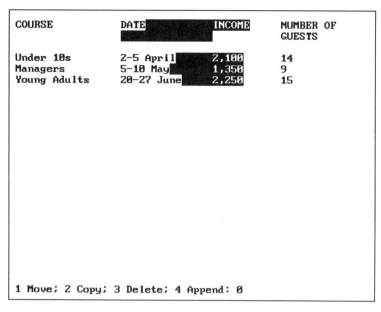

**Figure 5.5** Second stage of highlighting a column to be moved

- Extracting information from a document on disk to insert into the current document.
- Referring to your outline notes in one document while composing a report in another.

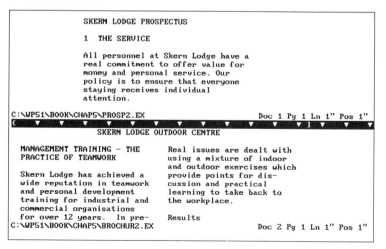

**Figure 5.6** Split screen

- Making notes as they occur to you while working on a document.
- Referring to earlier pages of a document while continuing to work on the same document (you can display the same document in both windows).
- Copying text and codes from one document to another.

The maximum number of lines available on the screen for the text of a document is 24. When you create a window, this is reduced to 22, as you have two status lines instead of one, and one line is occupied by the tab ruler line positioned where the screen is split between the two documents.

You can apportion this total as you wish between the two windows, when you open the window. The procedure is described in Section 57 of the Keystroke Guide, and involves pressing the Ctrl-F3 Screen key, choosing Window, and entering the number of lines you want for your current window (i.e. the Doc 1 window if you are in Doc 1, or the Doc 2 window if you are in Doc 2). If you wish to alter the size later, press Ctrl-F3 again and repeat the procedure, or enter 24 lines if you wish to return to a single window display.

## 5.12   The exercise: block operations

In the exercises on page 82 you corrected your PROSP2.EX file. The exercises below ask you to make further changes to this file. When you have completed them, you should save the revised file, replacing the previous version.

1   Use the Block and Move keys (Alt-F4/F12 and Ctrl-F4) to copy the first heading and paragraph ('THE SERVICE'). Start with the cursor on the first character, i.e. 'T', then press the Block key and select forwards with the down arrow key until the cursor is at the beginning of the next paragraph. (Alternatively drag over the block with the mouse.) Your block will be highlighted, and should include the two [HRt] codes at the end of the selected paragraph, as shown in Figure 5.7.

   Press the Move key, select Block, and then Copy. Move the cursor to the beginning of 'SAFETY FIRST', and press Enter. WordPerfect should retrieve the block from its memory and paste it at this point.

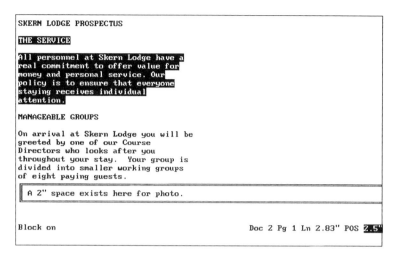

**Figure 5.7** Text highlighted, using the Block key

Use the Block and Move keys again to move this copied paragraph down one section so that it is retrieved above 'OUR TRANSPORT'. Finally use the Block and Delete keys to delete the copied paragraph.

2 Now try moving a single paragraph to a different position. In the 'Safety First' text, move the first paragraph below the second paragraph. Since the block you have to select is a whole paragraph, which function key can you use instead of Block which automatically selects the whole paragraph for you? Press this key, then choose 'Paragraph' and 'Move'. To move this paragraph so that it appears above the next heading ('OUR TRANSPORT'), place the cursor on the 'O' and press Enter. Note that WordPerfect has included the [ITALC] code at the beginning of the blocked text.

3 Sometimes you will need the Reveal Codes screen displayed so that you can include codes as well as text in your block.

The 'MANAGEABLE GROUPS' text is the second section and has to be moved below the third section (the 'SAFETY FIRST' text). However, the photograph has to be inserted immediately below the 'MANAGEABLE GROUPS' text and therefore the [Adv] and [Comment] codes must be moved as well.

Press the Reveal Codes key before you start and then use the Block and Move keys first to select the text *and* codes up to the beginning of the next paragraph ('SAFETY FIRST'). In the upper part of the screen you should see the text and the comment box highlighted. Now move the cursor to the next location for the text you have cut out ('OUR TRANSPORT') and press Enter. The 'MANAGEABLE GROUPS' text should be retrieved at this position with the space and the comment box below. Change the section numbering to compensate for this change in sequence.

4  Select the seventh and eighth sections with the Block key, and then use the Print key to print the highlighted text.

## 5.13  Further exercises: spell check and thesaurus

These exercises require you to amend your BROCHUR2.EX file. You should save this file, replacing the previous version, when you have completed them.

1  Retrieve your BROCHUR2.EX file and carry out a spell check on it.
2  Use Search (F2) to find each occurrence of the word 'team', then use the thesaurus to replace one of them by a suitable alternative.

## 5.14  Further exercises: block operations and creating a window

These exercises ask you to carry out a number of tasks on *your* PROSP2.EX file and your SUMMARY.EX file. You should *not* save the changes you make to these documents.

### PROSP2.EX

1  Block the text headed 'ARRIVALS' and save it as a new file called ARRIVALS.EX, using the F10 key. Then retrieve it into another of your files, using the Retrieve key.
2  Block the same text ('ARRIVALS') and append it to your SUMMARY.EX file. Use the F5 key to list your files and then use the Look option to view the contents of the SUMMARY.EX file; at the end of the document you should see the 'ARRIVALS' text.

WordPerfect does not always format text correctly in the Look option, but if you subsequently retrieve the SUMMARY.EX file the formatting will be correct. Since there was only one [HRt] code at the end of the file, you will need to insert one more to separate the appended text from the paragraph above.

If you get into the habit of pressing Enter twice to insert two [HRt] codes at the end of every file, you will always be able to append, move or copy extra paragraphs to this position without editing the line spaces.

Exit the SUMMARY.EX file without saving.

3 To copy text from one file to another, have PROSP2.EX retrieved in Doc 1 and BROCHUR2.EX retrieved in Doc 2. Before starting the copy operation, however, you are going to create a window so that both documents are displayed simultaneously, so proceed as follows:

a With the cursor in Doc 1, press Ctrl-F3 (Screen).
b Select Window. The prompt 'Number of lines in this window: 24' appears.
c Type '11' and press Enter.

You should then see on the screen 11 lines of PROSP2.EX in Doc 1 and 10 lines of BROCHUR2.EX in Doc 2. The Switch key moves the cursor between each document.

You are now going to copy the 'Outdoor Training' text from Doc 2 (BROCHUR2.EX) to Doc 1 (PROSP2.EX), so make sure the cursor is in Doc 2. Place the cursor at the beginning of the heading 'Outdoor Training', which is underlined. To match the headings in Doc 1 we wish to omit the underlining, so place the cursor *after* the [UND] code. Use the Block and Move keys to select the two paragraphs on 'Outdoor Training' as a block to copy.

WordPerfect then prompts you to move the cursor and press Enter to retrieve. Switch to Doc 1 (PROSP2.EX), move the cursor to 'GENERAL INFORMATION' and press Enter. The 'Outdoor Training' block should be copied in at this point. Note that WordPerfect formats the copied block according to the format of the current document; i.e. although in the original document the text was in newspaper columns, it is copied into the destination document using that document's format.

Note that by omitting the first [UND] code from your

selected block, WordPerfect automatically omits the second [und] code.

Now that you have completed your block operation, you want to close the window and return to a full screen display. To do this, proceed as follows:

a   With the cursor in Doc 1, press the Screen key.
b   Select Window.
c   Type '24'. You no longer have a split screen, but the two files are still retrieved in Doc 1 and Doc 2.

You wish to exit the Doc 2 file – BROCHUR2.EX – so switch to the Doc 2 screen and exit in the normal way. When you are prompted to exit Doc 2, type 'Y' for Yes and you will automatically be switched to Doc 1, leaving the Doc 2 screen empty.

4   In an earlier exercise, you used Replace to search for the text 'Skern Lodge' and replace it with italicized text. This replacement was confined to body text and did not change 'Skern Lodge' in the header text.

Look up WordPerfect's Help on Replace (F3, Alt-F2) and note how to extend your replacement to headers. Use this information to get 'Skern Lodge' in the header text changed to italics. The cursor will have to be at the beginning of the document in front of any codes before you start this operation – press Home, Home, Home, up arrow key to move to this position.

## SUMMARY.EX

5   For more block practice, retrieve SUMMARY.EX. This document has a number of paragraphs under headings such as 'Orienteering', 'Canoeing', 'Cliff Rescue', etc. Rearrange the text with the headings in alphabetical order, using the Block and Move keys.

6   Postpone the retrieval of a block by pressing Cancel (F1) instead of Enter. Then, with the cursor where the block should be retrieved, press Move and select Retrieve and Block.

7   Insert an [→Indent] code in front of each of the topic items at the beginning of this document as follows:

a   Place the cursor on the line *above* the first topic.
b   Use the Block key to select forwards to the end of the line containing the last topic.

```
            PROGRAMME FOR PERIOD APRIL-JUNE

COURSE              DATE          INCOME      NUMBER OF
                                              GUESTS

Under 10s           2-5 April     2,100       14
Managers            5-10 May      1,350       9
Young Adults        20-27 June    2,250       15
```

**Figure 5.8**  COLMOVE.EX

c Press the Replace key and type 'N' for automatic replacement.

d Press the Enter key to make [HRt] your search string, and press F2.

e Press the Enter key and the Indent key (F4) to make [HRt][→Indent] your replacement string, then press F2.

You should have restricted this indented effect to just your blocked text.

8 Use the Block key to select part of a page of this document, and do a limited spell check on it.

9 Practise moving a tabulated column in the file called COLMOVE.EX (see Figure 5.8). This file has four tabulated columns, and the exercise is to move the third column into fourth place. Retrieve COLMOVE.EX and reveal the codes to check that there is a single [Tab] code preceding each entry in the third column − 'INCOME'. Then proceed as follows:

a Place the cursor on the 'I' of 'INCOME'.

b Press the Block key.

c Highlight the whole column by pressing the down arrow key. The screen should look like Figure 5.4.

d Press 2 or T for Tabular Column. The screen should now look like Figure 5.5.

e Press 1 or M for Move.

f Move the cursor to the end of the line containing the column headings, i.e. after 'NUMBER OF', and press Enter. The 'INCOME' column should be copied.

# 6
# Tabulating and calculating business data

## 6.1   What you will achieve in this chapter

Many word processed documents include tables of numerical data, including totals and other calculated numbers. This chapter explores how WordPerfect can help you set up these tables and perform the calculations. When you have completed it, you should be able to:

- Create a table of figures, with the data formatted into rows and columns.
- Calculate totals down the columns and across the rows.
- Use formulas to carry out more complex table calculations.
- Insert quick decimal tabs.
- Change the alignment character.
- Import a spreadsheet file.
- Create a link to a spreadsheet file.

## 6.2   Routines you will use in this chapter

As you work through this chapter, you will be getting to grips with the following routines. The Keystroke Guide section number for each routine is given below in brackets.

- Use WordPerfect's Maths feature to calculate subtotals (31).
- Use the Maths Definition feature for formulas (31).
- Create and edit a table (63).
- Use the Maths feature in a table (63).
- Use Tab Align for quick decimal tabs (61).
- Change the decimal align character from a full stop to any keyboard character (61).

- Import all or part of a spreadsheet file (58).
- Create a link to a spreadsheet file for updating information (58).

## 6.3 Tables and calculations

It might seem strange to have a chapter on tabulating and calculating data in a book on word processing. To carry out this kind of task on a computer we normally use a spreadsheet package such as Lotus 1−2−3, Microsoft's Excel, or Borland's Quattro Pro. If you want to do any complicated calculations, you must indeed use packages such as these. However, many calculations on tables of figures are very simple, typically subtotals, totals and grand totals. And it's surprising how often you want to include such tables in a word processed document. So it makes sense to include simple calculating facilities in a package such as WordPerfect. And if you do want to incorporate more ambitious tables produced on a spreadsheet in a document, WordPerfect provides facilities for this too.

Skern Lodge, the outdoor activity centre we have been using as our example business, is typical. It generates data on all its various business transactions, and needs to include some of this data in word processed reports.

An important part of Skern Lodge's work is providing meals. In fact, it operates a large wholesale bakery business, supplying not just its own catering establishment but other businesses as well. In this chapter we'll be using WordPerfect to tabulate and analyse some of the data produced by this bakery business, such as its monthly sales of various products, the commission it pays to its salesmen, and its gross profits. A simple table showing its monthly sales figures for pastries is shown in Figure 6.1.

Before the days of computers and word processors, it was quite a job to produce by typewriter a large table of data. The typewriter's tab key allowed you to align entries easily, but you could not use the machine to calculate data, and if you decided later that you wanted to adjust the width of the columns, or reorder the columns, then you would have to start all over again. WordPerfect takes things like this in its stride.

**SKERN LODGE BAKERIES**

| Product | January | February |
|---|---|---|
| Apple Pie | 344.25 | 487.65 |
| Treacle Tart | 657.00 | (500.02) |
| Linzertorte | 783.15 | 657.75 |
| Blackberry Pie | 299.65 | 105.22 |
| | | |
| TOTAL | £2,084.05 | £750.60 |

**Figure 6.1**   Skern Lodge Bakery – pastry sales

## 6.4   Designing tables

The point about tables is they allow you to present data in a very clear way. Imagine trying to describe and present the bakery sales figures as ordinary paragraphs of text. So it's clarity you should aim for when thinking about presenting data of this sort.

First, if your table has a time component (such as months of the year), then these should run horizontally. The different products in the case of a sales table will normally be shown vertically. The table in Figure 6.1 is typical in this respect. Partly this is convention, partly it makes for a more sensible display of any subtotals and totals (i.e. they are calculated vertically downwards).

If you have a large table, with subtotals produced at various points as well as overall totals, it may make your table easier to comprehend if the totals are highlighted in some way, perhaps by the use of emboldening, or perhaps by the use of lines as shown in Figure 6.1. The eye is then drawn to these more important figures and away from the mass of more trivial detailed figures. In the case of large figures it also helps to draw lines between the rows and columns, as shown in some of the tables later in this chapter. WordPerfect's Table feature will do this automatically for you.

You may also need to think about the way in which you organize your column and row headings. A table showing the sales of all Skern Lodge Bakery's products might split them under the headings of bread, pastries, gateaux, etc., with the individual products listing under the appropriate heading, with subtotals for each heading. Column headings should also be logically arranged. If calculations are being performed, the headings should normally reflect the order of the calculations. For an example, see Figure 6.4.

Don't forget that your table should have a suitable heading, in a suitable font, and that it should located at a suitable position. Typically you will want to centre it on the page, but there is no reason why it should not be incorporated within a parallel column, for example, if you are producing that kind of document. Any notes on the table should be located immediately below it, perhaps in a smaller font.

You may want to make comparisons across a set of numbers in your table. For example, you may want to show how the total sales are growing (or declining) from month to month, or you may want to compare the sales of the different types of product (pastries, bread, etc.). Comparisons of this sort are best achieved using charts and graphs, and you may wish to include one or more of these in your document. In this case, it may be best to create the table in a spreadsheet package, and then have that package produce the chart for you. Both the table and the chart can then be imported into your WordPerfect document. We look at importing a spreadsheet table later in this chapter, and importing graphics such as charts are covered in Chapter 10.

If you are comparing sales across a number of months, a graph is best. This should show each monthly figure as a point plotted on the graph, and it should join these points by lines. Your spreadsheet package will look after these details for you. If you are comparing the sales of different products, then a bar chart or a pie chart is probably most appropriate. Most spreadsheet packages provide a generous range of charting options, and most produce files that can be imported into WordPerfect.

## 6.5   Simple Maths

All of WordPerfect's table and calculation features depend upon *columns* of figures, such as those shown in Figure 6.1. This table shows the sales of pastries during the months of January and February. (We have repeated this figure on the next page.)

In this table, the sales figures were entered first, then special operators were typed where the totals are required at the foot of the table, and then WordPerfect's Maths feature was used to convert the operators to the results shown.

**SKERN LODGE BAKERIES**

| Product | January | February |
|---|---|---|
| Apple Pie | 344.25 | 487.65 |
| Treacle Tart | 657.00 | (500.02) |
| Linzertorte | 783.15 | 657.75 |
| Blackberry Pie | 299.65 | 105.22 |
| | | |
| TOTAL | £2,084.05 | £750.60 |

**Figure 6.1** Skern Lodge Bakery — pastry sales

To create columns containing calculations, such as columns 2 and 3 in this table, you must precede every column entry by a tab. (Do not attempt to set up columns by pressing the spacebar to create the spaces between columns. In the first place, the figures may not line up when you print with a proportional font, and in the second place WordPerfect's Maths feature will not work.)

The procedure to create a table incorporating calculations is as follows.

1  Set tabs for your table, using the Shift-F8 Format key. This is explained in Chapter 2, and in Section 62 of the Keystroke Guide. Clearly the default tab positions (at half-inch intervals) will not be appropriate for most tables. Note that if your figures include decimals, then the tab position should be set where you want to locate the decimal point. If your figures are not decimal, set the tab stops immediately after the last digit in each column.

2  Press the Alt-F7 Columns/Table key, and choose Maths. The Maths menu appears, as shown in Figure 6.2. Then choose On. 'Maths On' has the following effects:

```
Maths: 1 On; 2 Off; 3 Define; 4 Calculate: 0
```

**Figure 6.2**  The Maths menu

**SKERN LODGE BAKERIES**

| Product | January | February |
|---|---|---|
| Apple Pie | 344.25 | 487.65 |
| Treacle Tart | 657.00 | (500.02) |
| Linzertorte | 783.15 | 657.75 |
| Blackberry Pie | 299.65 | 105.22 |
| | | |
| TOTAL | + | + |

**Figure 6.3** The operators used in the Bakery table

- It converts your tab settings to decimal. This means that the numbers will line up properly, either on the decimal point or, in the case of non-decimals, on the final digit.
- It allows you to insert special characters in your table to calculate subtotals, totals and other amounts.
- It inserts a [Maths On] code in your document, and the word 'Maths' appears on the message line at the foot of the screen.

3  Type your table. This could be a single column of figures, each one tabbed (i.e. with a [Tab] code preceding it).

4  Enter special characters, called *operators*, where you want calculations performed. The main operators are as follows:

+,  which adds up the numbers listed above it, to produce a subtotal;

=,  which adds up the subtotals above it (ignoring other numbers), to produce a total;

*,  which adds up the totals above it, to produce a grand total.

Other operators are t, T, and N. See Section 31 of the Keystroke Guide for details on these. Figure 6.3 shows the subtotal operator that was inserted in the Skern Lodge Bakery table in Figure 6.1.

5  When you want WordPerfect to perform the calculations, i.e. to insert results where you have typed the operators, press Alt-F7 again and choose Maths Calculate. Note that the

**SKERN LODGE BAKERIES**

| Product | January | February | Commission | Net Total |
|---|---|---|---|---|
| Apple Pie | 344.25 | 487.65 | 83.19 | 748.71 |
| Treacle Tart | 657.00 | (500.02) | 15.70 | 141.28 |
| Linzertorte | 783.15 | 657.75 | 144.09 | 1,296.81 |
| Blackberry Pie | 299.65 | 105.22 | 40.49 | 364.38 |
| | | | | |
| TOTAL | £2,084.05 | £750.60 | £283.47 | £2,551.18 |

**Figure 6.4**  Further Maths example

operators will still be displayed on the editing screen, to the immediate right of the results, but they will not print. If you alter any of the numbers in your table later on, simply choose Maths Calculate again to recalculate the results.

6   When you have finished typing your table, insert a [Maths Off] code below it by using the Alt-F7 key again and choosing Maths Off.

Note that any column headings used in your table should precede the [Maths On] code. Otherwise, any ts, Ts, or Ns in those headings will be treated by WordPerfect as operators and will not print.

```
┌─────────────────────────────────────────────────────────────────┐
│ Maths Definition        Use arrow keys to position cursor        │
│                                                                   │
│ Columns                 A B C D E F G H I J K L M N O P Q R S T U V W X │
│                                                                   │
│ Type                    2 2 0 0 2 2 2 2 2 2 2 2 2 2 2 2 2 2 2 2 2 2 2 2 │
│                                                                   │
│ Negative Numbers        ( ( ( ( ( ( ( ( ( ( ( ( ( ( ( ( ( ( ( ( ( ( ( ( │
│                                                                   │
│ Number of Places to     2 2 2 2 2 2 2 2 2 2 2 2 2 2 2 2 2 2 2 2 2 2 2 2 │
│   the Right (0-4)                                                 │
│                                                                   │
│ Calculation    1    C   .10*(A+B)                                │
│   Formulas     2    D   A+B-C                                     │
│                3                                                  │
│                4                                                  │
│                                                                   │
│ Type of Column:                                                   │
│     0 = Calculation    1 = Text    2 = Numeric    3 = Total       │
│                                                                   │
│ Negative Numbers                                                  │
│     ( = Parentheses (50.00)        - = Minus Sign  -50.00         │
│                                                                   │
│                                                                   │
│ Press Exit when done                                              │
└─────────────────────────────────────────────────────────────────┘
```

**Figure 6.5**  The Maths Definition screen, with the entries needed for Figure 6.4

## 6.6 Defined Maths

Figure 6.4 shows the Skern Lodge Bakeries data with two additional columns at the right. All the figures in these additional columns are calculated. In this case, the calculations are carried out horizontally across the columns rather than vertically downwards. The column headed 'Commission' contains figures calculated as 10% of the total sales for January and February. The Net Total column is the January column plus the February column minus the Commission column.

To perform this type of calculation in a WordPerfect table, you have to carry out a further step in addition to those outlined above, involving specifying the formulas. You do this on the Maths Definition screen. The important point to note is that the [Maths Def] code that is inserted in your document must be before the [Maths On] code. (It can be anywhere before; however, it is best to group similar codes together in case you wish to delete or move them later, so put it immediately before.) It's most convenient to carry out this additional step immediately after setting tabs in step 1 in the last section. If you do it later, make sure that the cursor is in front of the [Maths On] code.

Then:

• Press the Alt-F7 Columns/Table key, then choose Maths Define.

The Maths Definition screen appears (see Figure 6.5). You have to amend this by specifying which columns of your table are to contain formulas (enter a '0' in the 'Type' row, under the appropriate column, as shown in Figure 6.5), and you have to enter the appropriate calculation formulas. The formulas needed to produce the table in Figure 6.4 are shown in Figure 6.5.

```
SKERN LODGE BAKERIES
```

| Product | January | February | Commission | Net Total |
|---|---|---|---|---|
| Apple Pie | 344.25 | 487.65 | ! | ! |
| Treacle Tart | 657.00 | (500.02) | ! | ! |
| Linzertorte | 783.15 | 657.75 | ! | ! |
| Blackberry Pie | 299.65 | 105.22 | ! | ! |
| TOTAL | + | + | + | + |

**Figure 6.6** A Maths example (screen display)

For more detail on making entries on the Maths Definition screen, see Section 31 of the Keystroke Guide.

Having completed this additional step, you can then select Maths On from the Maths menu, and continue with steps 2 to 5 described in the last section. To create the calculated columns in the table, simply tab from column to column. WordPerfect will display a '!' at any point where a formula exists, as shown in Figure 6.6. This symbol behaves rather like the '+' used in simple maths: when you choose Calculate from the Maths menu, the results are worked out and inserted in the table.

## 6.7   The exercise: the monthly sales figures

Skern Lodge needs to produce a financial statement of income from the sale of pastries during the months of January and February. To achieve this, produce the table shown in Figure 6.1. The operator that you need to enter to produce the totals is shown in Figure 6.3.

You should be able to create this table from the information given in the 'Simple Maths' section of this chapter without any further guidance from us. However, to help you we have included the detailed steps below, though we suggest you only refer to these steps if you get stuck. The file that you create should be called MATHS1.EX.

1   Create a new document called MATHS1.EX, and change left and right margins to 0.5″. This document is going to contain the table shown in Figure 6.1.

2   Delete all existing tab stops, and insert new ones starting at 2.7″ and repeating every 1.4″. Remember that the 2.7 is relative to the left margin and not an absolute position. Remember also that you can easily set evenly spaced tabs (see Keystroke Guide, Section 62). This operation sets the tab positions for the decimal points in the two numeric columns.

3   Type the main heading.

4   Type the subheading 'Product' but leave the other two column headings until you have typed the column data.

5   Press Enter twice and turn on the Maths feature. 'Maths' will appear in the status line.

6   Type the rest of the table up to but not including the TOTAL line.

7   Type in the word 'TOTAL' and tab across to each of the two columns, typing in the + symbol in each.
8   Finish off with some more underlining under each total.
9   Use the maths key to calculate, and your document should look like that in Figure 6.3.
10  You can now type in the two missing subheadings, using the spacebar to move across the line.
11  Save the file, replacing MATHS1.EX.

If you look at your document on the View screen, you will see that the + operator does not print.

*Further exercises on this file*
Do not save any of the following:

1   Try changing some of the figures and then recalculate.
2   Insert some more figures below the TOTAL line and use the + operator for another subtotal. You can now put in the = operator below each subtotal to get WordPerfect to add the subtotals.
3   You can practise using the t, T and N operators by typing in the letters followed by numbers in a line above the = operator line. When you view the document, you will not see the letter operators.

## 6.8   The exercise: calculating the commission and net totals

Skern Lodge wishes to extend its financial statement to include the commission paid to its salesmen and the net total. For this, you should produce the table shown in Figure 6.4. Again, you should be able to complete this exercise without any further assistance from us, using the information in the section headed 'Defined Maths' earlier in this chapter. The entries that you will need to make on the Maths Definition screen are shown in Figure 6.5. The file that you create should be called MATHS2.EX.

Again, we include the detailed steps below, in case you get stuck. To get the maximum benefit from this exercise, try to do it without referring to these steps.

1   Retrieve MATHS1.EX and save as MATHS2.EX. You can

keep the current margins for this document, and the tab settings are already in place for two more columns. You can confirm this by revealing the codes and looking at the tab triangles on the separation bar between the two parts of the screen.

2   With the Codes screen still revealed, look for the [Maths On] code and place the cursor *on* the code.

3   Select Maths Def from the maths menu. This will display the Maths Definition menu as shown in Figure 6.5.

4   The columns for January and February are columns A and B. Move the cursor across to column C which will contain the commission data, and type '0' to make this a calculation column. Enter the formula:

.10*(A + B)

for this column and press Enter.

5   The cursor moves back up to the column line to column D. This will be the net total column so press '0' again and enter the formula:

A + B − C

and press Enter.

6   You can now exit the Maths Definition. Back at the document, the Maths menu is displayed in the status line. Since you already have a [Maths On] code in the document, simply exit from the menu. (You can now see in the Codes screen a [Maths Def] code preceding the [Maths On] code.)

7   Move the cursor down to the first line of figures and press the End key. Tab across to each of the last two columns. Word-Perfect inserts a ! in each column. Use the down arrow key to move down to each of the remaining lines and repeat the tabbing.

8   In the TOTAL line, use the Backspace key to delete the ! symbol and type instead the + symbol. Your document should look like Figure 6.6.

9   Select Calculate from the Maths menu. Save the document, replacing the previous version.

Again if you look at your document at the View screen, you will see that the operators do not print.

## 6.9   Tab Align

When you pressed the Tab key to move from column to column in the above exercises, you may have noticed that the status line displayed the message 'Align char =.'. This '.' indicates a decimal point, and the message appears because your tabs have become decimal tabs. Text typed before the alignment character (the '.') is right-aligned, and text typed after the alignment character is left-aligned. In the Reveal Codes screen, a [Dec Tab] code is inserted in the document each time the Tab key is pressed.

As was said earlier, turning Maths 'On' automatically makes your tabs decimal tabs. If you are not using this Maths feature, you can change your tab settings to decimals using the Shift-F8 Format key. However, if you want a quick decimal tab without doing any of these things, then simply press the Ctrl-F6 Tab Align key instead of Tab. So to enter a column of decimal numbers without using Maths or without changing the tab settings, use Ctrl-F6 to tab the column entries.

You can also use this Tab Align key to align text at characters such as a colon or a dash, or indeed any keyboard character. To do this, you must change the alignment character from a '.' to the

```
            To: Roger Carter
          From: Ann Gautier
          Date: 24 March 1993
           Ref: WordPerfect Book
```

**Figure 6.7**   Tab Align example

# MEMORANDUM

```
    To:

  From:

  Date:

   Ref:
```

**Figure 6.8**   Memo form

one you want, by pressing Shift-F8 (Format), 4, 3 (see Section 61 of the Keystroke Guide). In the example shown in Figure 6.7, the alignment character has been changed to a colon, forcing the memo labels to right-align and the fields to left-align.

Note that changing the alignment character using Shift-F8 will only affect the current document. To change the default alignment character for all future documents, use the Shift-F1 Setup key (Section 53 of the Keystroke Guide).

## 6.10   Further exercise: Tab Align

1   Create a simple memo form using the Font key for a variety of text size and appearance. An example is shown in Figure 6.8. The alignment character here is a colon, so you will need to change from a full stop to a colon using the Format key. This will insert a [Decml/Algn Char::,,] code in your document.

Save the document, calling it MYMEMO1.EX. This file is your master memo file.

2   Retrieve MYMEMO1.EX and save it as MYMEMO2.EX. You are going to send to the Skern Lodge accountant a memo

**MEMORANDUM**

     **To:** Skern Lodge Accountant

   **From:** Ann Gautier

   **Date:** 24 March 1993

    **Ref:** Sales Figures


Here is the sales data you requested on four of our bakery products.


**SKERN LODGE BAKERIES**

| Product | January | February | Commission | Net Total |
|---|---|---|---|---|
| Apple Pie | 344.25 | 487.65 | 83.19 | 748.71 |
| Treacle Tart | 657.00 | (500.02) | 15.70 | 141.28 |
| Linzertorte | 783.15 | 657.75 | 144.09 | 1,296.81 |
| Blackberry Pie | 299.65 | 105.22 | 40.49 | 364.38 |
| | | | | |
| TOTAL | £2,084.05 | £750.60 | £283.47 | £2,551.18 |

**Figure 6.9**   MYMEMO2.EX

which contains the sales figures for certain bakery items (i.e.
the information contained in the MATHS2.EX file).

3 Enter your own data in each of the memo fields. Figure 6.9
shows our example of this memo. Then, with the cursor
several lines below the last field, press the Retrieve key to
retrieve MATHS2.EX.

4 Look at the View Document screen and you will find that the
columns of figures do not format correctly. Why is this? To
achieve the correct format, place the cursor below the memo
labels and use the Format key to change the alignment character
from a colon to a full stop.

5 You can finish off the document by deleting the [L/R
Mar:0.5,0.5] code from the maths part of the document and
restoring it (with F1,1) at the top of the memo.

## 6.11 Table

Skern Lodge needs to produce regular course schedules such as
that shown in Figure 6.10. The Table feature, which we describe
now, is ideal for this purpose, as it allows you to create a master
schedule which is blank. This can then be retrieved each time a
schedule is needed, and saved under a new name.

Up to this point we have been using tabs to create tables of
numbers. However, WordPerfect's Table feature also does this
and more besides. Its advantages are:

● You do not have to change your tab settings.

| COURSE | DATE | NUMBER OF GUESTS |
|---|---|---|
| Handicapped Group | 2-5 April | 14 |
| Management Development | 5-10 May | 9 |
| Young Adults | 20-27 June | 15 |

**Figure 6.10** Tabulated data created with the Table feature

- Maths is automatically provided.
- If your table spans several pages, this feature ensures that the page breaks occur at convenient points, and it allows you to assign rows to be automatic headers on each page.
- Most of the table codes cannot be deleted, which eases subsequent editing of the table. (This is explained in the next section.)
- You can use this feature to create business forms, such as invoices and order forms, or the master schedule described below.

However, the Table feature does have a couple of disadvantages:

- You cannot break a table row entry at the foot of the page. Instead, WordPerfect shifts the whole row forwards to the next page. This can result in unsightly gaps at the foot of a page.
- You can't have ordinary document text flowing around a table (so that the table is set within text at the left and/or right). If you need a table to appear within some text at the left and/or right, insert it in a graphics box, as explained in Chapter 10.

When created, a table consists of (horizontal) rows and (vertical) columns. Like a spreadsheet, the rows are labelled numerically and the columns alphabetically. This creates boxes or *cells* in which you type your data. When the cursor is located on a cell, an extra item appears in the status line identifying the cell. For example, 'Cell C4' indicates that the cursor is in the third column from the left (C) and the fourth row from the top (4).

## 6.12  Creating a table

To create a table, press the Alt-F7 Columns/Table key, then choose Table Create. WordPerfect prompts you for the number of columns in your table (the default is 3). You can enter up to 32. WordPerfect then prompts you for the number of rows (the default is 1). You can enter up to 32,765. You then see the empty table on the screen with the Table Edit menu below, as shown in Figure 6.11.

You may have noticed that so far you have not had to enter the

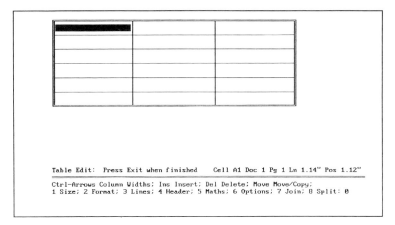

Table Edit:  Press Exit when finished    Cell A1 Doc 1 Pg 1 Ln 1.14" Pos 1.12"

Ctrl-Arrows Column Widths; Ins Insert; Del Delete; Move Move/Copy;
1 Size; 2 Format; 3 Lines; 4 Header; 5 Maths; 6 Options; 7 Join; 8 Split: 0

**Figure 6.11**   An empty table with the Table Edit menu

column widths. WordPerfect has in fact calculated what they should be by dividing the space between the left and right margins by the number of columns. However, you can set these and other aspects of your table's format by choosing Format from the Table Edit menu (Section 63 of the Keystroke Guide). We cover the Table Edit menu in the next section.

To make some entries in your table (text or numbers), you must exit the Table Edit menu for the ordinary editing screen (by pressing F7 or Alt-F7). (You can restore the Table Edit menu by pressing Alt-F7 again.)

Back at the editing screen, you can turn on Reveal Codes to examine the table codes that have been inserted in your document. The codes for Figure 6.11 are shown in Figure 6.12. They consist of:

- A definition code at the beginning which contains the table number as a Roman numeral, how many columns there are and the width of each column.
- [Row] codes for each row.
- [Cell] codes for each column.
- A [Tbl Off] code at the end.

Most of these codes cannot be deleted, which means that the table text is easy to edit − there's no chance of deleting invisible codes in error. The only deletable table code is the first one which sets up the table. If you delete this, the table changes to

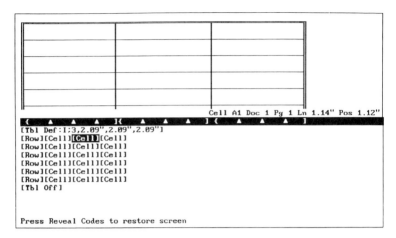

**Figure 6.12**   Empty table with the codes revealed

tabulated text, with each [Row] code converting to a [HRt], and each [Cell] code converting to a [Tab].

## 6.13   Entering text in the table

Pressing Tab moves the cursor right from cell to cell, Shift-Tab moves left, and the arrow keys can be used to move up and down. For other cursor movement keys, see Section 63 of the Keystroke Guide. If you need to enter a tab in a cell, press Home, Tab.

To enter text or numbers in a cell, simply type them in the usual way at the editing screen. If the amount of text you type in a cell exceeds the cell width, WordPerfect adds another line to the cell by increasing its height. Pressing Enter will have the same effect. You can use all your normal text formatting keys, such as emboldening or centring, and these will insert the usual codes in your document. However, the Table feature provides these features as well as additional formatting options at the Table Edit menu. These enhance your text but without inserting codes that can be deleted in error.

## 6.14    Editing a table

By 'editing a table' we mean changing its format. To do this, make sure your cursor is located somewhere on the table and press the Alt-F7 Table key. (If your cursor is off the table, you will have to press Alt-F7 then choose Table Edit.)

The Table Edit menu provides the following options. For details on how to use these options, see Section 63 of the Keystroke Guide.

1    *Size*. This enables you to add more rows or columns at the bottom/right of the table, or to delete rows or columns.
2    *Format*. This option allows you to change the format of a cell or its contents. Features such as bold and underlining are included, as well as adjusting the column width and row height.
3    *Lines*. This allows you to change the style of the border lines and also to add shading to cells.
4    *Header*. If your table is longer than one page, you can specify which row(s) can be used as headers on subsequent pages.
5    *Math*. This is an easy-to-use version of the ordinary Maths feature described earlier.
6    *Options*. These include changing the spacing between the text within cells and the lines bordering the cells; displaying negative results within parentheses; changing the horizontal position of the table on the page; and adjusting the degree of shading of cells.
7    *Join*. This allows you to join cells.
8    *Split*. This allows you to split cells.

In addition to these menu choices, there are short-cut keys as indicated in the line above the numbered menu on the Table Edit screen (i.e. one line up from the bottom − see Figure 6.11). For example, using the Ctrl key with the left or right arrow keys changes the width of the current column. The other keys shown there allow you to insert, delete and move/copy columns or rows.

Note the following additional operations that you can carry out on tables:

● To remove the table but not the text within it, remove the [Tbl Def] code at the start of the table. The [Cell] codes are converted to [Tab] codes, and the [Row] codes are converted to [HRt].

- To remove some or all of the text but keep the table, use the Block key to mark the text and then delete. Make sure you exclude the [Tbl Def] code from the block.
- To convert existing tabulated columns (created by pressing the Tab key) to table format, use the Block key to mark the columns, then press the Alt-F7 Columns/Table key, then choose Create, Tabular Column.

## 6.15   The exercise: creating a table

Create the table shown in Figure 6.10. When you've done this, extend the table so that it looks like Figure 6.13. Save the finished table as TABLE.EX.

In case you need help with the details, such as inserting the extra thick line below the header row, the steps are explained below. Note that step 2 onwards assume that you are at the Table Edit menu.

1   After typing the table entries shown in Figure 6.10, insert the heading shown in Figure 6.13 above it. To do this, locate the Table Definition code, place the cursor on the code, and press Enter twice. In the space you have created above the table, type the centred heading 'PROGRAMME FOR PERIOD APRIL–JUNE'.

PROGRAMME FOR PERIOD APRIL-JUNE

| COURSE | DATE | NUMBER OF GUESTS | INCOME |
|--------|------|------------------|--------|
| Under 10s Group | 2-5 April | 14 | 2,100 |
| Management Development | 5-10 May | 9 | 1,350 |
| Young Adults | 20-27 June | 15 | 2,250 |
| TOTAL | | 38 | 5,700 |

**Figure 6.13**   Extended table

2  Reduce the width of each column (at the Table Edit menu) so that it matches the example in Figure 6.10. You will notice that in doing so, the table width reduces from the right and is no longer centred on the page. Look at the View Document screen to confirm this.

3  In order to get the table centred horizontally on the page, choose Options and change the position to centre.

4  Change the alignment of the last column to centre. Place the cursor in the last column and choose Format, Column, Justify, Centre.

5  Change the alignment of the header row to centre. Block the whole row and follow the instructions in 4 above, except that you choose Cell instead of Column.

6  Change the header text from normal to emboldened. Block the row again, and choose Format, Cell, Attributes, Appearance, Bold.

7  Change the background of the header row to shaded by blocking the row and choosing Lines, Shade. You will have to view the document to see the effect of this.

8  Use the Lines option again to change the bottom line of the header row to extra thick. Don't forget to block the row first.

Your document should now look very similar to the one in Figure 6.10. Now edit it so that it looks like the table in Figure 6.13. The instructions for this are as follows; as before, they assume you have the Table Edit menu on your screen.

9  First of all, add an extra column to the end of your table: from the Table Edit menu, choose Size, Columns, and enter the total number of columns you want.

10  Now insert an extra row, again choosing Size then Row.

11  Type in the heading 'INCOME' and view the document. You will see that the format attributes of the previous column have been copied over to the new column, i.e. the header text is emboldened and centred, the cell background is shaded, and the bottom line is extra thick. Type the word 'TOTAL' in the bottom row but do not type either the income figures or the totals.

12  Again with the Table Edit menu displayed, we can use the Table Maths feature to insert a formula for calculating the income. Each guest pays £150 for his course, so with the cursor in the first income cell (D2) select Maths and insert the formula:

C2*150

This tells WordPerfect to multiply the contents of C2 by 150. You should then copy this formula down the column for the other courses.

13  Still using the Maths feature, insert the + operator in the TOTAL row for the last two columns.

14  Now use the Maths Calculate command. You will see the results inserted to 2 decimal places. Since you want whole numbers in the current table, block the last two columns and select Format, Column, Number Digits. Enter '0' to give you no decimal places. You will have to use the Maths Calculate command again to get WordPerfect to reformat the figures.

15  Block the bottom row and change the line attributes as shown in Figure 6.13.

## 6.16   Further exercises

Carry out the following exercises on your table. Do not save the results. Again, these exercises assume you are at the Table Edit menu.

1  Try forcing a new page. With the cursor in the Young Adults cell, press Ctrl-Enter. The table now flows over to a second page. In this case, it's a good idea to specify header rows so that they automatically repeat at the top of all table pages. With the cursor anywhere on the table, choose Header from the menu and type 1 to have the first table row specified as the header row. To see the effect of this, move the cursor to page 2 and view the document.

2  Try transposing the Course and Date columns. With the cursor in the Course column press the Move key (Ctrl-F4) and choose Column, Move. Move the cursor to the Date column and press Enter. The two columns should be transposed (and you would then need to edit the lines of the table). Try moving the two columns back as they were.

3  Practise joining and splitting rows and columns.

4  If you have an enhanced keyboard, try inserting an extra row without using the Table Edit menu by pressing Ctrl-Insert. The extra row is inserted at the cursor position. Also try deleting a row by pressing Ctrl-Delete.

Now try converting tabulated columns to a table:

1 Retrieve your TABS.EX document. This contains columns of tabulated text, with one [Tab] code between each column.
2 Use the Block key to select all the columns, including the column headings.
3 Press Alt-F7, then 2 (Tables), then 1 (Create), then 1 (Tabular Column).

WordPerfect carries out the conversion, inserting horizontal and vertical lines. You may find that you have an extra blank row after the headings row. You can delete this at the Table Edit menu, or, if you have an enhanced keyboard, by pressing Ctrl-Delete.

## 6.17   Spreadsheets

Spreadsheet software allows you to create tables of data incorporating powerful formulas and functions. With them, you can handle complex statistical calculations, keep financial accounts and manage many other business, scientific and engineering applications. However, spreadsheet programs do not provide much in the way of word processing capabilities, and it is useful therefore to be able to import spreadsheet files into WordPerfect, and sometimes to create links between the imported spreadsheet and the original file, in order to keep the data up to date.

This means that you can use the power of the spreadsheet program for calculations, and then use WordPerfect to incorporate the information within a larger document and to print it in an attractive form. You can also import spreadsheet graphs using WordPerfect's graphics feature. We describe this feature in Chapter 10.

WordPerfect can import spreadsheet files produced on any of the following spreadsheet programs:

Lotus 1−2−3 Version 2
Excel Version 2
Quattro
Quattro Pro
Symphony
PlanPerfect

It can also be used with any other spreadsheet software that is able to create spreadsheet files in the standard WK1 format used by Lotus 1−2−3 Version 2. This includes, for example, Lotus 1−2−3 Version 3. Check the Help screen on this feature for the spreadsheets WordPerfect can handle.

Note the following points:

- WordPerfect can import a spreadsheet file in either tabulated text or table format. Importing in tabulated text format can display up to 20 columns in a row; importing in table format can display up to 32 columns. To fit the spreadsheet onto a page, you may have to adjust the margins of your document, or even use the Table Edit menu to reduce the number of columns.
- There are two ways to bring in a spreadsheet file into Word-Perfect. You can retrieve it as you would a normal Word-Perfect text file, but entering the full pathname where the file is located. In this case WordPerfect automatically places it in a table. Alternatively you can import a spreadsheet into an existing (possibly empty) WordPerfect document. This is dealt with in the next section.

## 6.18   Import or link a spreadsheet

You can use the Import/Link feature to import all or part of a spreadsheet file, either as tabulated text or in table form, into an existing WordPerfect document. You can also use it to create a link to the original file for future updating.

The procedure is as follows.

1   Locate the cursor at the point in your document where you want the spreadsheet located, and press the Ctrl-F5 Text In/ Out key.

2   Press 5 for Spreadsheet, then 1 (Import) or 2 (Create Link). The Import menu appears, shown in Figure 6.14.

3   Choose Filename from this menu and enter the name of the spreadsheet file (this should be the full pathname if it is not in the default WordPerfect directory). WordPerfect enters the entire range of cells occupied by the spreadsheet in the Range option on the menu. If you wish to import only part of the spreadsheet, choose Range and enter the actual range of cells

```
Spreadsheet: Import

    1 - Filename

    2 - Range

    3 - Type                    Table

    4 - Perform Import








Selection: 0
```

**Figure 6.14** Spreadsheet Import menu

that you require. If the spreadsheet file contains named ranges,
you can display these using the List key (F5), and then select
one (by moving the cursor to it) for importing.

4 · Choose Type if you want to change the import type to tabulated
text form, then choose Perform Import (or Link).

If you have chosen Link rather than Import, WordPerfect will
insert a comment box above the spreadsheet containing the full
pathname of the spreadsheet file, and a second comment box
below the spreadsheet marking the end of the link. You then
have the choice of automatic updating of the spreadsheet data
each time you retrieve the WordPerfect file, or manual updating.
   For more information on importing or linking spreadsheets,
see Section 58 of the Keystroke Guide.

## 6.19   Exercise: retrieving a spreadsheet file

Before carrying out this exercise you will need to have a spreadsheet file stored on disk. This should be in a format that Word-

Perfect is able to import, e.g. the .WK1 format used by Lotus 1−2−3 V.2.

1  Retrieve the spreadsheet file, typing in the full pathname.
2  If necessary adjust the margins of the page to accommodate the spreadsheet.

## 6.20  Further exercise

1  Try importing a spreadsheet file using the Ctrl-F5 Text In/Out key, and create a link to the original file. Save this as SPREAD.EX.
2  Run your spreadsheet program, and alter some of the data in the original spreadsheet file, saving the result (under the same filename).
3  Retrieve SPREAD.EX into WordPerfect, and use the Text In/Out key to update the file.

# 7
# Merging and sorting

## 7.1 What you will achieve in this chapter

Many offices wish to use their word processor to merge data such
as names and addresses with a standard document in order to
carry out mass mailings and similar tasks with the minimum
effort. They may want to sort the name and address list into
alphabetical order, or to sort the paragraphs in a document. This
chapter shows you how to use WordPerfect for these tasks. When
you have completed it, you should be able to:

- Carry out mass mailing tasks, including producing mailing
  labels.
- Produce merge documents for regular use, allowing variables
  to be entered from the keyboard.
- Sort lists and paragraphs into alphabetical or numerical order.

## 7.2 Routines you will use in this chapter

As you work through this chapter, you will be getting to grips
with the following routines. The Keystroke Guide section number
for each routine is given below in brackets.

- Use WordPerfect's Merge commands to create a primary file
  (32).
- Use the Merge commands to create a secondary file (32).
- Name the fields in the secondary file (32).
- Change Setup to turn off the display of Merge commands
  (53).
- Complete the merge to the screen, and print (32).

- Complete the merge direct to the printer (32).
- Format the merged document by inserting formatting codes in the Initial Codes screen (32).
- Print the data in a secondary file (32).
- Produce mailing labels (32).
- Add a label form to WordPerfect's list of paper sizes and types (32).
- Create a merge document where the variables are entered from the keyboard (32).
- Sort lists, paragraphs, tabulated rows, and merge data into alphabetical or numerical order (54).

## 7.3 Merging

A word processor such as WordPerfect is much more than an efficient replacement for a typewriter. It allows you to perform business tasks that are completely impossible with a typewriter. One of the most valuable of these is merging a file containing, e.g. names and addresses with another document such as a standard letter.

Like so many scientific and engineering developments, this is open to misuse. We all suffer wastepaper baskets full of junk mail. However, the genuine benefits are considerable, and include mailing patients reminding them that a dental appointment is due, and mailing customers who haven't paid their bills.

An important use of merging for Skern Lodge is mailing potential customers with details of its activity holidays. Previous customers and enquiries from advertisements must all be mailed if Skern Lodge is to be successful in selling its holidays. It must also mail customers prior to their holidays to inform them of the arrangements that have been made on their behalf and to advise them on special clothing and other requirements. The exercises in this chapter are based on Skern Lodge's mailing requirements.

## 7.4 Merge files, records, and fields

Merging involves incorporating variable data — such as lists of names and addresses — with standard text held in a main document. Because the process is so often used to create documents for mailing, it is often called *mailmerge*.

The main document is called the *primary file*. It includes not only the text to be printed but also special *merge codes*, described in the next section, which tell WordPerfect where to insert the variable data. It also contains any document formatting codes. You can insert these in the normal way from the Format Line and Format Page menus (on Shift-F8), or you can insert them as initial codes. We deal with initial codes shortly.

The variable data are held in what's called the *secondary file*. Each name and address or other data items form a *record* in that file. The space occupied by a single item of data in a record, such as a name, is called a *field*. Note that:

- All the records in a secondary file must contain the same number of fields (though some of the fields in some records can be empty).
- Fields must be used in a consistent way across all the records. For example, if Field 3 in the first record contains a surname, then Field 3 in every other record in that file must contain a surname (or nothing at all).
- There is no limit to the number of fields you can use, or to the number of records that you can add to a file.

Having produced the primary and secondary documents, you are in a position to carry out the merge operation. When you do so, a new *merge document* is created consisting of many copies of the primary file with the merge codes replaced by the names, addresses and other items of data from each record in the secondary file. On printing this document, WordPerfect produces letters that look like they have been individually addressed and typed. Figure 7.1 illustrates the process.

## 7.5  The secondary file

We'll start with the secondary file containing the names, addresses and other variable data that you wish to include in the mailmerge. Of course, this can be a fairly general file containing data that are not only used in your current mailmerge task but also may be used in other mailmerges — such as producing mailing labels to stick on the envelopes containing the main merge document.

Creating the secondary file is like creating any other document in WordPerfect, except that you have to insert in it some special

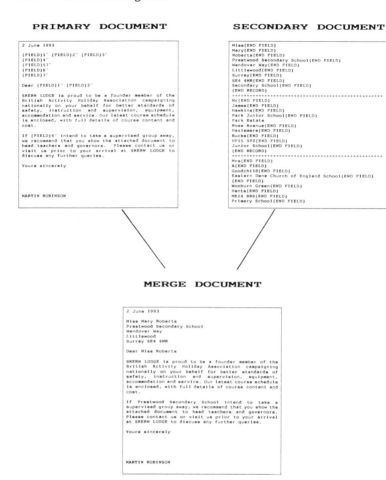

PRIMARY DOCUMENT

```
2 June 1993

(FIELD)1~ (FIELD)2~ (FIELD)3~
(FIELD)4~
(FIELD)5?~
(FIELD)6~
(FIELD)7~

Dear (FIELD)1~ (FIELD)3~

SKERN LODGE is proud to be a founder member of the
British Activity Holiday Association campaigning
nationally on your behalf for better standards of
safety, instruction and supervision, equipment,
accommodation and service. Our latest course schedule
is enclosed, with full details of course content and
cost.

If (FIELD)4~ intend to take a supervised group away,
we recommend that you show the attached document to
head teachers and governors. Please contact us or
visit us prior to your arrival at SKERN LODGE to
discuss any further queries.

Yours sincerely


MARTIN ROBINSON
```

SECONDARY DOCUMENT

```
Miss(END FIELD)
Mary(END FIELD)
Roberta(END FIELD)
Prestwood Secondary School(END FIELD)
Wendover Way(END FIELD)
Littlewood(END FIELD)
Surrey(END FIELD)
SE4 4MR(END FIELD)
Secondary School(END FIELD)
(END RECORD)
-------------------------------------------------
Mr(END FIELD)
James(END FIELD)
Hawkins(END FIELD)
Park Junior School(END FIELD)
Park Estate
Rose Avenue(END FIELD)
Haslemere(END FIELD)
Bucks(END FIELD)
HP15 9PZ(END FIELD)
Junior School(END FIELD)
(END RECORD)
-------------------------------------------------
Mrs(END FIELD)
A(END FIELD)
Goodchild(END FIELD)
Eastern Dene Church of England School(END FIELD)
(END FIELD)
Wooburn Green(END FIELD)
Hants(END FIELD)
ME24 8RS(END FIELD)
Primary School(END FIELD)
```

MERGE DOCUMENT

```
2 June 1993

Miss Mary Roberts
Prestwood Secondary School
Wendover Way
Littlewood
Surrey SE4 4MR

Dear Miss Roberts

SKERN LODGE is proud to be a founder member of the
British Activity Holiday Association campaigning
nationally on your behalf for better standards of
safety, instruction and supervision, equipment,
accommodation and service. Our latest course schedule
is enclosed, with full details of course content and
cost.

If Prestwood Secondary School intend to take a
supervised group away, we recommend that you show the
attached document to head teachers and governors.
Please contact us or visit us prior to your arrival
at SKERN LODGE to discuss any further queries.

Yours sincerely


MARTIN ROBINSON
```

**Figure 7.1**  The mailmerge process

merge command codes. These codes are not like normal Word-Perfect codes, which you can only see on the Reveal Codes screen. These appear as ordinary text on the editing screen, enclosed in curly brackets. Some of these codes are listed in Figure 7.2, which is a printout of the Merge Codes Help screen.

WordPerfect recognizes that these are not normal text for printing, and shows them in the normal code format (in square brackets) in Reveal Codes. As with other codes, you can't type these commands, you must insert them by pressing the appropriate function key. Although visible on the editing screen, these com-

```
Merge Codes
      FIELD: Inserts the contents of a specific field of the secondary file
             records into your merged document.  WordPerfect will prompt you
             for the field name.  The equivalent of ^F in WP 5.0.
  END RECORD: Marks the end of a secondary file record.  The equivalent of ^E in
             5.0.
      INPUT: Stops the merge and waits for keyboard input.  Terminate the
             input by pressing End Field (F9).  The equivalent of ^Omessage^O^C
             codes in 5.0.
   PAGE OFF: Instructs WordPerfect not to place Hard Pages after each primary
             file.  This takes the place of the ^N^P^P codes in 5.0.
 NEXT RECORD: Instructs WordPerfect to move to the next secondary file record
             during the merge.  The equivalent of ^N in 5.0.
       MORE: Where MORE displays a command access box for selecting the other
             merge code that aren't listed.  See the Reference Manual for
             details.

Note:  Secondary merge files created with previous versions of WordPerfect
require no conversion to be run with WordPerfect 5.1.  Primary merge files
created with WordPerfect 5.0 also require no conversion.

If a "Field:" message mistakenly remains on the screen after you have deleted a
merge code, you can erase the message by pressing Home, Home, Up.
Selection: 0                                        (Press ENTER to exit Help)
```

**Figure 7.2** WordPerfect's merge codes

mands will not appear on paper when you come to print your document.

Only two of these merge command codes are used in the secondary file: {END FIELD} and {END RECORD}. (The other codes are used in the primary file.)

- Each field in the secondary file must end with the {END FIELD} command. WordPerfect automatically inserts a hard return after this command.
- Each record in the secondary file must end with the {END RECORD} command, which must be on the line immediately below the last field in the record. WordPerfect inserts automatically a hard page break after this command.

Figure 7.3 shows a single record from an example secondary file. As you can see, this file contains five fields, three for the person's title, one for the address, and one for the postcode. In this file, why are the three components of the person's name separated into distinct fields, whereas the multiple lines of the address are grouped into a single field? Why not put the title and name in a single field, or why not break up the address into a street field, town field, county field, etc.? To make the right decisions on your field structure, you need to give some thought to what data you want to retrieve in the primary document(s) before creating the secondary file.

For example:

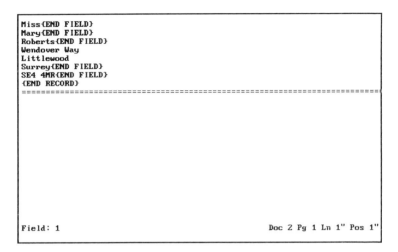

```
Miss{END FIELD}
Mary{END FIELD}
Roberts{END FIELD}
Wendover Way
Littlewood
Surrey{END FIELD}
SE4 4MR{END FIELD}
{END RECORD}
========================================================================


Field: 1                                        Doc 2 Pg 1 Ln 1" Pos 1"
```

**Figure 7.3**   Example secondary file record

- You may want to address a person formally by title and surname, or informally by forename. Both these are feasible if you use separate fields for each data item.
- You may want subsequently to sort your data file by postcode. This is easily done if the postcode is a separate field.

To be on the safe side, it might be best to create fields for each possible line of the address; however, this has the disadvantage of increasing the complexity of both the secondary file and the primary file. Figure 7.5 shows an address file with the addresses split into separate fields.

If you wish to sort the records in a secondary file, e.g. into alphabetical order, then WordPerfect's sorting feature, described later in this chapter, allows you to do this.

## 7.6   Creating a secondary file

To create the secondary file, follow the procedure described in Section 32 of the Keystroke Guide. After typing each field entry, press the F9 End Field key to insert the {END FIELD} command. You will note on the status line that WordPerfect keeps a track of the fields by numbering the first field '1', the second field '2', and so on.

To insert the {END RECORD} command at the end of each record, press the Shift-F9 Merge Codes key and choose End Record. Figure 7.4 shows the menu that appears when you press Merge Codes. Continue entering the data until your set of records is complete, then save the file in the usual way.

Note that the records in your secondary file may vary in the number of lines they contain. Addresses in particular are highly variable, some occupying only four lines, others occupying five or six. Figure 7.5 illustrates this, and it also illustrates what to do about these variations:

- If a record contains fewer lines than your basic record design, simply insert the {END FIELD} command by itself where a blank line occurs.
- If a record is exceptionally long, perhaps having more lines of address than other records, simply type in the extra lines without an {END FIELD} command.

You may find it easier to have WordPerfect refer to your fields by name rather than number. The status line will then prompt with the name rather than the number when you come to enter the data, so you are less likely to put an entry in the wrong field. Figure 7.6 shows a secondary document with named fields (listed at the top).

- To name your fields, press the Shift-F9 Merge Codes key, choose More, then choose Field Names from the list that appears.

## 7.7   The primary file

The primary file contains the main body of text for your document. It should also contain:

- merge codes telling WordPerfect where to merge (i.e. insert) the variable data from the secondary file,

---

1 Field; 2 End Record; 3 Input; 4 Page Off; 5 Next Record; 6 More: 0

---

**Figure 7.4**   The Merge Codes menu

```
Miss{END FIELD}
Mary{END FIELD}
Roberts{END FIELD}
Prestwood Secondary School{END FIELD}
Wendover Way{END FIELD}
Littlewood{END FIELD}
Surrey{END FIELD}
SE4 4MR{END FIELD}
Secondary School{END FIELD}
{END RECORD}
=======================================================
Mr{END FIELD}
James{END FIELD}
Hawkins{END FIELD}
Park Junior School{END FIELD}
Park Estate
Rose Avenue{END FIELD}
Hazlemere{END FIELD}
Bucks{END FIELD}
HP15 9PZ{END FIELD}
Junior School{END FIELD}
{END RECORD}
=======================================================
Mrs{END FIELD}
A{END FIELD}
Goodchild{END FIELD}
Eastern Dene Church of England School{END FIELD}
{END FIELD}
Wooburn Green{END FIELD}
Hants{END FIELD}
ME24 8RS{END FIELD}
Primary School{END FIELD}
{END RECORD}
=======================================================
```

**Figure 7.5**   Three records from a secondary document


- any formatting codes that are to be applied to the merged
  data.

Figure 7.7 shows an example of a primary document.

For detail on creating the primary document, see Section 32 of
the Keystroke Guide. Briefly, you type the text in the usual
way, but where you wish to merge variable data from the secondary
document you press the Shift-F9 Merge Codes key then choose
'Field' from the menu and enter the number of the field in the
secondary file. (In the secondary file shown in Figure 7.5 for
example, Field 1 is the title, Field 2 is the forename, and so on.
To check which number refers to which field, you could split the
screen, displaying the secondary file as Doc 1 and the primary file
as Doc 2.)

```
{FIELD NAMES}Title~Fname~Sname~School~Road~Town~County~Postcode~Type of
school~~{END RECORD}
===============================================================================
Miss{END FIELD}
Mary{END FIELD}
Roberts{END FIELD}
Prestwood Secondary School{END FIELD}
Wendover Way{END FIELD}
Littlewood{END FIELD}
Surrey{END FIELD}
SE4 4MR{END FIELD}
Secondary School{END FIELD}
{END RECORD}
===============================================================================
Mr{END FIELD}
James{END FIELD}
Hawkins{END FIELD}
Park Junior School{END FIELD}
Park Estate
Rose Avenue{END FIELD}
Hazlemere{END FIELD}
Bucks{END FIELD}
HP15 9PZ{END FIELD}
Junior School{END FIELD}
Field: Title                                      Doc 2 Pg 2 Ln 1" Pos 1"
```

**Figure 7.6**   Secondary document with named fields

```
6 April 1993

{FIELD}1~ {FIELD}2~ {FIELD}3~
{FIELD}4~
{FIELD}5?~
{FIELD}6~
{FIELD}7~

Dear {FIELD}1~ {FIELD}3~

SKERN LODGE is proud to be a founder member of the British
Activity Holiday Association campaigning nationally on your
behalf for better standards of safety, instruction and
supervision, equipment, accommodation and service. Our latest
course schedule is enclosed, with full details of course content
and cost.

If {FIELD}4~ intend to take a supervised group away, we recommend
that you show the attached document to head teachers and
governors.  Please contact us or visit us prior to your arrival
at SKERN LODGE to discuss any further queries.

Yours sincerely



MARTIN ROBINSON
```

**Figure 7.7**   A primary document

WordPerfect inserts the {FIELD} command at this point in your primary document, followed by the number of the field then a tilde (~). This is illustrated in Figure 7.7.

Note that if any of the records in your secondary document have blank fields, WordPerfect will insert a blank space for those fields when you come to perform the merge operation (described shortly). To tell WordPerfect not to insert this space, add a question mark after the relevant field number in the primary document (for example {FIELD}5?~).

When you have completed your primary document, save it in the normal way.

After you have completed your primary and secondary documents, you may prefer to turn off the merge commands display. This makes it easier to see how your document will print. You can turn off this display on the Shift-F1 Setup key (choose Display then Edit Screens, as explained in Section 53 of the Keystroke Guide).

## 7.8  Completing the merge

Having created and saved both the primary and secondary files, you are in a position to carry out the merge. Simply press the Ctrl-F9 Merge/Sort key, and enter the names of the primary file and the secondary file.

WordPerfect will carry out the merge, displaying on the screen the primary file merged with the last record in the secondary file. If you scroll up, you will see each of the previous records merged with the primary file and separated from each other by a hard page break. You can print this document in the normal way by pressing the Shift-F7 Print key. Or you could if you wish save it to print at a later date.

If your secondary file is very large, WordPerfect may not be able to complete the merge operation because of shortage of computer memory. To overcome this problem, you can either:

• split your secondary file into smaller parts by highlighting them (with the Alt-F4 Block key) and saving under different names (with the Save key); or

• merge direct to the printer, as explained in Section 32 of the Keystroke Guide.

If you wish to print to only a selection of names and addresses from your secondary file, use the Select feature on the Sort menu, described on page 147.

## 7.9  Printing the secondary document

You will probably want a printed record of the data in your secondary document. One reason would be to check for errors, which is easier to do on a printout than on a screen. However, since each record ends with a page break, the document as it stands will print each record on a separate page.

To print the records in a list without page breaks, proceed as follows:

1   Insert a {PAGE OFF} command at the beginning of the secondary document, then save it under a new name.
2   Create a primary file consisting simply of field numbers or names, with appropriate field labels. Figure 7.8 gives an example of this.
3   Carry out the merge in the usual way, using your revised secondary file.

An alternative way of removing the page breaks is to use the Replace key (Alt-F2) to search for each [END RECORD] code, replacing it with two hard returns. The result can then be printed, though without the field labels that the above method produces. If you save this altered file, do not overwrite the original. (Remember that you cannot type this [END RECORD] code, you must insert it at the search prompt by pressing Shift-F9.)

```
{FIELD}1~ {FIELD}2~ {FIELD}3~
School: {FIELD}4~
Address: {FIELD}5?~
{FIELD}6~
{FIELD}7~ {FIELD}8~
Type of School: {FIELD}9~
```

**Figure 7.8**  Primary document for printing merge data

## 7.10  The exercise: merging

Skern Lodge has produced a schedule of courses to be held during the coming months, and wishes to circulate this to schools in the south of the country. It therefore has to create a primary document containing the covering letter and a secondary document containing the names and addresses of interested schools.

1  Create the secondary document shown in Figure 7.5. Although there would be many names and addresses in real life, for the sake of this exercise we are including just three. Save the file, calling it DATA.EX.
2  Split the screen (using Ctrl-F3), and create as Doc 2 the primary document shown in Figure 7.7. By splitting the screen, you can check that you are typing the right field numbers in the primary file. Use the Date/Outline key to insert the date. Save the file, calling it LETTER.EX, and exit the file.
3  Complete the merge to the screen, and view the result. Then print it. Exit the file without saving.

## 7.11  Initial codes

Formatting codes that affect the entire document, such as margin codes, are inserted once at the start of the document. In the case of a primary file, these codes pose a slight problem. When you carry out the merge, these codes will be inserted repeatedly throughout the merged document, once at the start of each merged record. This will make the document larger than it need be, and also increase the time WordPerfect takes to execute the merge.

To avoid this, you can if you wish impose these whole-document formatting commands on a document without entering codes in it:

● In the case of a single document, enter the codes in the Initial Codes screen, using the Format Document menu (i.e. by pressing the Shift-F8 Format key and choosing Document).
● If you wish to impose these codes automatically on all future documents, using the Setup Initial Settings menu to enter the codes in the Initial Codes screen (i.e. press Shift-F1 Setup and choose Initial Settings). For more details, see Section 53 of the Keystroke Guide.

- Alternatively, you can omit such codes entirely from the primary document, and insert them instead, after completing the merge to screen, at the start of the merged document. This is not possible if the merged document is too large to merge to screen (in which case it must be merged direct to the printer, as described in Section 32 of the Keystroke Guide). Then, you will have to use the first option above.

The Initial Codes screen contains the two default codes which modify WordPerfect for use in the UK. They are explained in the Keystroke Guide, Section 25.

## 7.12 The exercise: more on merging

This exercise makes use of the primary and secondary files you created a couple of pages back (LETTER.EX and DATA.EX).

Change the field numbers to names in your secondary file, DATA.EX, saving the result as NAMES.EX. Merge it with the primary file LETTER.EX. Then print the data in the DATA.EX secondary file.

If you need help with this exercise, the detailed steps are as follows:

1 Retrieve DATA.EX, and place the cursor at its beginning.
2 Press Shift-F9 twice to display the merge commands box.
3 Press 'F' to move the cursor to that part of the commands list.
4 With the cursor on the {FIELD NAMES} command, press Enter. WordPerfect prompts you in the status line 'Enter field 1:'.
5 Type in the appropriate field name and press Enter. Word-Perfect then prompts you for each field name one by one.
6 Continue typing in each field name until you have completed your record, pressing Exit when you have finished.
7 Your document will then look like Figure 7.6, with the field names arranged across the top of the screen at the beginning of your secondary document. Exit this file, saving it as NAMES.EX.
8 Complete a merge with LETTER.EX.
9 To print the data in the DATA.EX secondary file, retrieve it and insert the {PAGE OFF} command at its beginning. Save

the file, calling it PRNTDATA.EX, and exit. Create a primary file as in Figure 7.8, and merge it with PRNTDATA.EX.

## 7.13   Further exercises

1   Create the primary file shown in Figure 7.8, making sure you insert two hard returns at the end of the field numbers: this will ensure some space between each of your records. (Alternatively, you could block the appropriate part of your LETTER.EX file and press F10 to save it under a new name.) If you wish, you can type in identifying labels for the data. Save the file, calling it RECORDS.EX, and exit. Then complete a merge with DATA.EX.

2   Change the margins of your letter by adding a margin code to the initial codes for the document. This exercise need not be saved. The details are:

   a   Retrieve LETTER.EX.
   b   Use the Format key and select Initial Codes from the Document Format menu.
   c   Use the Format key again to insert a code changing the letter's left and right margins to 2″. When you exit from the Format menu, the margin code should have been added to the initial codes.
   d   Back at the document, you should see the change of margin in the status line. If, however, you reveal the codes, you will not see a margin code.

3   Try turning off the merge commands display in primary and secondary documents by altering the display setup on Shift-F1. Retrieve a primary file and a secondary file to see the effect, then change the setup back again.

## 7.14   Printing mailing labels

Having produced all your letters for mailing to potential customers, you now wish to print address labels for sticking on the envelopes. Since you already have a secondary file containing the addresses (DATA.EX), all you need do is create a new primary file containing just {FIELD} commands for the name and address fields, and merge this file with DATA.EX. When you do so, WordPerfect will replace these merge commands with the name and address data to print the labels.

However, you must include a code instructing WordPerfect to print to a label form rather than to the default A4 paper size. This is the [Paper Sz/Type] code, with information included in it on the label size you are going to print to and the number of labels per page. You can insert this code using the methods described in the last section, i.e. either on the Initial Codes screen for the primary file or at the start of the merged document.

- To insert the code at the Initial Codes screen of the primary file, follow the procedure outlined in the last section and explained in detail in the Keystroke Guide.
- To insert the code at the start of the merged document, press Shift-F8 (Format), then 2,7, then choose the appropriate label form from the list that appears. If this is the first time you have printed to labels, this list will not contain a label form. You will have to create it and add it to the list, as described in Section 32 of the Keystroke Guide.

With this code inserted, the names and addresses in the merged document look, on the normal editing screen, as if each one is on a separate page. However, if you view the document (by pressing Shift-F7,6), you will see an entire sheet of labels, with the addresses arranged correctly.

## 7.15 The exercise: merging mailing labels to the screen

1  Using your DATA.EX file as the secondary file, create a primary file that prints the name and address from each record, as below. Save the file, calling it LABELS.EX, and exit.

      {FIELD}1~ {FIELD}2~ {FIELD}3~
      {FIELD}4~
  ~   {FIELD}5~
      {FIELD}6~
      {FIELD}7~ {FIELD}8~

2  Complete the merge to the screen. The first record from DATA.EX will come out like this:

Miss Mary Roberts
Prestwood Secondary School
Wendover Way
Littlewood
Surrey SE4 4MR

However, when you view the document, you will see one address per page. Exit the document without saving.

3   Add a label form to the list of paper sizes and types, using the Format key. Use real or imaginary labels for entering the measurements.

4   Repeat step 2 above to complete the merge to the screen. At the beginning of the document, select the label form. View the document to see the addresses arranged correctly on a label sheet. Exit without saving. (You can if you wish print some mailing labels from this file, provided you first insert some labels of the appropriate size in your printer.)

## 7.16   Further exercise: merging mailing labels to the printer

Try merging the documents created in the above exercise to the printer. First, you should insert the label form code in the initial codes for the primary file, LABELS.EX. Then, load your labels into the printer before carrying out the merge. Details on merging to the printer are in Section 32 of the Keystroke Guide.

## 7.17   Keyboard merging

Not all your merging requirements will necessarily involve mass mailings. You will probably need a method of merging which can be used for documents which are produced regularly, but only in small numbers. In other words, you have a document which you want to use from time to time where most of the text is standard, with variable data occurring within it. For these small-scale merge jobs it is more efficient to enter the variable data directly at the keyboard during the merge rather than create a secondary file.

You still need the primary file, of course, containing the standard text, but it will include {INPUT} merge codes for keyboard input. When you retrieve this file with the Merge/Sort key to perform the merge, WordPerfect prompts you as to what variable data to type in, displaying messages that you yourself previously entered when you created the file.

For example, Skern Lodge wants to send acknowledgements to everyone who enquires about their courses. Most of the text is standard, but variable data such as the name and address of the enquirer, the date of the enquiry, and the name of the course need to be included. Examples of more complex keyboard merge applications include legal contracts or agreements.

Figure 7.9 shows a keyboard merge primary file. To create it, type the standard text in the normal way, then press the Merge Codes key (Shift-F9) and 3 (Input) wherever you want to insert the {INPUT} code. For each input, WordPerfect will ask you what prompt message is needed at merge time. For details, see Section 32 of the Keystroke Guide.

The procedure for carrying out the keyboard merge is also explained in this section of the Keystroke Guide. In brief:

1   Press the Ctrl-F9 Merge/Sort key, enter the name of the primary file, but when prompted for the secondary file just press Enter.
2   WordPerfect will then display the primary file up to the first {INPUT} command, and will display your prompt message on the status line. In the case of the keyboard merge file shown

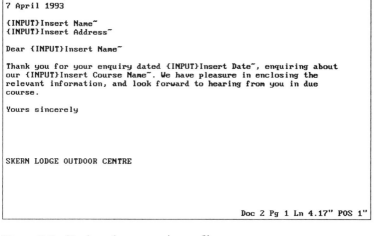

Figure 7.9   Keyboard merge primary file

in Figure 7.9, what appears is as shown in Figure 7.10. Enter the variable data, then press the F9 End Field key.

3 WordPerfect will display more of the file up to the next {INPUT} command. Continue entering the variable data, followed in each case by F9.

4 After completing the merge, you can print or save the merged document.

5 If you wish to send a second merged document, containing different variable data, repeat steps 1 to 4.

If you want the computer to beep at you whenever an input is required, include the {BELL} command, as explained in the further exercise below.

## 7.18 The exercise: keyboard merging

Create the keyboard merge primary file shown in Figure 7.9, saving it as KEYBOARD.EX. Then merge it with some variable data, such as that given below. You should be able to carry out this task without further assistance; however, in case you get stuck, the detailed steps are as follows:

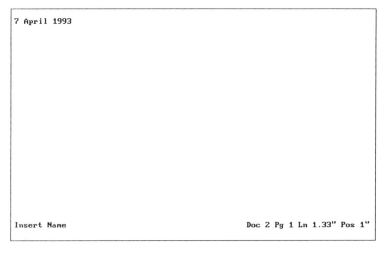

```
7 April 1993




















Insert Name                              Doc 2 Pg 1 Ln 1.33" Pos 1"
```

**Figure 7.10** Using a keyboard merge file

1 Use the Merge Codes key for each {INPUT} command and type in an appropriate message.
2 Save the file, calling it KEYBOARD.EX, and exit.
3 Use the document for a merge as follows:

    a Press the Merge/Sort key and choose 1 (Merge).
    b Type in KEYBOARD.EX when prompted for the primary file, and press Enter when prompted for the secondary file.
    c Enter the following data when prompted:

        Name: Mr J Bates
        Address: J Bates Manufacturing PLC
        Forest Industrial Estate
        Birmingham
        BE3 3EB
        Salutation: Mr Bates
        Date: 18 November
        Course: Management Development Course

    Don't forget to press F9 after each input to move on to the next input command.
4 Exit the file without saving.

## 7.19 Further exercise: inserting an audible prompt

Retrieve KEYBOARD.EX and insert an audible prompt command at each input point by adding a {BELL} command after each {INPUT} command. (Do this by pressing Shift-F9 twice and choosing {BELL} from the list.) To hear the effect, carry out a keyboard merge.

## 7.20 Sorting

WordPerfect's sorting feature lets you sort lists, paragraphs, or secondary merge files into alphabetical order. It also lets you select certain records from those lists, useful if you wish to merge a primary file with only some of the records in a secondary file. For example, your name and address records can be automatically sorted in alphabetical order of surname, company, town, or county; and you can select from the records just those of a particular county, for example, prior to sorting them.

Since sorting radically changes your file, and since it is easy to make a mistake when deciding how to sort, you should save your document before each sorting operation, just in case things go wrong.

You should be aware of the following terms, used in connection with sorting. You have already met most of them earlier in this chapter.

- *Data* — items of information.
- *Records* — the units which are sorted. A record can be a *line record*, i.e. data entered line by line, each line ending with a hard return. In this case the data may occur in a single column, or multiple columns separated by a single tab code. Or a record can be a *paragraph record*, ending with two or more hard returns. In the case of a secondary merge sort, records are separated by the {END RECORD} command. In a table, a row is a record.
- *Fields* — each piece of information within a record. In a line record, a column is a field; in a paragraph record, the entire paragraph is a field; in a secondary merge record, each line ending with {END FIELD} is a field; in a table, each cell is a field.
- *Words* — combinations of alphanumeric characters (letters and/or numbers) in a field.
- *Keys* — the words or numbers within a field which will be used to sort the text.
- *Key numbers* — sort priority indicators. Key1 has first priority, key2 has second priority, and so on.

The use of keys and key numbers is explained in the next section.

## 7.21 How to sort

To carry out a sort:

1 Press the Ctrl-F9 Merge/Sort key and choose Sort.
2 WordPerfect then asks whether you want to sort the file

already displayed on the screen, or whether you wish to enter the name of a file to be retrieved from disk. Press Enter for the former, or type the name and Enter for the latter.

3  WordPerfect asks whether you want to sort to the screen, or whether you wish to sort to a file saved on disk. As before, press Enter for the former, or type the filename for the latter.

4  The Sort menu shown in Figure 7.11 appears in the lower half of the screen. This menu is explained below. The default settings are to sort lines alphabetically in ascending order, sorting each line by the first word in the first column.

5  Make appropriate choices from this menu, including the sort type. The default type is 'Line', but by choosing 7 (Type) you can change this to Paragraph or Merge.

6  Press 1 (Perform Action) to carry out the sort. You can then either save the file under its current name, replacing the previous version, or under a new name.

The various Sort menu options are as follows:

1  *Perform Action* − carries out the sort.
2  *View* − lets you scroll through the file in the upper half of the screen.
3  *Keys* − allows you to choose your sorting criteria. This defaults to a single sort key, sorting alphabetically on the first field (or column) by the first word in the field (or column). So the

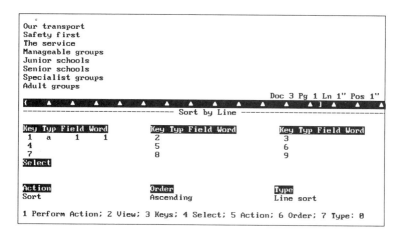

**Figure 7.11**  The Line Sort menu

default key settings are 'a 1 1'. You can change this to sorting numerically, on any field (column) and any word in the field. You can also have up to nine keys (i.e. nine priorities of sort). So if you want to sort names by surname and then forename (so that Adam Jones comes before Beverley Jones), you would use key1 for the main sort on surname, and key2 for the secondary sort on forename. To add key values, press the right arrow key; to delete unwanted keys, press Delete followed by the left arrow. The Keystroke Guide, Section 54 gives the detail.

4  *Select* — Lets you enter a statement that specifies records to be selected from the file before sorting. This is described in the next section.

5  *Action* — Allows you to specify whether you wish both to select records and to sort them, or just select. If you are only sorting, you will not need to use this option.

6  *Order* — Gives you the choice of ascending or descending order.

7  *Type* — Changes the type of sort, offering the choice of 'Merge' for secondary merge records, 'Line' for line records, and 'Paragraph' for paragraph records.

The changes you make to the criteria in the Sort menu remain in force until you change them again. So if your sorting efforts don't produce the expected result, check the entries at this menu. You may, for instance, have overlooked a 'Select' statement left over from the previous sort.

In the rest of this section line record sorting, multi-column line sorting, and sorting a block are described, then there is an exercise involving these three kinds of sort. In the next section, paragraph sorting, merge sorting, and table sorting are covered, followed by an exercise, and then selecting records for sorting is explained.

## Line record sorting

If your file consists of a single-column list, as in Figure 7.11, you need make no changes to the Sort menu since key1's defaults are appropriate. Simply select 1 (Perform Action), and the list is rearranged into alphabetical order.

## Multi-column line record sorting

If your list consists of several tabbed columns, like that shown in Figure 7.13, you can sort on any of these columns (fields) by entering the appropriate field number in the Keys section of the Sort menu. For example, if you have a five-column list and you wish to sort on the third column, change the 'Field' entry in key1 from 1 to 3.

## Sorting a block

If you wish to sort just part of a document rather than the whole document, select that part with the Block key, then press Merge/Sort. You can then choose the type of sort you wish to carry out within the block. If you don't select a block but sort the whole document by mistake, it could ruin your entire day. Every line and every heading will be rearranged.

## Variable lines and words

Some fields may contain a variable number of lines or words. For example, in Figure 7.18 the second field — the county — contains both single word entries (such as 'Surrey') and double word entries (such as 'N Yorks'). If you sorted this field by specifying word 1, N Yorks and S Yorks would be separated in the list. If you sorted by word 2, the single word entries would not be sorted. The solution is to count the words from the right of the field rather than the left, by preceding the number with a minus (i.e. a hyphen). In this case we want to sort by the first word, counted from the right of the field, so enter '-1'.

## 7.22  The exercise: sorting lists and blocks

The three exercises here give you practice in sorting a single-column list, sorting a block, and sorting a multi-column list.

1  The file used in Chapter 1 — TOPICS.EX — contained a list of topics to be covered in the Skern Lodge prospectus. This list is currently in random order. Rearrange it into alphabetical order. You will need to delete the heading first, otherwise that will be included in the sort. You should be able to carry

this out without further help, but in case you get stuck here's the detailed list of steps.

a   Retrieve TOPICS.EX.
b   Delete the heading so that you are left with just the list.
c   Press the Merge/Sort key then press Enter twice.
d   The defaults for key1 are appropriate for this sort, so press 1 (Perform Action).

Afterwards, exit the file without saving.

2   Retrieve TOPICS.EX again in its original (unsorted) state. This time, don't delete the heading, but use the Block key to highlight the list (excluding the heading), as shown in Figure 7.12, then sort.

3   In a file called TABSORT.EX, Skern Lodge has a four-column (i.e. four-field) list containing names of school contacts, the county, the type of school, and the telephone number. Part of this file is shown in Figure 7.13. As you can see, this list is in random order. You should sort this list in order of surname (on key1), with forenames sorted within surnames (i.e. on key2). When you have completed this sort, try sorting in order of county. If you get stuck, the detailed steps are as follows.

a   Retrieve TABSORT.EX.
b   Press the Merge/Sort key then press Enter twice.

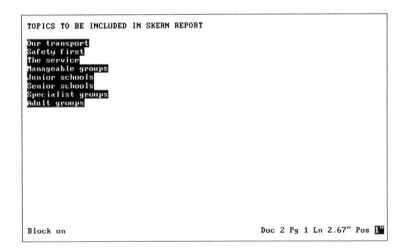

Figure 7.12   TOPICS.EX with the list highlighted

c  The key1 defaults are appropriate for sorting by surname, so if necessary remove any previous sorting entries, and press 1 (Perform Action). The list should be rearranged into alphabetical order of surname, but where a surname is repeated – e.g. 'Smith' – the forenames will not be in order.

d  Return to the Sort menu and choose 3 (Keys).

e  Leave key1 as it is (you still want the surnames sorted alphabetically) and press the right arrow key to move to key2.

f  Change the Word from '1' to '2', and press F7 to exit.

g  Press 1 (Perform Action). Now, where there is a repeated surname, the forenames should be arranged alphabetically.

h  Return to the Sort menu again in order to sort by county. Notice that your last sorting specification is in place, so choose 3 (Keys), then press Delete to restore the default specification. Change the Field in key1 from '1' to '2', and the Word to '-1'. Press F7 to exit.

i  Press 1 (Perform Action). Your list should be sorted correctly into county order.

## 7.23  More on sorting

In this section we cover paragraph sorting, merge sorting, and table sorting.

### Paragraph sorting

This kind of sort can be carried out on paragraphs of any length. However, they must meet WordPerfect's criterion for a paragraph – each paragraph must end with two or more hard returns, as illustrated in Figure 7.14.

```
Smith, George        Surrey     Secondary   0992 76366
Hawkins, Eric        N Yorks    Junior      0625 234899
Roberts, Mary        Surrey     Secondary   0992 84564
Hawkins, James       Bucks      Junior      0494 561233
Smith, S             S Yorks    Secondary   0683 375711
Goodchild, A         Hants      Primary     0256 842020
Parker, John         Surrey     Secondary   0992 32678
Adams, Robert        Devon      Secondary   0451 871234
Carlton-Brown, E J   Surrey     Secondary   0992 54890
```

**Figure 7.13**  TABSORT.EX

When the Sort menu is displayed, you must change the type to a paragraph sort, not forgetting to remove all previous sorting criteria from the menu. Notice in Figure 7.14 that there is an extra entry in the Keys section, i.e. 'Line'. This allows you to identify the paragraph line you would like to sort by; in practice, this will usually be line 1. The Field option is for items separated by a tab or indent code; if the paragraph heading is separated from the paragraph text by a tab or indent code, the heading is Field 1 and the paragraph text is Field 2.

## Table sorting

In a table, each row is a record and each cell in a row is a field within the record. For best results, you should only sort rows with the same number of cells; WordPerfect is unable to sort other rows correctly.

To sort a table, make sure the cursor is on one of the table cells and press Merge/Sort. You will not be asked for input or output files, but will be taken directly to the Sort menu with the table type already selected, as illustrated in Figure 7.15.

However, if the table has headings which you do not want included in the sort, you must highlight the cells below the headings (by pressing the Block key and selecting them) before pressing Merge/Sort.

To perform the sort, choose 1 (Perform Action) in the usual way. The table rows will be sorted on the screen.

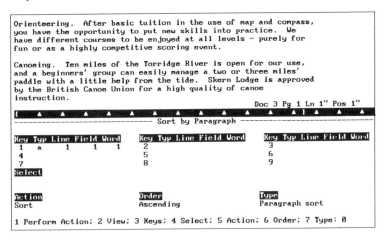

**Figure 7.14** The Paragraph Sort menu

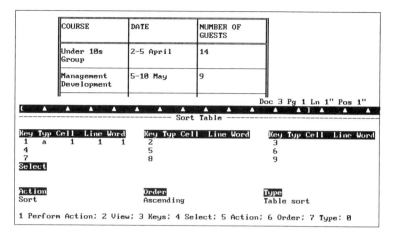

**Figure 7.15** The Table Sort menu

## Merge data sorting

If you have created a secondary merge document containing names and addresses, you can sort the data in a number of ways. For instance, you can have one version with the names in alphabetical order, another version with the same data sorted in alphabetical order of town, and so on. When you change the Type (in the Sort menu) to a secondary merge file, the Keys section changes slightly, as shown in Figure 7.16. In the figure, the values for key1 are set for sorting Field 8, the postcode field.

The extra item in this menu, 'Line', allows you to specify which line to sort in a field which has more than one line. For example, if the address field contains all parts of the address, you can still sort on one of the lines within the address, so long as this line is used consistently (e.g. for the town) throughout the records.

As explained in the next section, you can use the Select option to pick out records which can then be used for your mass mailing. For example, you could restrict your mailing to a particular town or postcode.

## 7.24 The exercise: sorting paragraphs and tables

For this exercise you should first sort the paragraphs in the file PARASORT.EX on your disk, sorting into alphabetical order of the paragraph headings. Then you should sort the table in the file

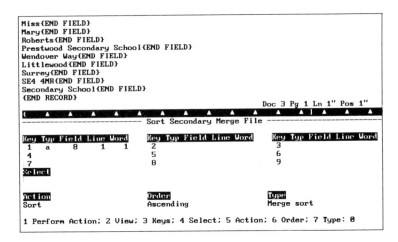

```
Miss{END FIELD}
Mary{END FIELD}
Roberts{END FIELD}
Prestwood Secondary School{END FIELD}
Wendover Way{END FIELD}
Littlewood{END FIELD}
Surrey{END FIELD}
SE4 4MR{END FIELD}
Secondary School{END FIELD}
{END RECORD}
                                         Doc 3 Pg 1 Ln 1" Pos 1"
```

**Figure 7.16** The Secondary Merge Sort menu

TABLSORT.EX, sorting on the first column in alphabetical order, then on the last column in numerical order. In both cases you should exit without saving the sorted file. You should be able to carry out these exercises without further assistance, but detailed instructions are given below in case you get stuck.

1  Retrieve the file PARASORT.EX which contains a number of paragraphs, each of which starts with a heading. These paragraphs require sorting into alphabetical order of the headings.

   a  Use the Block key to highlight the paragraphs so that you can omit the main heading at the start of the document from the sort.

   b  From the Merge/Sort menu, remove all the previous sorting criteria before you start.

   c  Change the Type to paragraph. The screen should look like Figure 7.14.

   d  Perform the action.

   e  Exit without saving the file.

2  Retrieve the file TABLSORT.EX which contains a table of three columns and four rows. The first row is a headings row.

   a  Block the text in the table below the headings row, starting in cell A2 and finishing at the end of the text in C4.

b   Set the sort criteria as in Figure 7.15, to sort the first column into alphabetical order.

c   Exit without saving the file.

d   Now retrieve the file again and sort the last column into numerical order.

e   Exit without saving the file.

## 7.25 Selecting

In this section we deal with the Select option on the Sort menu (Figure 7.11). This allows you to pick out specific records from your file. You can apply this with the mailmerge feature described earlier to print letters to a selection of addresses in a secondary file. In the case of the school contacts shown in Figure 7.13, for example, you may want to select the secondary schools from the list.

Suppose you do want to make this selection. The procedure is as follows:

1   Enter '3' as the Field in key1 on the Sort menu, since 'Secondary' appears in the third column. Press F7 to exit.

2   Choose Select from the Sort menu. WordPerfect changes 'Action' for 'Sort' to 'Select and Sort'. A list of selection operators is displayed at the foot of the screen. These are listed and described in Figure 7.17, and allow you to enter your selection conditions. In this case, you use the '=' operator: enter 'key1=Secondary'. Press F7 to exit.

3   Press 1 (Perform Action). This performs a simple selection. If sorting is also needed on another field, e.g. on surnames, this must be entered as a key. If you wish, you can save this list, either under a new name (if you wish to retrieve the original at a later date), or under the same name to replace the original.

Now look at Figure 7.18. In this, the first priority sort is on surname (key1), the second priority sort is on forename (key2), and the third sort (key3) is on type of school. To select the secondary schools, the selection condition is now 'key3=Secondary'.

Suppose 'Secondary' can occur in other fields besides column 3. How would you then select records containing this word?

| | |
|---|---|
| +(OR) | Select records that meet either condition |
| *(AND) | Select records that meet both conditions |
| = | Equal to |
| <> | Not equal to |
| > | Greater than |
| < | Less than |
| >= | Greater than or equal to |
| <= | Less than or equal to |

**Figure 7.17** List of selection operators with functions

```
Smith, George          Surrey      Secondary    0992 76366
Hawkins, Eric          N Yorks     Junior       0625 234899
Roberts, Mary          Surrey      Secondary    0992 84564
Hawkins, James         Bucks       Junior       0494 561233
Smith, S               S Yorks     Secondary    0683 375711
Goodchild, A           Hants       Primary      0256 842020
Parker, John           Surrey      Secondary    0992 32678
Adams, Robert          Devon       Secondary    0451 871234
Carlton-Brown, E J     Surrey      Secondary    0992 54890


                                          Doc 3 Pg 1 Ln 1" Pos 1"
[             ▲               ▲                ▲              ]
--------------------------- Sort by Line ------------------------
Key Typ Field Word         Key Typ Field Word        Key Typ Field Word
 1   a    1     1           2   a    1     2          3   a    3     1
 4                          5                         6
 7                          8                         9
Select
key3=Secondary

Action                     Order                     Type
Select and sort            Ascending                 Line sort

+(OR), *(AND), =, <>, >, <, >=, <=;  Press Exit when done
```

**Figure 7.18** Sort menu showing a Select statement

WordPerfect allows you to perform a *global* select, across all fields, by entering 'g' instead of a key number in your selection condition. In this case you would enter:

'keyg=Secondary'.

When entering selection conditions, note that:

- You can only enter a single word, e.g. 'Secondary'.
- The selection is not case-sensitive, i.e. it doesn't matter if you enter it in upper or lower case.

## 7.26 The exercise: selecting and sorting merge data

In this exercise you should sort your DATA.EX file in order of
postcode, and then select the junior school records from this file.
In case you get stuck, the detailed instructions are as follows:

1  Retrieve your DATA.EX file which contains three records.
2  Set up your sorting criteria as shown in Figure 7.16, and carry
   out the sort. The records should be rearranged in order of
   postcode.
3  Now select the junior school records (in this file there is only
   one such record). Don't forget to remove the previous sort
   criteria first. You will find that if you type in 'Junior School'
   as the data to select, you will see an error message; this is
   because you can only type in one word to select. Delete the
   word 'School' and then proceed.

# 8
# Automating with macros

## 8.1 What you will achieve in this chapter

This chapter is mainly concerned with setting up macros to automate your word processing tasks. When you have completed it,
you should be able to:

- Execute macros.
- Create and edit macros.
- Insert special characters in documents.


## 8.2 Routines you will use in this chapter

As you work through this chapter, you will be getting to grips
with the following routines. The Keystroke Guide section number
for each routine is given below in brackets.

- Run a macro (30).
- Make changes to an existing macro (30).
- Define a new macro on both the normal editing screen and
  the Macro Editing screen (30).
- Use WordPerfect's Compose feature to insert special characters
  in a document (55).


## 8.3 Becoming a WordPerfect power user

Word processing is mainly about automating routine text entry
tasks and producing good looking results. As you've worked
through this book, you've practised many aspects of these. In

these final three chapters you will explore the limits of Word-Perfect's power in these areas. They will help you become what some call a 'power user', able to make the most of WordPerfect's automation and document publishing capabilities.

We start in this chapter with *macros*, which allow you to add customized automation features to WordPerfect.

## 8.4 Macros

Although WordPerfect provides many built-in automation features, it cannot provide comprehensive automation for all your needs. So you find yourself repeating certain tasks endlessly, such as typing 'Yours faithfully' at the foot of letters, or choosing a certain sequence of menu commands. Macros allow you to automate these tasks.

A macro is a stored sequence of keystrokes − which may include pressing function keys to activate a command − which can be replayed at any time at the press of a single key combination (usually Alt plus another key). It is the same principle as the redial facility on your telephone: not only does it save you time and effort, you know that the sequence of keystrokes will be error-free (because the computer, in effect, is pressing them for you).

A couple of the macros that Skern Lodge needs, that you will be setting up in this chapter, are:

- Applying suitable formats to subheadings in reports.
- Incorporating a standard footer which includes the page number together with the total number of pages in the report (e.g. 'Page 3 of 12').

It is important that you think about and plan the macros that you are going to set up for your own work. Make a list of the tasks that you find yourself repeatedly doing, such as:

- Entering the same commands time and again, e.g. to change your left and right margins.
- Entering the same text repeatedly, such as your address.
- Entering a combination of commands and text, such as a change of margins and your address.

All these are suitable candidates for macros. You will also find that you are repeatedly entering certain combinations of formatting codes for certain types of documents. These could also be assigned to macros, but you may find it better to store them in *styles*. Styles are described in Chapter 9.

Having arrived at this list of tasks, you then have to turn them into macros, and this chapter shows you how. Of course, you can add further macros to this list at any time, and you can delete macros from it that you no longer need.

The first step is to write down against each macro on your list a suitable name.

## 8.5 Macro names

You need to name your macros in order to replay them. Word-Perfect provides two naming conventions.

1 For frequently used macros the most convenient naming method is a combination of the Alt key plus a single letter from A to Z. The macro is then replayed by pressing Alt plus the letter. You can choose whichever letter you like for a macro, though it's best to use a letter that's easily remembered, e.g. Alt-M for your margins macro. You can't use the same letter twice − having used 'M' for 'margins', you can't use it again for 'main heading format'. When you are planning your macros, think about and write down the names you are going to use, so that suitable letters are used for each one.

2 For macros that you use less often, a descriptive name is probably best. It's easy to forget what 'Alt-M' does, but you are less likely to forget what a macro file called 'MARGINS' does. Like any filename, a descriptive macro name can be no more than eight characters in length. The disadvantage of this descriptive naming method is it's not so quick and easy to replay the macro: you have to press the Alt-F10 Macro key, then enter the macro name.

## 8.6 Macro files

WordPerfect stores macros on disk in macro files, permanently available to you at the press of a key. The filename is the macro name, followed by the .WPM extension. So your Alt-M macro is stored as ALTM.WPM.

Sometimes, though, you will want to set up a temporary macro that carries out a task that's needed for the current document only, e.g. to enter a particular client's name repeatedly in a long report you are about to type. In this case you can store it in a special temporary macro file called WP{WP}.WPM. This is replaced as soon as you create another temporary macro. There is no need to name a temporary macro, as it is replayed simply by pressing the Macro key (see later).

A number of macro files are supplied with the WordPerfect program ready for you to use. They should appear in the list of files for your default directory. Have a look in your directory to see if any macro files already exist: press your List key (F5), change the extension * to 'WPM', then press Enter. If you cannot find any macro files, look in Setup − Location of Files, and see which directory has been assigned to macros.

### The supplied macros

The macro files supplied with WordPerfect are as follows. You will note that some of these are 'chained', meaning that when one macro in the chain ends, the next starts.

- ENDFOOT.WPM. This changes endnotes in a document to footnotes.
- FOOTEND.WPM. This changes footnotes in a document to endnotes.
- LABELS.WPM. This macro lets you choose a label form from a list of label types manufactured by 3M and Avery. The form is then added to your list of paper size/type definitions.
- CODES.WPM. This chains REVEALCO.WPM and REVEALTX.WPM to print merge codes in addition to text and codes from the Reveal Codes screen.
- REVEALCO.WPM. This is chained by CODES.WPM to print merge codes in addition to text and codes from the Reveal Codes screen. Do not run this macro by itself; run CODES.WPM instead.
- REVEALTX.WPM. This is chained by CODES.WPM to print merge codes in addition to text and codes from the Reveal Codes screen. Do not run this macro; run CODES.WPM instead.

## Using the List menu with macro files

You will find the following List menu options useful with macros:

2 Delete — use this to delete a macro.
3 Move/Rename — use this to move the macro to another drive or directory, or rename the macro.
6 Look — use this to see the macro description. You cannot retrieve macro files, so Look is useful to remind you what a macro file contains.
8 Copy — use this to copy the macro to a floppy disk so that you can use it on another computer.

## 8.7 Defining a macro

There are two ways to define (i.e. create) a macro:

1 Enter the keystrokes you want recorded on the normal editing screen, while WordPerfect records them for you in the background. This is the easiest way to create a macro, and is dealt with in this section.
2 Type the keystrokes as a sequence of commands on the Macro Editing screen. This is more difficult, but it gives you more power as you can include special macro programming commands. This is described later in this chapter.

We'll start with the easy (keystroke recording) method first. The procedure is:

1 At the normal editing screen press the Ctrl-F10 Macro Define key. The following prompts appear in the message line:

a *Define macro*. Enter the name you wish to give the macro either by pressing Alt and a letter, or by typing in a descriptive name.
b *Description*. Type a description of what the macro will do. You can use up to 39 characters.
c *Macro Def*. Type the keystrokes that make up your macro, whether text, or commands, or both. WordPerfect will respond to these keystrokes in the normal way, but it will at the same time record them, indicating this by flashing the 'Macro Def' message.

2   When you have finished entering the keystrokes you want recorded, press Ctrl-F10 again. WordPerfect will save the recorded keystrokes in the macro file.

Here's one example of a macro. When we've typed a heading for a section of this book, we like to embolden it and also to insert a conditional end-of-page on the preceding line to ensure that it is not left hanging at the foot of a page with no text following it. All this takes a number of keystrokes, and would be quite a chore to do for every heading. So, we have set it up as a macro: when we've typed a heading, we merely press Alt-H and the job's done. You will be creating this macro in the next exercise.

## 8.8   Exercise: defining and executing a macro

1   At Skern Lodge you would like to create a macro similar to the Alt-H macro described above. You would then use it for formatting subheadings in various reports. On a blank screen, type a couple of words to represent a typical subheading. Leave the cursor at the end of this heading (so don't press Enter or any other keys), and define the macro as follows:

   a   Press the Macro Define key, and at the first prompt name the macro Alt-H (press the Alt key and H). At the next prompt type in a meaningful description.
   b   Your recording can now begin. Enter the keystrokes as shown below (and repeated in Figure 8.1), then stop the recording by pressing Macro Define again.

> Block key; Home,left arrow; Bold key; up arrow; Format key,4,2; 4, Enter; Exit; down arrow; End; Enter, Enter

This will embolden your sample subheading and position the cursor ready for typing in a new paragraph. In the Codes screen, you should see the [Condl EOP: 4] code above the subheading.

2   Try out this macro by typing in some more text as another subheading, then pressing Alt-H to execute the macro.
3   Look for the macro file (ALTH.WPM) in your list of files. (If

you cannot see it, look in Setup — Location of Files, and see which directory has been assigned to macros, and switch to that directory.) Alongside the filename you should see its size, date, and time of creation.

4  Use the Look feature in List to see the description of the macro.

5  Use the Copy feature to copy the macro to a floppy disk.

6  Create another macro, called 'ADDRESS', which inserts your home address at the top of a page. It should use the Tab key to place each line at the right of the page; and it should add the date as a code beneath, followed by two hard returns.

7  Retrieve the SUMMARY.EX file, which has footnotes in it. Try running the FOOTEND macro to change the footnotes to endnotes. Then run the other macro, ENDFOOT, to change the endnotes back to footnotes. Exit the file without saving.

## 8.9  Defining and executing a temporary macro

Defining a temporary macro is similar to defining a permanent macro described in the last section, except that when the prompt 'Define macro:' appears, you press the Enter key by itself instead of entering a name. You will not then be asked to enter a description, but will be able to start recording the keystrokes. To run the temporary macro, press the Alt-F10 Macro key then Enter.

## 8.10  Exercise: a temporary macro

Before you start, list your macros and look for the default macro filename — WP{WP}.WPM. The file will not exist until the first time you create a temporary macro. If it does exist, execute it to see what it does. If it does something useful which you would like to keep, use the List menu to rename it.

Now create a temporary macro containing the name of a new client which is constantly cropping up in a long report you are due to type. (So that you need to use the name repeatedly during the next day or so, but not thereafter.) Then execute the macro to check that it works.

In case you get stuck on this exercise, here's the detailed list of steps:

1   On a blank screen, press the Macro Define key. Press Enter
    when prompted 'Define macro'.
2   Record the keystrokes by typing in the client's name –
    'Buckinghamshire County Council Education Department' –
    and press Macro Define to end the recording.
3   Look in the default directory for the WP{WP}.WPM file.
4   Execute the macro by pressing the Macro key and Enter.

Try creating a replacement temporary macro using another client
name, e.g. 'Avon and Somerset County Council Education
Department'. Then run the macro. Notice that WordPerfect
replaces the previous macro without asking you to confirm that
this is what you want.

## 8.11   Replacing a macro

If you make a mistake while recording a macro, simply press the
Macro Define key to end the recording, and record the macro
again. When you type in the macro name at the 'Define macro:'
prompt, e.g. Alt-H, WordPerfect will display the message:
'ALTH.WPM already exists; (1) Replace; (2) Edit or (3) Descrip-
tion:0'. Type 1 (Replace), then continue defining the macro in
the usual way.
   In the same way you can replace an earlier macro with a new
one if your macro requirements change.

## 8.12   Editing a macro

If you wish to edit an existing macro rather than replacing it
completely, perhaps because the change is only minor whereas
redoing the whole thing is rather complex, then you should display
the macro on the Macro Editing screen, as shown in Figure 8.1.
(You could also use this screen to create a new macro.)
   Notice how commands, menu choices, and ordinary text are
displayed on the Macro Editing screen:

●   Any commands, such as function keys or editing key com-
    mands, are in curly brackets – e.g. {Format} for the Shift-F8
    Format key and {Enter} for the Enter key.

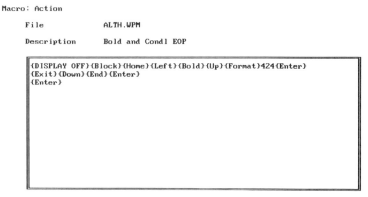

**Figure 8.1**   ALTH.WPM displayed on the Macro Editing screen

- Any menu choices, such as pressing 4 then 2 after the Format key, appear as regular text: '42'.
- Ordinary text is displayed in the normal way, except for spaces which are shown as dots.

Whether you wish to use the Macro Editing screen to edit an existing macro or to create a new macro, the procedure is as follows:

1  Press Home, then the Ctrl-F10 Macro Define key. The prompt 'Define macro:' appears at the foot of the screen.
2  Enter the name of the macro. In the case of an existing macro, the macro description is displayed at the foot of the screen. If you wish, you can enter a new description.
3  Press Enter. The Macro Editing screen appears. If you are editing an existing macro, the sequence of commands together with any text that may comprise it is displayed on this screen, as shown in Figure 8.1.
4  You can now edit your macro. You are in 'editing mode', so all the editing keys such as the arrow keys, Enter, Backspace, etc. work in the way you would expect. If you wish to insert an edit key command, e.g. {Enter}, you can't type it in, either by attempting to type the characters '{', 'E', etc., or by pressing Enter. You must instead switch to 'command insert mode' by pressing Ctrl-V, and then press the appropriate edit

key, e.g. Enter. If you wish to insert a succession of such commands, press the Ctrl-F10 Macro key, then the keys, then Ctrl-F10 again to return to editing mode. For details, see Section 30 of the 'Keystroke Guide'. You can also insert special macro commands, such as {DISPLAY OFF}, displayed in the box at the top right of the screen. You will be learning about these shortly.

5   When you have finished, press the F7 Exit key (while in editing mode) to save your macro and return to the normal editing screen.

## 8.13   Exercise: editing the ADDRESS macro

1   Edit the ADDRESS macro you created on page 156 by inserting three additional hard returns below the date. With such a minor alteration, it is best to use the macro editor rather than to recreate the macro by recording all the keystrokes again.

a   Retrieve the macro into the Macro Editing screen as described above. The screen will look something like Figure 8.2.

b   Move the cursor to the end of the keystrokes and press Enter several times to add these hard returns. You will find that instead of inserting the {Enter} command, the cursor moves down several lines.

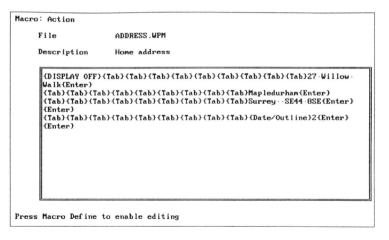

```
Macro: Action

    File            ADDRESS.WPM

    Description     Home address

    ┌─────────────────────────────────────────────────────────────────┐
    │{DISPLAY OFF}{Tab}{Tab}{Tab}{Tab}{Tab}{Tab}{Tab}{Tab}27 Willow    │
    │Walk{Enter}                                                        │
    │{Tab}{Tab}{Tab}{Tab}{Tab}{Tab}{Tab}{Tab}Mapledurham{Enter}        │
    │{Tab}{Tab}{Tab}{Tab}{Tab}{Tab}{Tab}{Tab}Surrey SE44 8SE{Enter}    │
    │{Enter}                                                            │
    │{Tab}{Tab}{Tab}{Tab}{Tab}{Tab}{Tab}{Tab}{Date/Outline}2{Enter}    │
    │{Enter}                                                            │
    │                                                                   │
    │                                                                   │
    │                                                                   │
    │                                                                   │
    └─────────────────────────────────────────────────────────────────┘

Press Macro Define to enable editing
```

**Figure 8.2**   ADDRESS.WPM on the Macro Editing screen

   c  Delete these unwanted returns (with Backspace), then press Ctrl-F10 to switch to the command insert mode, then the Enter key three times to insert the additional hard returns.

   d  To exit the macro, press the F7 Exit key. However, this just inserts an {Exit} command, as you are still in the command insert mode. So press Ctrl-F10 to return to the editing mode, delete the unwanted {Exit} command, then press F7 to exit.

2  Execute the macro on a blank screen to check that it does what you wanted. To demonstrate how economical macros are of disk space, save the address that this macro creates as a file, and look in the list of files to compare the size of the macro file with the size of the text file. You will probably find that the former is only a quarter of the size of the latter − quite a difference. So storing this as a macro rather than a text file − which could also be inserted in the document − saves disk space.

## 8.14   Macro programming commands

If you wish to include macro programming commands in your macro, you have to use the macro editor. You can either add these commands to an existing macro, or you can create the entire macro from scratch in the editor.

One program command is automatically added by WordPerfect to every macro that you create. That is the {DISPLAY OFF} command, which turns off the screen display of any commands that execute when the macro runs. To see this display would be rather disconcerting for the user, and would also slow down the macro considerably.

Other program commands are available at the macro command box at the top right of the Macro Editing screen. To move the highlight to this box in order to scroll through and select commands, you need to press Ctrl-PgUp. For details on the various commands, refer to the programming command appendix in the WordPerfect manual.

In the next exercise, you will be using the following commands:

•  {SYSTEM} − used to determine a state of the system, such

as the current filename, the current page number, or the path to the current document. It must be followed by the appropriate system variable specifying which of the possibilities is required. These system variables are described in the programming command appendix to the manual. They are typed in immediately after the {SYSTEM} command. In the case of our macro in the next exercise, the system variable is 'page', which gives the current page number.

- {ASSIGN} – this allows you to set up a variable of your own, by typing a suitable name for it after this command. The value you give this variable is determined by the expression that you type after it. So in the example in Figure 8.3, the value of {SYSTEM}page is assigned to a variable that we've called 'numbers'.

- {VARIABLE} – this is followed by your chosen variable name, and can be placed wherever you wish the value of this variable to appear. In our example, it will appear after the words 'Page {^B} of'.

## 8.15 Exercise: creating a standard footer

Skern Lodge finds it useful to include a standard footer in reports, containing the page number together with the total number of pages in the document. A simple macro can be created to insert the page number as a footer, but the total number of pages has to be entered as a program command.

Figure 8.3 shows this macro. It carries out the following sequence of tasks. It:

- Moves the cursor to the end of the document (Home,Home, Down).
- Looks at the page number.
- Returns to the top of the document in front of any existing codes (Home,Home,Home,Up).
- Moves to the footer A screen.
- Enters a centred footer as 'Page *n* of *n*', where the first *n* is the current page number and the second *n* is the last page number.
- Exits back to the text editing screen.

Note that we have put in hard returns between the different parts of the macro to make it easier to read. These will have no effect when the macro runs.

The exercise is as follows:

1  Go to the macro editor by pressing Home, Macro Define. Move the cursor beyond the {DISPLAY OFF} command and enter the keystrokes and commands shown in Figure 8.3. Remember that you have to be in command insert mode to enter the cursor movement commands — such as {Home} {Home}{Up} in the second line — so press Macro Define before pressing these keys. You will have to move in and out of command insert mode several times in creating this macro.

2  Exit the macro editor, and retrieve a multi-page document (the W&O.EX file would be suitable). Execute the macro from any point in this document (it has been created so that it will run correctly from any cursor position). In the Codes screen, you should be able to see that the appropriate footer code has been entered in the document, and you should be able to see its effect if you view the document. Exit the file without saving it.

## 8.16  Special characters

We conclude this chapter with a note about the special characters that WordPerfect provides which are not available on the normal

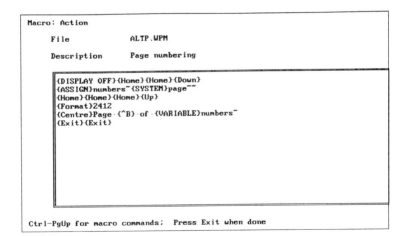

```
Macro: Action

    File          ALTP.WPM

    Description   Page numbering

    {DISPLAY OFF}{Home}{Home}{Down}
    {ASSIGN}numbers~{SYSTEM}page~~
    {Home}{Home}{Home}{Up}
    {Format}2412
    {Centre}Page {^B} of {VARIABLE}numbers~
    {Exit}{Exit}







Ctrl-PgUp for macro commands;  Press Exit when done
```

**Figure 8.3**  ALTP.WPM on the Macro Editing screen

keyboard, such as the ½ or the ¼, or special foreign language characters. These can be accessed via its Compose feature. (Characters from the IBM extended character set can be inserted without using Compose, as explained at the Help screen for Compose.)

Over 1,000 characters are available with WordPerfect. These are contained in 13 different sets, denoted Character Set 0, Character Set 1, etc. Within these sets, each character has its own identifying number. A list of all the character sets is contained in an appendix in the WordPerfect manual. Before you use a character, you normally have to know the number of its character set, and its identifying number within that set. The more common symbols, however, can be simply typed in by pressing an appropriate sequence of two keys, as explained on the Help screen for Compose.

To use Compose, proceed as follows:

1  Press Ctrl-V or Ctrl-2 (Compose). If you press Ctrl-V a 'Key =' prompt appears; if you press Ctrl-2 there is no prompt.
2  Type the character set number, a comma, then the character identifying number.
3  Press Enter to enter the character in your document at the current cursor position.

Note that the characters you insert may not display properly on the editing screen, so you will have to view the document to see how they will print. Note too that your printer may not be able to support all these characters. To see what it can support, print the WordPerfect file CHARMAP.TST.

■  The following words have been borrowed from other languages and are in common use in the UK. What do they mean?

passé; mañana; bête-noire; lèse-majesté

■  ¼ + ½ + ¾ =

■  Name the four suits in a pack of cards:

♥ ♦ ♣ ♠

**Figure 8.4**  Children's quiz

## 8.17   Exercise: composing special characters

Skern Lodge is putting together a quiz for a children's course. Some of the questions are shown in Figure 8.4. Retrieve a file called QUIZ.EX, and insert into it the special characters shown in this figure, including the bullets, using the Compose key. Exit the file without saving.

# 9
# Styles and outline

## 9.1 What you will achieve in this chapter

This chapter shows you how to apply pre-set formatting styles to your document, including automatic paragraph numbering styles. When you have completed it, you should be able to:

- Create styles and apply them to documents.
- Edit styles.
- Create a style library.
- Use WordPerfect's Outline feature to apply automatic numbering to paragraphs.
- Change the numbering style.
- Move, copy, and delete outline paragraphs.
- Create an outline style.

In this chapter, you will be applying what you learn to a Skern Lodge report.

## 9.2 Routines you will use in this chapter

As you work through this chapter, you will be getting to grips with the following routines. The Keystroke Guide section number for each routine is given below in brackets.

- Create open and paired styles (59).
- Apply these styles to both new and existing text (59).
- Change the contents of a style (59).
- Create a style from existing codes (59).
- Delete a style (59).

- Create a file containing a library of styles (59).
- Use the Outline feature to number paragraphs automatically (37).
- Select and apply a different style of paragraph numbering (37).
- Define a numbering style (37).
- Use the 'family' feature to move, copy, and delete outline (i.e. numbered) paragraphs (38).

## 9.3 Styles

In your job, you probably create regularly letters with a particular formatting style — margin sizes, line spacing, fonts, and so on. You might also create reports with another formatting style, including not just different margin settings but also perhaps a standard heading such as 'Skern Lodge Outdoor Centre', paragraph numbering conventions, page numbering conventions, and so on.

It's not much fun to have to enter a number of formatting codes each time you want to create a different style of document. With WordPerfect, you don't have to, as you can store all these settings in what are called *styles*. When you apply a style to a document, you automatically apply the formats stored in the style. Not only does this save you time, it also ensures that you are consistent in your formatting.

You can have styles that apply to the whole document (e.g. to set margins), or styles that apply to small sections of a document (e.g. to enhance some characters). You can also store text in a style. For example, the standard heading 'Skern Lodge Outdoor Centre' could be stored in this way. This can either be part of the same style that provides the report format parameters, or it can be stored in a separate style.

There is nothing to stop you applying several styles to the same document: when you write a report, you might first apply the style that sets its margins and other format parameters, and then apply a second style that provides the heading. You might then apply further styles for particular paragraphs.

As you learned in the last chapter, it's possible to set up macros to do much the same thing. For this particular task, however, styles provide a major advantage over macros: a style is inserted as a single 'style' code in the document. When Word-

Perfect encounters this code, it looks in the style for individual format codes. This means that:

- You avoid the clutter of a large number of individual codes in the Codes screen.
- If you want to make changes to these individual codes, it's merely a matter of editing the style, then applying the revised style instead of the old one. Wherever that style is applied in the document, the changes you have made are applied automatically. This is rather easier than searching your document for the codes to change.

Imagine you have used a macro 50 times in a document to apply a particular text enhancement, and you want to make a change. You will have to edit 50 occurrences of the formats inserted by the macro. If you use a style, you need only make a single change, by editing the style.

Note that changing a style in this way affects only the current document. Previous documents that used the style are not affected. As with macros, you need to think about and list the styles that you could create to help you in your word processing work. As you work through this chapter, you will get a better idea of the kinds of things that styles can do for you, and you will pick up some hints on what styles you might create, how to name them, and so on.

## 9.4 Saving styles

Any styles you create are stored as part of the document when that's saved. So the next time you retrieve the file, any styles you created within it are available. However, this automatic method of saving styles does not allow you to use them with other documents.

If you wish to use those styles with other documents, you must save them as a separate style file (see below). That file can then be retrieved into other documents, and the styles in it will then be available. To help identify style files it's a good idea to give them a standard extension when naming them – for example .STY. WordPerfect will save them in the directory specified in Setup – Location of Files.

## 9.5   Creating and applying a style

Creating, applying, saving, or retrieving styles are all carried out using the Alt-F8 Styles key. When you press it, the Styles menu is displayed at the foot of the screen together with a list of the styles that have been created for the current document (see Figure 9.1). From the menu you can create a new style (option 3), edit the highlighted style on the list (4), delete the highlighted style from the list (5), save the list of styles as a file (6), retrieve a list of styles stored as a file on disk (7), and apply a style to the document (1).

When you choose 3 to create a style, you are taken to the Styles Edit screen (Figure 9.2). Here, you specify:

- A name for your style (up to 12 characters).
- A type (open or paired — see below).
- A description (up to 54 characters).
- The codes that comprise the style. To insert these codes, you are taken to the Codes screen, where you apply codes in the normal way.

When you've completed this, you exit back to the Styles menu, where you can apply the style by choosing 1 (On).

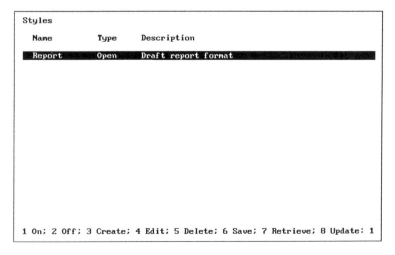

```
Styles

  Name         Type      Description

  Report       Open      Draft report format




















  1 On; 2 Off; 3 Create; 4 Edit; 5 Delete; 6 Save; 7 Retrieve; 8 Update: 1
```

**Figure 9.1**   The Styles menu

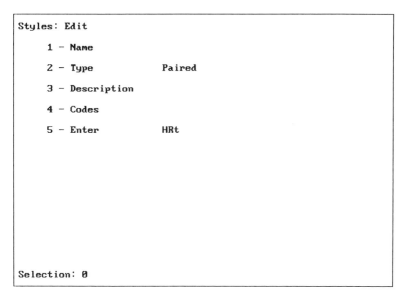

```
Styles: Edit

    1 - Name

    2 - Type            Paired

    3 - Description

    4 - Codes

    5 - Enter           HRt




Selection: 0
```

**Figure 9.2** The Styles Edit menu for a paired style

Note that the styles are listed alphabetically at the Styles menu. If you have a number of styles, it's a good idea to give those you frequently used names whose first letter lies near the beginning of the alphabet, so that they appear towards the top of the list. The names should be reasonably descriptive, although you can augment this by adding a description.

The problem with creating a style in this way is that you can't actually see what it looks like until after you have applied it to your document. If it doesn't produce quite the effect you wanted, you will have to go back to the Styles Edit menu and change it. An alternative way of creating a style is to:

● Insert the codes directly into the document, check that they produce the desired effect, and then copy them into a style.

Later on in the chapter you will be trying this out. Note that the codes that you want to copy must be contiguous (next to each other), and not separated by any text. (You cannot copy text into a style.)

## 9.6   Open and paired styles

WordPerfect provides two kinds of style:

1   *Open* styles, i.e. styles which insert a single style code in the document, and which cannot therefore be turned off by inserting a second style code later in the document. (However, their effect can be negated by applying other format parameters later in the document, e.g. in the case of a margins style by resetting the margins.) These styles are used for formats that affect the whole document.
2   *Paired* styles, i.e. styles which insert a Style On code at one point in the text (where they are turned on) and a Style Off code at a later point in the text (where they are turned off). These are normally used to store format codes or text that are to be inserted at specific places within a document. One example of such a style would be the formats you wish to apply to main headings, e.g. centred, emboldened, and in large-size text. Another example is the text of a report heading, mentioned in the last section. Paired styles are also used to store outline and paragraph numbering styles, described later in this chapter.

You will practise using open styles first, then paired styles. Section 59 of the Keystroke Guide provides the detail on creating these styles.

## 9.7   Exercise: creating and applying an open style

When producing reports at Skern Lodge, you normally create a draft which eventually, after much editing, becomes the final version. A number of format codes are inserted at the start of the report, and you want to incorporate these in a style.

1   Retrieve the file STYLE1.EX, which is a two-page document.
2   Place the cursor at the top of the document, press Style (Alt-F8), then choose Create. The menu in Figure 9.2 is displayed.
3   Choose 1 (Name) and type 'Report'. Choose 3 (Description) and type 'Draft report format'. Choose 2 (Type) and select 'Open'. The menu should appear as in Figure 9.3.

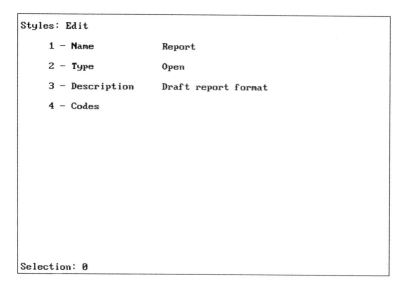

```
Styles: Edit

    1 - Name           Report

    2 - Type           Open

    3 - Description    Draft report format

    4 - Codes














Selection: 0
```

**Figure 9.3** The Styles Edit menu for an open style

4    Choose 4 (Codes). You should now be placed in the Style
     Codes screen. Insert the following format codes:

          Top-bottom margins 0.5″
          Left-right margins 0.5″
          Left justification
          Line spacing 2
          Header A: Every page, flush right, small, 'Draft at [Date
          code]'
          Footer A: Every page, centre, small, 'Page ^B'.

     Use the Format key to insert these, apart from the small size
     for the header and footer (Font), the date code in the header
     (Date/Outline), and the page code in the footer (Ctrl-B).
     When you've finished, the Style Codes screen should appear
     as in Figure 9.4.
5    Exit back to the styles list, which should now look like Figure
     9.1.
6    Now that you have created a style, you can apply it to the
     current document. With the cursor on the Report style in
     the style list, select On. You should be placed back in the

```
Style:  Press Exit when finished              Doc 2 Pg 1 Ln 1" Pos 1"
▲    {    ▲    ▲    ▲   ▲    ▲    ▲    ▲    ▲    ▲    ▲    ▲ ] ▲    ▲
[T/B Mar:0.5",0.5"][L/R Mar:0.5",0.5"][Just:Left][Ln Spacing:2][Header A:Every p
age;[Flsh Rgt][SMALL]Draft at  ... ][Footer A:Every page;[SMALL][Centre]Page ^B]
```

**Figure 9.4** Style codes for Skern Lodge report style

STYLE1.EX file with the [Open Style:Report] code inserted in the document.

7 At the Reveal Codes screen, move the cursor onto the style code. You will see the contents of the code, as in Figure 9.5. If you move the cursor off the code, its contents will be hidden again. Exit the file, saving it as STYLE2.EX.

## 9.8 Using a paired style

As explained already, paired styles allow you to apply some enhancement to just a few words or paragraphs. In this case two codes are inserted in your document, the first 'Style On' marking the start of the enhancement, the second 'Style Off' code marking its end.

When you apply the style, using the Alt-F8 Style key, the following sequence of events occurs:

1 WordPerfect inserts both codes, side by side, in your document.

```
SKERN LODGE ACTIVITIES


Orienteering.


After basic tuition in the use of map and compass, you have the

opportunity to put new skills into practice.  We have different courses
C:\WP51\BOOK\STYLE2.EX                        Doc 2 Pg 1 Ln 1" Pos 1"
▲    {    ▲    ▲    ▲   ▲    ▲    ▲    ▲    ▲    ▲    ▲    ▲ ] ▲    ▲
[Open Style:Report;[T/B Mar:0.5",0.5"][L/R Mar:0.5",0.5"][Just:Left][Ln Spacing:
2][Header A:Every page;[Flsh Rgt][SMALL]Draft at  ... ][Footer A:Every page;[SMA
LL][Centre]Page ^B]]SKERN LODGE ACTIVITIES[HRt]
[HRt]
Orienteering.[HRt]
[HRt]
After basic tuition in the use of map and compass, you have the[SRt]
opportunity to put new skills into practice.  We have different courses[SRt]
to be enjoyed at all levels [-] purely for fun or as a highly competitive[SRt]
scoring event.[HRt]

Press Reveal Codes to restore screen
```

**Figure 9.5** Style code in STYLE2.EX

2   You type the text that is to be enhanced by the style; it is inserted automatically between the two codes.
3   You exit the style, either by pressing the right arrow key to move beyond the Style Off code, or Alt-F8 (Style) and choose Off, or the Enter key if you have defined it to exit the style (see below).

What if you want to apply the style to some existing text? As you might imagine, you simply block the text (with Alt-F4 or dragging with the mouse), then press Alt-F8 to apply the style.

Creating a paired style is much the same as creating an open style, with two differences: you have to define how you use the Enter key immediately after applying the style, and you have to make entries at the end of the style, in the Style Off code, to turn off formats that were applied at the start of the style in the Style On code. You set both of these at the Styles Edit menu, when you create the style.

- There is an extra option on the Styles Edit menu, namely *Enter*. This allows you to define what the Enter key will do when you first press it after applying a style. There are three possibilities. It can:

  a   Retain its normal function of giving a hard return – use this if you want to type in text between the Style On and Style Off codes that contains returns, e.g. several paragraphs.
  b   Exit the style – use this if you want to apply the style to just a few words, such as a heading. (This saves you having to use other keys, described above, to exit the style.)
  c   Exit the style, and then apply it again – use this if you want to type some text in the style, then some more text in the default document format, and then some further text in the style.

  Once you have moved the cursor beyond the Style Off code, the Enter key behaves normally.

- At the Style Codes screen there is an On and an Off section. You are asked to enter the codes that you wish to apply in the On section, then the codes that are to end the style in the Off section. Almost always, you will want to enter Off codes that simply negate the effects of the first set of codes you entered in the On section. If this is the case, you needn't bother — WordPerfect will automatically do this for you as soon as it encounters the Style Off code.

## 9.9    Exercise: creating and applying paired styles

Skern Lodge wishes to create styles for enhancing the headings and subheadings of its reports. Figure 9.6 shows how the report you worked on in the last exercise (STYLE2.EX) will look with the main heading and subheading styles applied to it. In this exercise, you should create these two (paired) styles, then apply them to this report to achieve this effect.

When you have finished, save the collection (list) of styles you have created as DRAFT.STY, so that they can be applied to other documents. Also save STYLE2.EX with these styles applied to it.

Then try using your DRAFT.STY styles with a new document. Type in any appropriate text which includes a main heading and subheadings, and apply the styles. Also apply the Report open style that you created earlier. Save the result as STYLE3.EX.

Try to carry out this exercise without referring to the detailed instructions that follow, which are included to help if you get stuck.

```
SKERN LODGE ACTIVITIES


Orienteering.


After basic tuition in the use of map and compass, you have the
opportunity to put new skills into practice.  We have different courses
C:\WP51\BOOK\STYLE2.EX                      Doc 2 Pg 1 Ln 0.833" Pos 0.5"
[  ▲   ▲    ▲     ▲     ▲    ▲    ▲    ▲    ▲    ▲    ▲    ▲    ▲ ] ▲
[Open Style:Report][Style On:Heading 1:[LARGE][BOLD]]SKERN LODGE ACTIVITIES[Styl
e Off:Heading 1][HRt]
[HRt]
Orienteering.[HRt]
[HRt]
After basic tuition in the use of map and compass, you have the[SRt]
opportunity to put new skills into practice.  We have different courses[SRt]
to be enjoyed at all levels [-] purely for fun or as a highly competitive[SRt]
scoring event.[HRt]
[HRt]

Press Reveal Codes to restore screen
```

**Figure 9.6**   STYLE2.EX with open and paired styles applied

Start by creating a style for the main heading, as follows:

1  Retrieve STYLE2.EX, the file where you applied an open style.

2  Select Style, and Create. Enter a name − Heading 1 − and a description − Main heading style.

3  Select Codes, so that the Style Codes screen appears. Use the Font key to insert Large, and then the Bold key to insert emboldening before the Comment. There is no need to enter Off codes for these enhancements. Figure 9.7 shows the completed style codes.

4  Now create the subheading style, which you should name 'Heading 2' with description 'Subheading style'. At the Style Codes screen, in the On section, insert italics using the Font key, and emboldening using the Bold key. There is no need to insert any Off codes for these enhancements.

5  Now exit back to the styles list, which will now have 'Heading 1' and 'Heading 2' added to it. Since you want to use these styles in other documents, save the styles list as DRAFT.STY, and exit back to the STYLE2.EX document.

Now try applying these new styles to STYLE2.EX:

1  Since the text for the main heading already exists, you will have to block it first, so use the Block key to highlight the

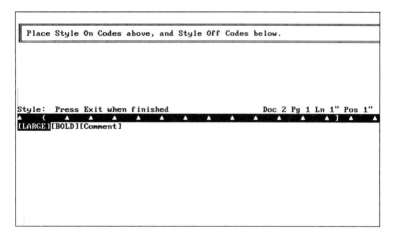

**Figure 9.7**  Completed Style Codes screen for Heading 1

main heading, and then press Style. With the cursor on the Heading 1 style, select On. You should be placed back at the text editing screen, with the following codes inserted at the beginning and end of the heading:

[Style On:Heading 1] [Style Off:Heading 1]

When the cursor is on the On code, you see the contents of the style — [LARGE][BOLD], as in Figure 9.6. When the cursor is on the Off code, you see the equivalent Off codes — [large][bold].

2  Now use the Block key to highlight the first subheading, and proceed as in step 1 where you applied the Heading 1 style, but applying Heading 2 instead. Back at the text editing screen, you have inserted a pair of style codes as follows:

[Style On:Heading 2] [Style Off:Heading 2]

at the beginning and end of the subheading text. When the cursor is on the Style On code, you see the [ITALC][BOLD] codes; when the cursor is on the Style Off code, you see the corresponding [italc][bold] codes.

3  Apply the Heading 2 style to the rest of the subheadings.

4  Now add in an extra section (see below) at the end of the document, applying the Heading 2 style to the heading as you type it in. To do this, with the cursor starting a new paragraph at the end of the document, turn on Heading 2 style. Then type the subheading 'Sailing'. Press the right arrow key to move past the Off code. Type in the rest of the text:

Sailing.

Our large open sea boats are the best possible for sailing in the Taw and Torridge estuary. During the tuition all on board can have an opportunity to take command themselves, under the watchful eye of an instructor.

5  Save your revised STYLE2.EX file and exit.

Now try using your styles in a new document:

1  On a blank screen, press Alt-F8 and select Retrieve. Type in

the style name — DRAFT.STY — and you will see the style names listed for you to choose from.

2    Turn on each style in turn, typing in some appropriate text. Note that the Report open style you created earlier should also be applied.

3    Save the document as STYLE3.EX and exit.

Look for the name of your style file — DRAFT.STY — in the directory allocated for style files. Although it contains a lot of formatting codes, the size of the file is quite small — only 589 bytes on my machine. You cannot retrieve or look at a style file.

## 9.10    Deleting a style

You can remove a style from your style list by choosing Delete from the Style List menu. WordPerfect gives you the following options:

- *Leaving codes.* This deletes the style, and replaces the style codes that you've inserted in the document by the codes contained in the style. Therefore, the document is unchanged, because the style codes have been converted to ordinary format codes.

- *Including codes.* This deletes the style from the style list, and its codes from the document. This changes the document, removing the effects of the style from it.

- *Definition only.* This deletes the style from the style list, but leaves its codes in the document, so that the document is not affected by the deletion. As its codes are present in the document, WordPerfect will recreate the style for you, restoring it to the style list. The purpose of this is to allow you to remove styles indiscriminately from large style lists, cutting it down to a manageable size, knowing that WordPerfect will restore any that are actually needed by the document.

## 9.11    Editing a style

If you want to change the contents of style, you can edit them by selecting the style name from the style list and choosing Edit from the menu. You are taken to the Styles Edit menu, where you can make your changes at the Style Codes screen. You can also change the style's name and description at this menu.

When you exit back to your document, every occurrence of the style within the document is updated, so that its appearance is changed. However, this change only affects the current document. Other documents that use this style are unaffected, unless you retrieve your modified style into them.

## 9.12  Exercise: editing an open style

In this exercise you should retrieve your STYLE2.EX document and edit the Report open style you created earlier by deleting the margin code. Resave your style list (DRAFT.STY), and save your changed document. Then retrieve STYLE3.EX, and retrieve into it your modified DRAFT.STY. If you now check the margins in STYLE3.EX, you will see that they have been automatically changed to reflect the changes in your Report open style.

In case you get stuck, here's a detailed list of steps you need to carry out for this exercise.

1  Retrieve your STYLE2.EX document and press Alt-F8 to go to the Styles screen.
2  Highlight 'Report' in the style list, and choose Edit.
3  Delete the left and right margin code so that the margins change back to the default 1″.
4  Exit the Style Codes screen, choose Save, and confirm the replacement of the previous version of DRAFT.STY.
5  Exit back to the document. WordPerfect should update the Report style in the document automatically, so that the left/ right margin code is removed from the style. (In practice this may not happen immediately, but if you scroll forwards and then back to the style code, the code should be updated.) Exit the document, saving it.

Now retrieve the STYLE3.EX document containing the previous version of the Report style. To update the style in this file, proceed as follows:

1  From the Styles menu, select Retrieve.
2  Type 'DRAFT.STY', the name of the style file, and confirm

that you wish to replace the current list of styles with the saved list.

3   Exit back to the document from the Styles menu. The Report style should be updated in STYLE3.EX. Save the document and exit.

## 9.13   Exercise: editing a paired style

In your DRAFT.STY style file you have a paired style called Heading 2 containing italics and emboldening. You decide you want to add a further font change – small capitals, and you want the changed style applied to your STYLE2.EX and STYLE3.EX files. Do this, then save both these documents with these changes.

In case you need help with this, the detailed steps are as follows.

1   Retrieve STYLE2.EX and edit the Heading 2 style codes by adding to it small capitals (Ctrl-F8, Appearance).
2   Save the style file, replacing the previous version (DRAFT.STY).
3   Exit back to the document, and you should see that all your Heading 2 styles are updated. You will have to look at the View Document screen to see the small capitals.
4   Save the document and exit.
5   Retrieve STYLE3.EX and retrieve into it the style file DRAFT.STY.
6   Confirm that you wish to replace the current styles with the new list, and then exit back to the document. As you will see, all Heading 2 styles have been automatically updated. Save the document and exit.

## 9.14   Exercise: creating a style from existing codes

One of your earlier files – BROCHUR2.EX – contains a large number of codes at the beginning of the document, including left/right margin, top/bottom margin, header, and footer. You would like to use these four codes in an open style. Create this style, saving it as BROCHURE.STY.

The detailed steps are:

1   Retrieve BROCHUR2.EX and reveal the codes. Use the
    Block key to select the following codes:

>    left/right margin
>    top/bottom margin
>    header
>    footer

    Do not include the codes or text of the main heading.
2   Press the Style key and select Create. Enter the name BRO-
    CHURE for the style, and BROCHURE FORMAT for the
    description. Change the type to Open. You should see all the
    above codes in the Style Codes screen.
3   Save the style as BROCHURE.STY, and exit the document.
4   On a blank screen, retrieve the BROCHURE.STY style file.
    You should have all the formatting in place for starting a new
    brochure. Exit the document without saving.

## 9.15   Overwriting styles

Your STYLE2.EX file exists at the moment as a draft. It contains
various styles which you use in draft reports, in a style file called
DRAFT.STY. Imagine, for the sake of the exercises that are
coming up shortly, that this report has been edited and now exists
in its final form, and you want to apply different styles to the final
text. The way to approach this is to create another style file
containing the new styles, and then as long as the style names are
the same in both style files, you can retrieve the new ones into
the document and replace the old ones automatically.

   When you retrieve styles which have the same name as existing
styles, WordPerfect will display the 'Style(s) Already Exist.
Replace?' message. If you type 'N', WordPerfect retrieves only
those styles whose names do not match current style names. If
you type 'Y', WordPerfect retrieves all of the styles, replacing
current styles with the incoming styles of the same name.

## 9.16   Defining a default style file

When you press the Style key in a new document, the style list
that appears is normally empty. You have to choose Retrieve

from the Style menu to retrieve a style file with its list of files. However, you can specify that WordPerfect treats one of your style files as the *default list*. Then, whenever you press Style in a new document, this list is automatically retrieved into it.

To do this:

- Go to the Location of Files menu in Setup (press Shift-F1,5), then type the name of the style file as the library filename.

For this book, we have set up a style file called BOOK.STY; since we are constantly using it, we have made it our default style file, as shown in Figure 9.8.

Note that:

- If you wish to use another style file instead of the default, you should use the Retrieve option on the Styles menu. If any styles have the same name, WordPerfect will display the 'Styles already exist' message described in the last section.

- If, on the other hand, you wish to use the default file as well as some other styles that are used in a document, you should use the Update option on the Styles menu. Any existing

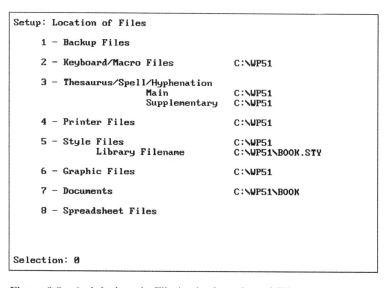

```
Setup: Location of Files

    1 - Backup Files

    2 - Keyboard/Macro Files           C:\WP51

    3 - Thesaurus/Spell/Hyphenation
                         Main          C:\WP51
                         Supplementary C:\WP51

    4 - Printer Files                  C:\WP51

    5 - Style Files                    C:\WP51
            Library Filename           C:\WP51\BOOK.STY

    6 - Graphic Files                  C:\WP51

    7 - Documents                      C:\WP51\BOOK

    8 - Spreadsheet Files


Selection: 0
```

**Figure 9.8**   A default style File in the Location of Files menu

styles of the same name are then automatically overwritten. The 'Styles already exist' message will not in this case be displayed.

## 9.17   Exercise: creating a new style file for reports

In this exercise you will be creating a new style file for reports. You will do this by amending the styles contained in your DRAFT.STY file:

| Report | Open | Draft report format |
|--------|------|--------------------|
| Heading 1 | Paired | Main heading format |
| Heading 2 | Paired | Subheading format |

1   Retrieve STYLE2.EX; this is your draft report containing the DRAFT.STY styles.
2   Edit each style in the list as follows:

   a   Report: Delete all margin codes, line spacing, justification and header, leaving just the footer code for page numbering. Change the description to 'Report format'.
   b   Heading 1: Change the [LARGE] code to [VRY LARGE].
   c   Heading 2: Delete the [ITALC] code.

Save the revised list as SKERNREP.STY.
3   When you exit the style list, the document should be updated with the new styles. Save the document and exit.

You now have two style files which you have created – DRAFT.STY and SKERNREP.STY.

## 9.18   Exercise: defining a default style file and updating

In this exercise, you should define SKERNREP.STY as your default file, and then retrieve STYLE3.EX and update the styles in it with your new defaults.
The detailed steps are as follows:

1   Select the Location of Files menu from Setup, and enter SKERNREP.STY as the library filename.
2   Now check that this default appears on new documents. On a

blank screen press the Style key. The styles list should display the SKERNREP style names. Exit without saving.

3  Retrieve your STYLE3.EX report. This currently has the DRAFT.STY style file attached. Choose Update from the Styles menu. This will retrieve the default style file, automatically overwriting any existing styles of the same name. Your STYLE3.EX document should now contain styles for a final report, rather than a draft. Check its appearance.

## 9.19  Outline

WordPerfect provides an automatic paragraph labelling facility called 'Outline'. When this is turned on, all subsequent paragraphs in your document are numbered, or lettered, with a style of your choice. If you subsequently delete numbered paragraphs or insert extra ones, WordPerfect automatically updates the numbering.

You can insert subparagraphs below main paragraphs, and subsubparagraphs, down to eight levels, all appropriately labelled. Main (Level 1) paragraphs are aligned at the left margin, Level 2 paragraphs are aligned at the first tab stop, and lower level paragraphs at subsequent tab stops.

This outlining facility is obviously very useful if you wish to create e.g. reports with paragraph numbering. Not only is the numbering itself handled completely automatically, WordPerfect provides you with the facility for moving, copying, or deleting complete outline families. (A 'family' is a paragraph together with all its subordinate (lower level) paragraphs.) You can thus, with a few keystrokes, extensively reorganize your document.

Figure 9.9 shows a document with three levels of paragraph, illustrating WordPerfect's default 'Outline' numbering style. The full eight levels of numbering that this style provides are:

    I.  Level 1
        A.  Level 2
            1.  Level 3
                a.  Level 4
                    (1)  Level 5
                        (a)  Level 6
                            i)  Level 7
                                a)  Level 8

```
SKERN LODGE OUTDOOR CENTRE

How to get there

I.   BY ROAD

     A.   If approaching the West Country by the M5 Motorway
          (south towards Exeter), exit at Junction 27
          Tiverton.

          1.   Follow signs to North Devon, Barnstable and
               Bideford.
          2.   Turn right at roundabout.
          3.   Follow A386 signs.

II.  BY RAIL OR COACH

     A.   Barnstable is the nearest train station.

     B.   Coaches run from most places in the country to
          Bideford.

SKERN LODGE transport can collect you from Barnstable or
Bideford.
```

**Figure 9.9**   Example of automatic paragraph numbering

## 9.20   Outlining a document

To turn on the automatic outlining (paragraph numbering) facility, press the Shift-F5 Outline key and, from the menu that appears, choose Outline, On. An [Outline On] code is inserted in your document, and 'Outline' appears in the status line.

After this code, the first time you press Enter a Level 1 paragraph number is inserted. If you immediately press Tab, this changes to a Level 2 number indented at the first tab stop. Press Tab again, and it changes to a Level 3 number at the next tab stop. Subsequent Tab presses reduce the level further. If you reduce the level too far, you can press Shift-Tab to increase it back. Having tabbed to the required level, you can type your paragraph in the normal way. If you wish to indent the paragraph (to offset it from the number), press the F4 Indent key in the normal way at the start of the paragraph.

Each automatic paragraph number is created by pressing Enter followed, if necessary, by pressing Tab or Shift-Tab. Each time, a [Par Num:Auto] code is inserted in your document. If you are working in Outline mode but do not want the Enter key to insert a paragraph number, then you can delete the appropriate [Par Num:Auto] at the Codes screen; it's easier, though, to press the key that WordPerfect provides for this purpose:

• Press Ctrl-V immediately before pressing Enter to turn off the Outline feature temporarily. This does not affect subsequent presses of Enter.

(If you want to number only some of the paragraphs in your document, then you may find it more convenient to use the alternative paragraph numbering feature instead of outlining, as this avoids the need to use Ctrl-V repeatedly. This is described later in this chapter.)

Note that to change the level of an existing outline paragraph, you should place the cursor immediately after the outline number and press Tab or Shift-Tab.

When you have finished using Outline, press Shift-F5 and choose Outline, Off.

## 9.21 Defining the outline numbering style

Besides its default outline numbering style, WordPerfect offers you three other styles plus the option of defining your own style. You can see these other styles by pressing the Shift-F5 Outline key then choosing Define.

The Paragraph Number Definition menu shown in Figure 9.10 appears. The default Outline style is number 3 in the list of styles, the others being:

2  Paragraph
4  Legal
5  Bullets
6  User-defined (described in the next section).

You can choose any of these from the list as a replacement for the default Outline style. When you do so, your choice appears in the 'Current Definition' section of the menu, and a [Par Num Def] code is placed at the current cursor position in the document. Any outline paragraph numbers after this code are displayed in your chosen style. This doesn't affect the way the outline facility works.

```
Paragraph Number Definition

    1 - Starting Paragraph Number                 1
        (in legal style)
                                           Levels
                        1     2     3     4     5     6     7     8
    2 - Paragraph       1.    a.    i.    (1)   (a)   (i)   1)    a)
    3 - Outline         I.    A.    1.    a.    (1)   (a)   i)    a)
    4 - Legal (1.1.1)   1     .1    .1    .1    .1    .1    .1    .1
    5 - Bullets         *     o     -     ■     *     +     .     x
    6 - User-defined

    Current Definition  I.    A.    1.    a.    (1)   (a)   i)    a)
    Attach Previous Level     No    No    No    No    No    No    No

    7 - Enter Inserts Paragraph Number            Yes

    8 - Automatically Adjust to Current Level      Yes

    9 - Outline Style Name



Selection: 8
```

**Figure 9.10** The Paragraph Number Definition menu

This facility is very flexible:

● You can have several [Par Num Def] codes in your text if you wish, the style defined by each taking effect up till the next code.
● You can insert a [Par Num Def] code after you have created the paragraphs if you wish. Simply position the cursor at the point in your document where you want the new style to begin, and define it. (If your code is a straight replacement for the default Outline style, position the cursor on the [Outline On] code at the start of the numbered paragraphs.) To see the effect of your changes, either update the screen by pressing Ctrl-F3,3, or scroll through the document.
● You can delete a [Par Num Def] code if you wish, in which case the style reverts to the previous code or, if there is none, to the default Outline style.

## 9.22  Defining your own numbering style

If you choose 'User-defined' at the Paragraph Number Definition menu, the screen changes to that shown in Figure 9.11 allowing you to create your own outline numbering style.

The list of choices at the bottom of the screen allows you to include letters, numbers, and punctuation in your definition. You can also use the Compose key (Ctrl-2) to insert other WordPerfect characters.

After typing in your choices, you can enter 'Y' or 'N' in the Attach Previous Level field. If you enter 'Y' here, WordPerfect will incorporate the numbers of higher-level paragraphs in the labels it gives lower levels. The legal style, for example, has this automatically set to 'Y', so the first Level 1 paragraph in this case will be numbered '1.', the third subparagraph under this will be '1.3.', and the second subsubparagraph under this will be numbered '1.3.2.'.

## 9.23 Manipulating outline families

An outline *family* is the outline level on the line where the cursor is located, plus any subordinate (lower) levels. WordPerfect allows you to treat a family as a single entity for the purposes of moving, copying or deleting, so allowing you to carry out major surgery on your document quickly and easily.

To use this facility, position the cursor on the first line of the family, press the Shift-F5 Outline key, choose Outline, then choose one of the editing options: Move, Copy, or Delete. In the case of Move or Copy, you must then press the arrow keys to move the cursor to where you want to put the family, then Enter.

```
Paragraph Number Definition

    1 - Starting Paragraph Number               1
        (in legal style)
                                        Levels
                              ▌1▐  ▌2▐  ▌3▐  ▌4▐  ▌5▐  ▌6▐  ▌7▐  ▌8▐
    2 - Paragraph            1.   a.   i.   (1)  (a)  (i)  1)   a)
    3 - Outline              I.   A.   1.   a.   (1)  (a)  i)   a)
    4 - Legal (1.1.1)        1    .1   .1   .1   .1   .1   .1   .1
    5 - Bullets              *    o    -    ■    *    +    ·    x
    6 - User-defined

    Current Definition       1)   A)   i)   (a)  (1)  (A)  (i)  (a)
    Attach Previous Level         No   No   No   No   No   No   No

    7 - Enter Inserts Paragraph Number           Yes

    8 - Automatically Adjust to Current Level     Yes

    9 - Outline Style Name

1 - Digits, A - Uppercase Letters, a - Lowercase Letters
I - Uppercase Roman, i - Lowercase Roman
X - Uppercase Roman/Digits if Attached, x - Lowercase Roman/Digits if Attached
Other character - Bullet or Punctuation
```

**Figure 9.11** User-defined Numbering menu

Note that the Move and Copy options will only be successful if the family ends with two hard returns.

## 9.24 Exercise: applying outline numbering

In this exercise you should create the document shown in Figure 9.9, using the default Outline numbering style. You should then change its numbering style to legal, saving the file as OUTLINE.EX. You should also define your own numbering style, and apply it to the document. You should then try the effect of inserting an additional paragraph in the middle of the document, and you should practise using the 'family' features provided by WordPerfect by moving the 'BY RAIL OR COACH' family in front of the 'BY ROAD' family.

If you need help with any of this, the detailed steps are given below.

1   Type the first two lines of the document shown in Figure 9.9, then press Shift-F5 and choose Outline. The word 'Outline' appears at the left of the status line.

2   Press Enter. WordPerfect inserts the first level of number – 'I.' – at the left margin. If you switch on the Reveal Codes screen, you will see the code [Par Num:Auto], and above it [Outline On].

3   Press F4 (Indent) to indent the left margin of your paragraph, and type the first numbered paragraph in Figure 9.9.

4   Press Enter to start a new paragraph. WordPerfect treats this as a first level paragraph, numbering it 'II.'. Press Tab if you want to change it to a lower-level subparagraph. (Further Tab presses reduce the level. Shift-Tab reverses this, so increasing the level.)

5   Repeat step 4 for each numbered paragraph that you wish to type.

6   For the final unnumbered paragraph you can either turn off the Outline feature, or you can delete the [Par Num:Auto] code.

7   Under paragraph number I.A., add in a new item 2 as follows:

   a   With the cursor at the end of item 1, press Enter. This inserts a new item numbered '2.', and updates the other item numbers.

b   Type in the following text:

Cross the new high-level Bideford Bridge.

8   Under paragraph II, find the [Par Num:Auto] code for B. Delete it and the [Tab] and [Indent] codes. Join up the text with the previous paragraph. You should now have items A and B. Save the document.

9   Now change the style of numbering, as follows:

a   Place the cursor at the beginning of the document, and reveal the codes.

b   Look for the [Outline On] code and place the cursor on that code.

c   Press Shift-F5 and choose Define. The menu in Figure 9.10 will display.

d   Choose style number 4 – Legal. This inserts a [Par Num Def:] code in the document. Use the Rewrite option on Ctrl-F3 to display the numbering.

10   Save the document as OUTLINE.EX.

11   Using OUTLINE.EX, place the cursor at the beginning of the document and reveal the codes.

12   Look for the [Par Num Def:] code and delete it.

13   Press Shift-F5, select Define, and User-defined. Use the menu at the bottom of the screen to create your own style. Use the Enter key to move forward through the settings.

14   Exit back to the document and rewrite the screen. You should see the document with its new style of numbering.

15   Exit the document without saving.

16   Now retrieve OUTLINE.EX and practise rearranging your numbered paragraphs. This exercise need not be saved.

a   We are going to move section 2 up to become section 1, and for a successful move, make sure that there are two [HRt] codes at the end of the text in OUTLINE.EX.

b   Place the cursor on the line '2. BY RAIL OR COACH'. Select Outline, and Move Family. The screen should look like Figure 9.12.

c   Press the up arrow key to move the 'family' and press Enter.

## 9.25   Paragraph numbering

Besides its standard Outline feature, WordPerfect offers an alternative paragraph numbering facility which allows you to mix numbered and unnumbered paragraphs. Like outlining, it allows up to eight levels of numbering and the same choice of numbering styles. It differs from Outline, however, in that you must give the paragraph numbering command each time you want to insert a number. This is rather more cumbersome than using the Outline facility, but it has the advantage that the Enter and Tab keys behave normally on other occasions.

To give the paragraph number command, move the cursor to where you want the number inserted, press the Shift-F5 Outline key, then choose Para Num. The following message will appear:

Paragraph Level (Press Enter for Automatic)

This gives you the choice of two numbering methods:

1   Enter the paragraph level, e.g. '1' for a top level paragraph number, '2' for the next level down, and so on; this number is

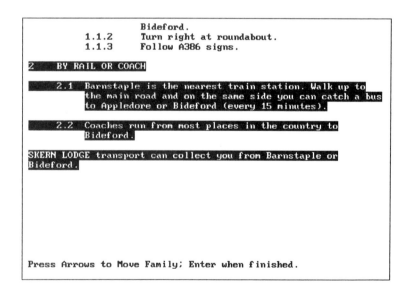

**Figure 9.12**   Outline text highlighted for moving

then unaffected by any tabs that you may apply to it in order to indent it.

2  Press Enter by itself if you wish WordPerfect to determine the level automatically. WordPerfect does this by looking at the position that you have tabbed to on the line. For example, no tabs will produce a top level paragraph number, one tab will give a second level paragraph number, and so on.

## 9.26 Exercise: applying paragraph numbering

1  Retrieve the W&O.EX file containing numerous paragraphs with subheadings.
2  At the beginning of each subheading, press Shift-F5 and select Para Num. At the paragraph level prompt, press Enter.
3  Use the Tab key to insert spaces between the number and the heading. Repeat this all the way through the document.
4  Change the style of numbering by moving the cursor to the beginning of the [Par Num:Auto] codes and selecting the legal style of numbering.
5  Exit the document without saving.

## 9.27 Outline styles

WordPerfect's Outline Style feature allows you to apply automatic enhancements and alignments to your paragraph numbers, as well as allowing you to store your own user-defined numbering definitions. Like the document styles described earlier, outline styles are displayed (and stored) in an outline style list, which can be saved as a separate file and applied to other documents.

The Outline feature forces you to have subparagraphs indented, whereas the Outline Style feature defaults to all levels of numbering appearing at the left margin. However, you can if you wish insert indenting codes at step 2 below.

To create an outline style:

1  Choose Outline Style Name from the Paragraph Number Definition menu (you get to this by pressing Shift-F5,6). You then see an outline styles list, similar to that in Figure 9.13.

This contains no named styles, only the default which stores the default numbering style you used earlier.

2   Choose Create from the menu at the foot of the Outline Styles screen, and the Outline Styles Edit menu will appear, shown in Figure 9.14. Like the document Styles Edit menu you used earlier in this chapter, this allows you to enter a name and description for your outline style. It also allows you to enter codes for up to eight levels of paragraph number. Entering the codes and other information at this menu (including the function of the Enter key) is little different from making the entries required at the document Styles Edit menu, and is described in Section 38 of the Keystroke Guide.

The style you create will be incorporated in both the outline style list and the main style list for the current document. It can be saved from the Outline Styles menu and then retrieved into other documents. It can also be retrieved into your main style list (using Alt-F8 — Style, and choosing the retrieve option there), where you can edit it or save it as part of another style file. However, you cannot apply it from the main style list; when you retrieve it to this style list it is also retrieved into the outline style list, and you must use the Outline Define option to apply it from there.

```
Outline Styles

   Name                    Description

 -- NONE --         Use paragraph numbers only




















1 Select; 2 Create; 3 Edit; 4 Delete; 5 Save; 6 Retrieve; 7 Update: 1
```

**Figure 9.13**   Outline Styles menu

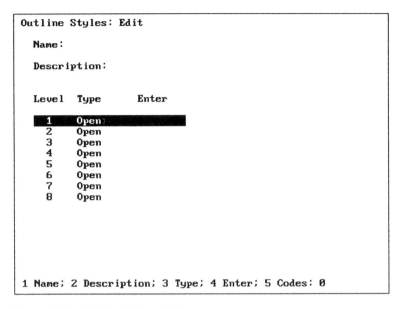

```
Outline Styles: Edit

  Name:

  Description:


  Level   Type        Enter

    1     Open
    2     Open
    3     Open
    4     Open
    5     Open
    6     Open
    7     Open
    8     Open





  1 Name; 2 Description; 3 Type; 4 Enter; 5 Codes: 0
```

**Figure 9.14**  Outline Styles Edit menu

## 9.28  The exercise: using an outline style

Skern Lodge wishes to develop an outline style for use with certain documents which uses the bullet style of paragraph labelling, and which inserts some emboldening, tabs, and indents. Develop a suitable style.

If you wish to use our suggestions for this style, follow the steps given below.

1  Start with a blank screen, and press the Outline key and choose Define, Outline Style Name. You will see the menu shown in Figure 9.13.
2  Choose Create, and you will then see the Outline Styles Edit menu as in Figure 9.14. Enter the name 'DIRECTIONS' and the description 'Bullet style'.
3  Then start entering codes for each level you intend to use, as follows.

    a  Level 1 codes should appear as in Figure 9.15. The first code is inserted by selecting 5 (Bullets) from the Paragraph

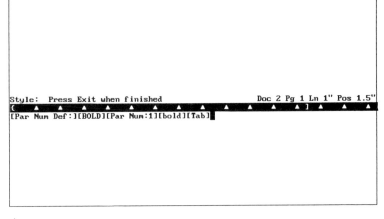

**Figure 9.15**  Codes for Level 1 outline style

Number Definition menu. Press Bold before and after the [Par Num] code. Finally insert a [Tab] code.

b  Level 2 codes should be
   [Tab][BOLD][Par Num:2][bold][Indent]
c  Level 3 codes should be
   [Tab][Tab][BOLD][Par Num:3][bold][Indent]

```
SKERN LODGE OUTDOOR CENTRE

How to get there

•    BY ROAD

     o    If approaching the West Country by the M5 Motorway
          (south towards Exeter), exit at Junction 27
          Tiverton.

               -    Follow signs to North Devon, Barnstable and
                    Bideford.
               -    Turn right at roundabout.
               -    Follow A386 signs.

•    BY RAIL OR COACH

     o    Barnstable is the nearest train station.

     o    Coaches run from most places in the country to
          Bideford.

SKERN LODGE transport can collect you from Barnstable or
Bideford.
```

**Figure 9.16**  OUTSTYLE.EX

4 Exit back to the outline style list, and save the outline style as 'DIRECTS.STY'. Choose Select and exit to the Paragraph Numbering Definition menu, where your style name 'DIRECTIONS' should be entered as the current outline style name.

5 Exit back to your document screen, and start typing the text in Figure 9.16. When you reach the first outline level, choose Outline, On; 'Outline' displays in the status line.

6 Press Enter and you should see the first outline bullet emboldened, and the cursor at the next tab position. Use the Tab and Shift-Tab keys to insert lower and higher levels as with normal outline.

7 Save the file, calling it OUTSTYLE.EX.

# 10
# Desktop publishing

## 10.1  What you will achieve in this chapter

This chapter shows you how to add that professional finish to your documents, using WordPerfect's powerful graphics and desktop publishing capabilities. When you have completed it, you should be able to:

- Apply different fonts and point sizes to text, both manually and using styles.
- Change the default font.
- Include graphics in a document.
- Use graphic lines in a document.
- Create a table of contents.
- Create an index.

In the chapter, you will be applying what you learn to some of the Skern Lodge documents you created earlier in the book. The particular skills you will learn are how to produce a good looking desktop published document with WordPerfect.

## 10.2  Routines you will use in this chapter

As you work through this chapter, you will be getting to grips with the following routines. The Keystroke Guide section number for each routine is given below in brackets.

- Use the Font key to select a font (15).
- Use the Style key to create a paired style containing a font code (57).

- Change the default font (15).
- Use the Font key to select a different point size (15).
- Insert a graphic (17).
- Edit a graphic (17).
- Insert a horizontal graphics line (18).
- Insert a vertical graphics line (18).
- Edit a graphics line (18).
- Use the Mark Text key to create a table of contents (64).
- Use the Mark Text key to create an index (24).

## 10.3   What is desktop publishing?

Desktop publishing (DTP) means using the capabilities of your personal computer and printer to create documents that look like they have been typeset and printed in the conventional way, with fonts, graphics, and other effects, all properly laid out on the page. For this, you need suitable DTP software, and a high quality computer printer such as a laser printer.

Desktop publishing took off in the latter half of the 1980s, following the development of low-cost laser printers small enough to occupy just the corner of a desk, and DTP software such as PageMaker and Ventura. The trouble was, you had to word process your document using another package, and then import it into the DTP package to lay it out on the page with whatever graphics and other features were required.

So word processing packages such as WordPerfect introduced DTP features (and DTP packages introduced some WP capabilities), so that today you carry out the entire text creation and publishing task with a single package. You have already made use of some of WordPerfect's features to enhance the presentation of your work — different sizes and appearance of text, alignment, columns, and so forth — but these only scratch the surface of its DTP capabilities. In this chapter, you will learn how to make the most of these to produce attractive newsletters and brochures.

If you don't have a suitable printer, offering a range of fonts and with graphics capabilities, then some of this chapter will be of little relevance to you, and you will not be able to complete all the exercises. For example, if you only have access to a daisy wheel printer then there is little that you can accomplish in the way of DTP. A laser printer is obviously best, though ink jet printers can give excellent results, as can some dot matrix printers.

This chapter compresses into a few pages what is a very large subject, for DTP involves all kinds of typographical and page layout skills. We start by discussing DTP design principles; then we explore how to make the most of WordPerfect's font capabilities; then how to incorporate graphics in your documents. Then you create a DTP document. Finally, we deal with how WordPerfect can create tables of contents and indexes for your documents.

## 10.4   Designing DTP documents

This is an extensive subject, and we can only provide a brief summary of the principles here. Some basic design rules are as follows:

- Make sure the text is easily legible, and the eye is not distracted from it by too many fancy effects. Choose a suitable font and font size, don't mix too many fonts on the page (keep to a maximum of two or three), and be sparing with enhancements such as bold and italics.
- As a related point, make sure the lines are not too long; if necessary, split the page into columns.
- If you have several articles or sections on a page, organize them visually by means of horizontal or vertical lines. Study newspapers and magazines to see how the professionals do it.
- Organize the page around a single dominant visual element, such as a graphic or a headline.
- Use subheads to provide a transition from the main headline to the body text and to provide a visually more interesting page.
- Use white space to make design elements stand out from the page. Avoid too much white space in the centre of the page, and avoid too little at the margins.

And, of course, the text itself must be well written. This means it must be coherent and organized properly; sentences must be short and crisp; and paragraphs short. Use techniques such as bulleted paragraphs to list points, and subheads to organize and break up text.

## 10.5   Fonts

Many modern computer printers allow you to use a variety of

fonts (or 'founts' as they used to be called) for your documents. Laser printers are particularly good in this respect. Used prudently, fonts can give your document the appearance of being typeset professionally. Most word processing packages now allow you to take advantage of fonts, and WordPerfect is no exception.

The fonts that are normally used for typewritten and word processed work are called 'Courier' and 'Elite'. In these, each character occupies a fixed amount of space on the page. The amount of space used is called the pitch. Typical pitch settings are:

- 10-pitch (meaning that each character occupies $\frac{1}{10}''$, giving 10 characters to the inch).
- 12-pitch (giving 12 characters to the inch).
- 15-pitch (giving 15 characters to the inch).

For typesetting work, the Times Roman font is often used. This does not have a fixed amount of space per character. Instead, the space depends on the shape of the character, how it fits in with adjacent characters, and the spacing that has to be added between characters to make sure that each line is justified at the right margin. Some other fonts used in typesetting also have these characteristics. They are called proportionally spaced fonts. Clearly this type of font cannot be used on ordinary typewriters or daisy wheel printers, but it can be used on laser printers.

Besides this division into fixed-space and proportionally spaced fonts, there is a further division into serif and sans-serif:

- 'Serif' refers to embellishments that are added to each letter, such as horizontal lines at the top and bottom of the capital T. The typeface used in this book (Times) is a serif font.
- 'Sans-serif' refers to the absence of such embellishments. The section headings in this book are in a sans-serif font.

## 10.6   The base font

The *base font* is the font that is applied automatically to your document, except where you specify other fonts. It is also called the *current font*.

However, there are several varieties of base font, accessed from different function keys, and it is important that you understand the differences between them:

- The *default initial base font*, set using the Shift-F7 Print key. We shall refer to this simply as the 'default base font'. This is the font that WordPerfect automatically applies to all your documents. When you install a printer, WordPerfect selects Courier as the default font unless you specify something else.

- The *document initial base font*, set using the Shift-F8 Format key. We shall refer to this simply as the 'initial base font'. This sets the base font for the current document, negating the default base font set via Shift-F7. No code is inserted in your document when you set this.

- The *base font*, applied using the Ctrl-F8 Font key. This inserts a code in the document, and affects all text after the code, taking precedence over previous base font settings.

In the exercises on the next pages you will practise setting all of these.

We have already seen how using WordPerfect's Font key allows different sizes and appearances of text to be selected, using the base font. In this chapter we go beyond this to experiment with different fonts. To see what fonts are available with your printer, press the Ctrl-F8 Font key and choose Base Font, and the fonts should be listed.

## 10.7   Exercise: changing the initial base font

In Chapter 2 you created the first version of your brochure in a file called BROCHUR1.EX. In Chapter 3 you made font attribute changes to this file which altered the size and appearance of text, but retained the original base font of Courier. This changed version was saved as BROCHUR2.EX.

Retrieve BROCHUR1.EX − the original brochure file − and see how effective a change of base font can be. Press the Format key and choose Document Initial Base Font. (Your cursor can be in any position when you do this, as this operation does not insert a code into the document. It also changes the base font for the current document only.) You then select a design from a list of fonts, and also specify the point size. For this exercise you should specify Helvetica, using a point size of 12. Points specify the vertical size of the characters; there are 72 points to the inch. Then save your document as FONT.EX and print it.

If you need detailed help with this, the steps are as follows:

1 Press the Shift-F8 Format key and choose Document.
2 Select 3 (Initial Base Font). A list of available fonts will display.
3 Move the cursor to Helvetica and choose Select. You are then prompted 'Point size:', followed by the current point size which is probably 12.
4 Press Enter to retain the point size of 12.
5 Press Exit to return to the normal editing screen.
6 Save the document, calling it FONT.EX.
7 Print the document.

When you exit back to the document, you will find that your lines are longer. A proportionally spaced font takes up less room on the page. View the document to see how your text would print. Is Helvetica a serif or a sans-serif font?

Compare the printed copy of FONT.EX with BROCHUR2.EX, and note the improved presentation of body text in the FONT document.

## 10.8 Further exercise: changing the initial base font

Retrieve your MENU.EX file which contains a menu. Change the initial base font from the current one, probably Courier, to a proportionally spaced font. Try something new from the list – perhaps Avant Garde or Palatino – and print the result. Whichever font you choose, it almost certainly will look a lot more attractive than the same menu printed in Courier. Don't save the changed document.

## 10.9 Exercise: changing the font and point sizes

Some printers provide different font styles giving italics and emboldening. Examples include Helvetica Bold and Helvetica Oblique. In this exercise, you are going to try some of these on parts of the text on your FONT.EX file. Since you will not be applying this change to the whole document, you will be selecting fonts using the Ctrl-F8 Font key.

1 Retrieve FONT.EX and reveal the codes.
2 Place the cursor on the first letter of the main heading. Using

the Font key, choose Base Font, and choose Helvetica Bold if available, and change the point size of the main heading to 24. If this style is not available to you, block the main heading and embolden it.

3   Again selecting Base Font, change the point size of the first subheading – 'MANAGEMENT TRAINING – THE PRACTICE OF TEAMWORK' – to 16 point.

Your FONT document now contains two font codes:

- one at the beginning of the main heading for 24 point;
- one at the beginning of the subheading for 16 point.

Since the 16 pt font code is the last one in the document, all the text forwards from the code is currently in 16 pt. This is too large for body text which should normally be no more than 12 pt, so insert a Helvetica 12 pt code at the start of the body text. To do this:

4   With the cursor at the beginning of the first paragraph ('Skern Lodge has achieved...'), use the Font key to change the base font from Helvetica 16 pt to Helvetica 12 pt. Check on the View Document screen to see the effect of these codes.

## 10.10   Exercise: using fonts in a style

In the above exercise, you inserted font codes before and after text in order to restrict the effect to that text. Why not try creating a paired style which will do the same thing more easily? Once created, a paired style can be applied to lots of headings. Specifically, you would like to create a style in order to apply the Helvetica Narrow Bold Oblique 14 pt font to further headings in the FONT.EX brochure. Do this now for the headings listed at step 5 below, saving the changed brochure, and saving the style as FONT.STY.

The detailed steps are as follows:

1   Retrieve FONT.EX. Press the Style key and choose Create.
2   Call the style 'Fonts' and enter the font name and point size as the description.
3   Press Codes and use the Font key to enter a base font code of Helvetica Narrow Bold Oblique 14 pt before the comment.

This is the On code. Don't enter anything after the comment. With this blank, WordPerfect will insert automatically whatever is your initial base font as the Off code. In the case of your current file, this will be Helvetica 12 pt.

4 Exit to the Style menu and save the style as FONT.STY. You can now use it in other documents. Exit back to the document.

5 Block each of the following subheadings and apply your font style to them:

> Outdoor Training
> Results
> SAMPLE ADULT WEEKEND PROGRAMME

6 Have a look at the contents of the Style Off code and you will see that WordPerfect has inserted your initial base font of Helvetica 12 pt. View the document to see the effect of the style. Save the document, replacing the previous version.

## 10.11 Further exercise: applying the font style

Retrieve the latest version of the prospectus file – PROSP2.EX. Retrieve your font style with the Font key, and apply it to each of the nine subheadings. Save the file again as PROSP2.EX and exit the document.

## 10.12 Exercise: changing the default base font

You may wish to change your default base font for all future documents. This exercise shows you how to do this.

1 With a blank screen, press the Print key and choose Select Printer. You should then see a list of printers installed on your machine.

2 With the cursor bar on your default printer, choose Edit. You will then see the Select Printer Edit menu.

3 Choose 5 (Initial Base Font) which currently displays your default base font. You should then see the list of fonts available.

4 Select the font and point size you require – Helvetica and 12 pt if available – and exit back to the editing screen.
    If you now type in some text and view the document, you

204 Word Processing Skills

should see that the text is formatted according to your new default base font. Press the Font key and look at the list of possible base fonts, and you should see your new base font as the current one. Note that any existing documents will not change, since the font that's the default at the time of saving is saved to the document.

5 Now change the default back to the original base font. When you exit back to the editing screen, you should see no change in the current document. However, any new files you create will use the original default base font.

## 10.13 Graphics

WordPerfect lets you incorporate a variety of graphics effects in your documents, such as pictures ('images') created with drawing software or computer-aided design (CAD) software, or scanned into your computer using a scanner. You can also incorporate graphs created using a spreadsheet package. This chapter does not tell you how to create these images − for this you will have to refer to the appropriate software documentation − merely how to use them in WordPerfect. (For a list of graphics software that is compatible with WordPerfect, see the Graphics Formats and Programs section of the manual.)

WordPerfect incorporates images in documents by enclosing them in what it calls *graphics boxes*. These are described in the next sections.

## 10.14 Graphics boxes

A graphics box acts as a holder for an image, allowing you to place it at an appropriate position in your document. It also provides a number of effects, such as a border, shading, a caption, and a caption numbering style. So, if you wanted to apply some of these effects to some text, you could place that text within a graphics box.

You can have any number of graphics boxes in a document, and you can set them up in the main body text, or in headers, footers, footnotes, endnotes and styles. (You would include a graphics box in a header, for example, if you want an image repeated on the top of every page.) Normally, a graphics box will contain a graphics image, though it could hold text, or it could be empty.

The steps in setting up a graphics box are described below. They fall into two stages:

1 Choose the type of graphics box.
2 Define the graphics box, i.e. specify its appearance and what it should contain.

Once you have created a graphics box, you can see its outline on the normal editing screen, as in Figure 10.1. However, you do not see the graphic itself. As with other graphics effects, you have to view the document to display the page as it will print. Figure 10.2 shows the same document on the View screen.

## 10.15 Selecting the type of graphics box

You can choose between five different types of graphics box. Your choice determines the border that surrounds the box, whether or not the box has background shading, and various other elements. The five box types are Figure, Table, Text, User-Defined, and Equation.

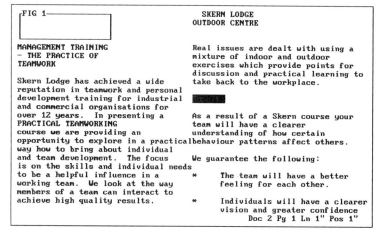

**Figure 10.1** Outline of a graphics box on the normal editing screen

# SKERN LODGE
# OUTDOOR CENTRE

## MANAGEMENT TRAINING - THE PRACTICE OF TEAMWORK

Skern Lodge has achieved a wide reputation in teamwork and personal development training for industrial and commercial organisations for over 12 years. In presenting a PRACTICAL TEAMWORKING course we are providing an opportunity to explore in a practical way how to bring about individual and team development. The focus is on the skills and individual needs to be a helpful influence in a working team. We look at the way members of a team can interact to achieve high quality results.

Real issues are dealt with using a mixture of indoor and outdoor exercises which provide points for discussion and practical learning to take back to the workplace.

*Results*

As a result of a Skern course your team will have a clearer understanding of how certain behaviour patterns affect others.

We guarantee the following:

* The team will have a better feeling for each other.

* Individuals will have a clearer vision and greater confidence

**Figure 10.2**   The Figure 10.1 document displayed on the View screen

The Figure graphics box, for example, has a thin border all the way round and no background shading. The Text graphics box has thick top and bottom borders and background shading. The type that you choose does not limit your use of the box; a Text box, for example, could be used to hold an image (although the shaded background may not look very good for this).

You can insert captions in boxes, in which case WordPerfect automatically numbers the boxes consecutively. The numbering style depends upon the type of graphics box you have selected.

Figures 10.3 to 10.6 show the different default box displays for the Figure, Table, Text, and User boxes. The Equation box is more appropriate for the creation of equations and is not covered in this book.

The Figure box defaults displayed in Figure 10.3 include a narrow border, the caption displayed below the image, and the 'Figure 1' caption text emboldened.

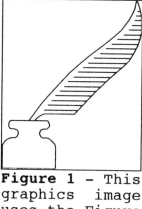

**Figure 1** – This
graphics image
uses the Figure
d e f a u l t
options.

**Figure 10.3** Defaults for a Figure box

The Table box default options shown in Figure 10.4 include a wide border above and below the graphics image, and the caption above the graphics image.

The Text box default options shown in Figure 10.5 include a wide border above and below the graphics image, and a shaded background.

**Table I** – This
graphics image
is created
using the Table
d e f a u l t
options.

**Figure 10.4** Defaults for a Table box

SKERN LODGE OUTDOOR
CENTRE

OUR BUSINESS
IS PEOPLE!

Appledore
Bideford
N Devon
EX39 1NG

(023 72) 75992)

1 - This graphics image uses
the    Text    Box    default
options.

**Figure 10.5**  Defaults for a Text box

The User box defaults as displayed in Figure 10.6 have no border around the graphics box.

Any of these border, shading and numbering style options can be changed for a single graphics box, or for all graphics boxes, and we will be explaining later on how to do this. You can also change the defaults for these options from the Initial Settings in the Setup menu.

1       -       This
graphics   image
uses   the   User-
Defined default
options.

**Figure 10.6**  Defaults for a User box

To select a graphics box:

1 Press the Alt-F9 Graphics key and make your choice from the Graphics Type menu that appears.
2 After selecting a type of box, a further menu appears, headed by the graphics box style (in this case 'Figure'):

1 Create; 2 Edit; 3 New Number; 4 Options

Choose Create. Now, you can specify the position, contents, and size of the graphics box. This is covered in the next section.

Later sections in the chapter cover the other options on the Graphics Box menu.

## 10.16  Defining the graphics box

Having selected the type of graphics box, you must now define it (i.e. specify its position in your text, its size, and its contents).

```
Definition: Figure

     1 - Filename

     2 - Contents        Empty

     3 - Caption

     4 - Anchor Type      Paragraph

     5 - Vertical Position   0"

     6 - Horizontal Position  Right

     7 - Size             3.13" wide x 3.13" (high)

     8 - Wrap Text Around Box Yes

     9 - Edit



Selection: 0
```

**Figure 10.7**  The Definition menu

Having selected 'Create' above, the Definition menu shown in
Figure 10.7 appears, headed by the graphics box style, in this
case 'Figure'. Some of the choices in this menu have default
values already entered, while others are blank. We deal with
each one in turn, using the menu numbering as shown in the
display.

1  *Filename*. Enter the name of the image or document that you
   wish to retrieve from disk into this graphics box. Later on, if
   you wish to replace this image or document with another,
   simply enter the new filename. WordPerfect will remove the
   original file and insert the new one. If you want the box to
   remain empty, leave the filename blank.
2  *Contents*. This displays a menu that enables you to choose the
   type of information to be placed in the box, as follows:

   Contents: 1 Graphic; 2 Graphic on Disk; 3 Text; 4 Equation

   In practice, once you retrieve a file into the box, WordPerfect
   inserts the appropriate entry in the box, either 'Text' or
   'Graphic'. If you subsequently retrieve a different type of file
   into the graphics box, WordPerfect will update the type of
   file.
   If the retrieved file is a graphic, you may wish to choose the
   Graphic on Disk option instead of Graphic. This lets you
   store a 'pointer' to a graphics image on disk rather than
   retrieving that image into a graphics box. This reduces the
   size of the document, since the graphics image is not saved as
   part of the document, only the pointer is saved. It also means
   that various WordPerfect operations connected with the graphic
   will be speeded up. However, if you copy your document to
   floppy disk to use on another machine, you must also copy
   any graphics files which are pointed to in the document.
   When you choose Graphic on Disk, you can save the graphic
   in WordPerfect's own format, as a .WPG file. This saves time
   later, as it means that WordPerfect does not have to keep
   converting the graphic from some other format each time it is
   displayed or printed.
   For details on the Graphic on Disk option, see Section 17
   of the Keystroke Guide.
3  *Caption*. This menu option takes you to a special editing
   screen where you type in the caption for your box. You can

use enhancements in your captions such as bold or italics. WordPerfect has already inserted for you the graphics box number, but you can delete this if you wish. If you retain the number, it is updated automatically as you insert more boxes of the same type. Numbering can begin with 1, I, or A. The default numbering styles are:

Figures — Figure 1
Tables  — Table I
Text    — 1
User    — 1

You can change the numbering style from the Graphics Options menu, as explained later.

4 *Anchor Type*. This option allows you to anchor a graphics box to a paragraph, a page, or to a character, so that it stays with that paragraph, page or character regardless of any changes you may subsequently make to the document.

5 *Vertical Position*. You can set the vertical alignment of the graphics box here, depending on the type of anchor selected.

6 *Horizontal Position*. This allows you to set the exact horizontal position of the graphics box in the paragraph or page.

7 *Size*. Graphics box sizes are measured in decimal inches unless you have changed the unit of measurement in the Setup menu. If you have entered a filename in Option 1, WordPerfect reads the size of the graphic from the disk file and automatically inserts the measurements needed to display the image. If you wish, you can change the size of the graphics box, and Word-Perfect will scale the image up or down automatically.

8 *Wrap Text Around Box*. You would normally want the text in the document to flow around a graphics box, as in Figure 10.1. However, if you select 'No' at this option, the text will be superimposed on top of the box. So why would anyone want to select 'No'? The reason is to give the graphics image within the box an irregular outline created by line endings: having selected 'No', you then put in your own hard returns in each line of text as it approaches the image. This is rather time consuming, as you have to keep switching between the normal editing screen to type the words, and the View Docu-ment screen to see the results.

(Note that if you place a box in the centre of a page, text flows only to the left of the box and you have blank space to the right. If you want text appearing on the right of the graphics box as well as the left, you will have to change the format to columns. Note too that WordPerfect can wrap text around a maximum of 100 boxes on any one page.)

9 *Edit.* When you select this option, your next screen display will depend on the contents of the graphics box.

   a If the box contains a text file, you will see the text. If the box is empty, the screen display will be blank. In both cases the prompt 'Press Exit when done, Graphics to rotate text' will be displayed. You can now type text and enhancement codes into the box, and edit any text. By pressing the Alt-F9 Graphics key, you can rotate your boxed text.

   b If the box contains a graphics image, you will see the image, together with menus at the bottom of the screen, as shown below. These menus allow you to rotate, or scale, or move, or display a mirror image of it.

      Arrow keys Move; PgUp/PgDn Scale; +/− Rotate; Ins % Change; Goto Reset
      1 Move; 2 Scale; 3 Rotate; 4 Invert; 5 Black and White; 0 (10%)

The main menu is the last line at the bottom of the screen. Its options take you through a sequence of operations to achieve a desired rotation, scaling, or move effect. These sequences can be rather long winded so short-cut keystrokes are provided

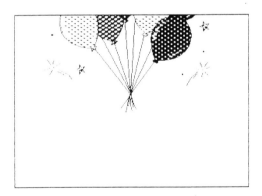

**Figure 10.8** A cropped image

in the line above this menu. Both menus are described in Section 17 of the Keystroke Guide. Another short-cut is provided by the Insert key: press this, and you can change the rate of rotation, scaling, or moving.

Note that:

a    If you *move* the image past the border of the box, then the image is 'cropped' as shown in Figure 10.8.

b    Any changes made here can be abandoned and the image restored to its original state by pressing Ctrl-Enter (Goto).

Some of the effects that can be achieved by this menu are shown in Figures 10.8, 10.9, and 10.10.

**Figure 10.9**    A scaled image

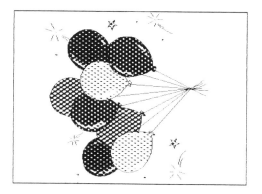

**Figure 10.10**    A rotated image

## 10.17 Exercise: defining a graphics box

The Skern Lodge logo has been used in the brochure shown in the book. In place of this logo, let's use instead a WordPerfect graphic to improve the appearance of the brochure. You will find a number of these graphics in the directory designated for graphics file (probably the WP51 directory). They all have the WPG extension and examples of them are shown in an appendix on graphics images in the WordPerfect manual.

1 Retrieve FONT.EX and place the cursor on the font code at the beginning of the document, after the margin codes.
2 Press the Graphics key, select Figure, and Create.
3 Enter the graphics filename, and change the contents to Graphic on Disk.
4 Change the Anchor Type to page, the Horizontal Position to left, and the Size to 1.5″ width (WordPerfect will calculate the height).
5 Exit back to the document and look at the View Document screen.

Your text after the logo may need moving down the page with the Enter key. Make sure that you insert the hard returns in front of the newspaper column codes and font code which immediately precede the text (MANAGEMENT TRAINING ...). Save the file, calling it GRAPHICS.EX.

## 10.18 Moving, deleting, and editing a graphics box

Once created, your graphics box can be moved, deleted, or edited.

- To move a graphics box from one place to another in your text, find the graphics box code and delete it. Then move the cursor to the new position and use the Cancel key to restore the box at that point.
- To remove the graphics box, find the code and delete it.
- Editing a graphics box means changing its definitions, i.e. its position, the filename of its contents, the caption, etc., or altering the box style. To do this, there is no need to move the cursor to the box before you begin, though you do need

to know the box number. To change the definition, select the correct graphics box from the Graphics Type menu, and then choose Edit from the Graphics Box menu. You will be placed in the Definition menu for that graphics box. If you wish to change the graphics box style, press the Graphics key (Alt-F9) when you reach the Definition menu and choose from the different graphics boxes on display.

## 10.19   Exercise: editing a graphics box

Retrieve GRAPHICS.EX, and change the style of the graphics box from Figure to User box. This will remove any outline from the logo. Then save the file.

  The detailed steps are as follows.

1   With the cursor anywhere in the document, press the Graphics key, choose Figure, and type '1' for the number of the box you want to edit. You should see the Definition menu for Figure 1.
2   Press the Graphics key again and select User box. The Definition menu should now be headed 'User box'.
3   Exit back to the document, where you should see 'USR 1' in the outline of the graphics box. View the document to check the effect of this.
4   Save the file, replacing the previous version.

## 10.20   Further exercise: defining and editing a graphics box

Retrieve GRAPHICS.EX, which contains some text together with a logo in a graphics box. Insert a text box so that it appears centred on page one between the two columns. The steps are:

1   Place the cursor immediately after the User box code, press the Graphics key, and choose Text box and Create.
2   Make the following changes to the Text Box Definition menu:

> Filename − None
> Contents − None
> Anchor Type − Page

outdoor centres

# SKERN LODGE
# OUTDOOR CENTRE

## MANAGEMENT TRAINING - THE PRACTICE OF TEAMWORK

Skern Lodge has achieved a wide reputation in teamwork and personal development training for industrial and commercial organisations for over 12 years. In presenting a PRACTICAL TEAMWORKING course we are providing an opportunity to explore in a practical way how to bring about individual and team development. The focus is on the skills and individual needs to be a helpful influence in a working team. We look at the way members of a team can interact to achieve high quality results.

*Call us on 0237 465992! We are always pleased to answer any queries.*

*Outdoor Training*

This form of training can be very enjoyable and rewarding. The benefits, however, can be difficult to translate into the workplace and therefore we focus heavily on applying the learning to daily work. This is the constant message of PRACTICE TEAMWORKING.

Real issues are dealt with using a mixture of indoor and outdoor exercises which provide points for discussion and practical learning to take back to the workplace.

*Results*

As a result of a Skern course your team will have a clearer understanding of how certain behaviour patterns affect others.

We guarantee the following:

* The team will have a better feeling for each other.

* Individuals will have a clearer vision and greater confidence in the future.

* All members will have improved their ability to listen and identify each other's strengths and skills.

At Skern the team will laugh a lot and share emotions that will develop a powerful synergy.

**Figure 10.11** GRAPHICS.EX with two graphics boxes

Vertical Position — Centre
Horizontal Position — Columns 1–2, Centre
Size — No change
Wrap Text Around — No change

3   Choose Edit and select centre justification with the Format
key. Type in some text as follows, with either italics selected
or Helvetica Narrow Oblique:

> Call us on 0237 465992! We are always pleased to
> answer any queries.

4   Exit back to the document and look at the View screen. You
should see the text in a graphics box with a shaded background,
centred on the page between the two columns.

## 10.21   New Number

So far, we have looked at the first two options on the Graphics
Box menu discussed on page 209. The third option is New Number,
which allows you to advance the numbering of graphics boxes at
any point in the document. You might want to do this, for
example, if you wish to leave a gap. For details, see Section 17 of
the Keystroke Guide.

```
Options: Figure

    1 - Border Style
            Left                        Single
            Right                       Single
            Top                         Single
            Bottom                      Single
    2 - Outside Border Space
            Left                        0.167"
            Right                       0.167"
            Top                         0.167"
            Bottom                      0.167"
    3 - Inside Border Space
            Left                        0"
            Right                       0"
            Top                         0"
            Bottom                      0"
    4 - First Level Numbering Method    Numbers
    5 - Second Level Numbering Method   Off
    6 - Caption Number Style            [BOLD]Figure 1[bold]
    7 - Position of Caption             Below box, Outside borders
    8 - Minimum Offset from Paragraph   0"
    9 - Grey Shading (% of black)       0%

Selection: 0
```

**Figure 10.12**   The Options menu

## 10.22   Box style options

These are on the fourth option of the Graphics Box menu. If, after selecting the type of graphics box you want, you then select Options, the menu shown in Figure 10.12 will appear.

Any changes you make here to these current definitions of border style, border spacing, etc. take effect from your current cursor position (as codes are inserted at this point). So graphics boxes earlier in the document are not affected, but later boxes are. If you want the changes to affect the whole document, position the cursor at the start of the document before using the Options menu.

## 10.23   Graphics lines

One of the options on the Graphics key allows you to draw horizontal and vertical lines. These can enhance the appearance of your document, e.g. by vertical lines between columns, or horizontal lines to emphasize a major heading.

Graphics lines do not appear at all on the text editing screen. They can only be seen on the View Document screen.

You can create these lines in much the same way as you create graphics boxes. You define their appearance in a similar way − they can be shaded, or black, and of different widths − and you place them similarly on the page. Graphics lines can also be edited.

When you create a horizontal line, you make your choices from the following menu:

1   *Horizontal position*. This allows you to fix the starting and finishing points of the line.
2   *Length of line*. Enter a value here for your line length.
3   *Width of line*. Enter the width (thickness); your entry can have up to two decimal places so it can be defined quite accurately.
4   *Grey shading*. Enter a percentage for the amount of shading you would like: the smaller the percentage, the lighter the result.

The Vertical Line menu is much like the Horizontal Line menu.

Like graphics boxes, you can include graphics lines in headers

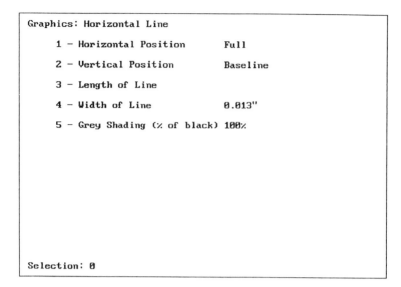

```
Graphics: Horizontal Line

     1 - Horizontal Position       Full

     2 - Vertical Position         Baseline

     3 - Length of Line

     4 - Width of Line             0.013"

     5 - Grey Shading (% of black) 100%

Selection: 0
```

**Figure 10.13** The Horizontal Line menu

and footers. Use lines if you want to add emphasis to a header or footer.

## 10.24 Exercise: creating a masthead

Skern Lodge wishes to create a master document to use for important reports. This master document will consist of a masthead containing text, a graphic, and graphic lines. When it is finished, it will look like Figure 10.14.

The Skern Lodge logo has been used, and the footer contains a graphic line and page numbering below.

Create this document, using a WordPerfect graphic where the logo should appear. You should start from a blank screen, and you will need to keep viewing the document in order to check its appearance. Save it as MASTHEAD.EX.

Then use this masthead file to produce a report. You should retrieve it, renaming it REPORT.EX, and you will need to retrieve into it a report contained in another file — we suggest the file W&O.EX.

If you need help with any of this, the detailed steps are as follows:

**Figure 10.14**   The masthead

1   Change the document initial font to Helvetica 12 pt (on the Format key).
2   Insert a footer on every page as follows:

> Horizontal line .03″ wide; keep other defaults
> 2 hard returns
> Centred text − 'Page ^B', in italics

3   Insert a Figure graphics box as follows:

   Filename – any WPG graphics file
   Graphic on disk
   Anchor type – Page
   Horizontal position – Left
   Size – 2″ wide
   Keep all other defaults

4   Now enter the text, applying a different font to the main heading. Select Helvetica Bold Oblique 24 pt, centre, and type 'REPORT'. Press Enter three times.

5   Change the font to Helvetica Narrow Bold Oblique 16 pt and use the Date key to insert the date as a code. Press the Flush Right key and type in your name. Press Enter three times. The cursor should now be at the left margin under the graphics box outline.

6   Insert a horizontal graphics line, changing the width to .03″, and retaining all other defaults. Press Enter three times.

7   Insert a final font code for the body text of the report – Helvetica 12 pt.

8   You may need to insert more or fewer hard returns in some places to get the text and graphics lines appearing in the right place on the page. Finally, save the document and exit.

9   Now use the masthead file to produce a report. First, retrieve MASTHEAD.EX and rename it REPORT.EX. Press Home, Home, Down arrow, and retrieve W&O.EX. The text should be inserted below the masthead, using the last font code in the document – Helvetica 12 pt.

Always rename MASTHEAD.EX every time it is retrieved, just as you would any other masterfile.

## 10.25   Exercise: including a graphics line in a footer

Retrieve your GRAPHICS.EX file (the latest version of the brochure), and add a footer containing a horizontal graphics line, two hard returns, and centred page numbering. Save the file, replacing the previous version.

## 10.26  The DTP exercise

This is your major exercise in this chapter, leading to the Skern Lodge document shown in Figure 10.15.

It uses the following files from your disk:

- Text files: SKI.EX; INSET.EX;
- Graphics files: SKI1.PCX; SKI2.PCX.

Two more graphics files are needed − one for the logo at the top of page 1, the other for the beach scene on page 3. We suggest that you use WordPerfect graphics in each case: the WordPerfect graphic file BKGRND-1.WPG for the beach scene, and one of your own choice for the logo.

(If at any time you cannot load a file into a graphics box because the file cannot be found, type in the full pathname or use the List key to look through directory lists for the filename. It may be that you have not copied all files needed in graphics boxes into the directory designated for graphics files.)

Note that all graphics boxes should be set for 'Graphic on Disk'. The document should be saved as HOLIDAYS.EX.

(Part of this exercise involves displaying text with a shaded background. The options on the Alt-F7 Table key are an easy way to achieve this, but since they cannot be used with newspaper columns they cannot be applied in this case.)

The detailed steps are as follows.

1  *Page one.* Insert the following on a blank screen:

- Initial base font Helvetica 12 pt (on the Format key).
- Footer every page − horizontal graphic line, .03″ width, centred page numbering below (Format, Graphics).
- Widow/Orphan Protection on (Format).
- Table graphics box (Graphics), as follows:

    Anchor type − Page
    Horizontal position − Margin, left
    Size 2″ wide
    Keep all other defaults

- Masthead heading 1 font − Helvetica Bold Oblique 24 pt (Font).

outdoor centres

# *SKERN LODGE HOLIDAYS*

*20 May 1993*                    *ANN GAUTIER*

## Learn to Ski Weeks at Risoul, Puy St Vincent and Les Orres

**Figure 1** Monetier

We have put together these LEARN TO SKI WEEKS for all those people who don't know what a snowplough turn is. It's a lot more fun to learn to ski with a group of people who are all in the same situation.

Our friendly ski guide will be on hand to sort out all your ski and boot hire problems and along with our courier introduce you to the rest of your group at the welcome meeting over a few drinks.

These weeks are ideal for the absolute novice to get an introduction to the fun sport that skiing really is.

### Dates Available

January 11, March 8, March 15

Cost

£490 for 10 days.

### Cost Includes

* A Ski Travel Centre sweatshirt
* 6 days ski, sticks and boot hire
* 2 hours instruction for 6 days
* Basic French Federation ski test

### Cost of Accommodation

| Resort | Hotel | Cost |
|---|---|---|
| Risoul | Chalet Geneve | £269 |
| Monetier | Les Ecrins | £284 |
| Les Orres | Le Montaigne | £228 |

**Figure 10.15**   The DTP document [1]

## Ski-ing for the Experienced

### Serre Chevalier

**Figure 2** The village of Serre Chevalier

We are very pleased to be able to introduce for 1987/8 season the outstanding French ski resort of Serre Chevalier. The ski-ing here is outstanding and offers numerous runs to suit all grades of skier.

Serre Chevalier is the name given to the ski area of the Guisane Valley which is made up of the three villages of Chantemerle, Villeneuve and Monetier. This superb resort boasts a total of 61 ski lifts with 200 km of pistes. It rates high in the top 20 French ski centres.

### Villeneuve

Villeneuve boasts the biggest and most modern telepherique in Europe. In addition, the higher slopes of Villeneuve offer outstanding runs for the intermediate and expert skier. The Clot Gautier has excellent red and black runs. The superb ski-ing at Villeneuve can be supplemented by the ski-ing offered by Chantemerle and Monetier

This vast interconnecting complex i due to be finally linked up this winte when 3 new lifts will be installed t connect Villeneuve and Chantemerle with the ski area of Monetier.

### Instruction

Instruction will be provided by a team c Travel Centre Instructors. Equipmen will be brand new and up to our usua high standard.

### Local Facilities

Serre   Chevalier   offers   exceller facilities both for apres ski and for the non-skier. The village of Villeneuve ha a superb indoor heated swimming poo floodlit ice skating rink, an indoor winte horse riding centre and 2 cinemas.

### Accommodation

We are pleased to offer the Hote Frejus. This modern hotel is decorate to a high standard and ha accommodation for 60 persons Adjacent to the hotel is the Telecabine de Frejus which gives immediate access to the outstanding higher slope of Serre Chevalier.

## Winter in Mauritius!

**Figure 4** A typical
Mauritius beach

A thousand miles south of the
Seychelles and about 1200 miles off
the east of Africa lies the island of
Mauritius. Just 40 miles long and 30
miles wide, the island is encircled by
soft white sandy beaches protected by
offshore coral reefs.

Mauritius is perfect for a beach holiday
with superb resort hotels, lovely
beaches, sophisticated entertainment
and excellent watersports. It also has
places of interest to visit from botanical
gardens to nature reserves as well as
colonial Port Louis. Be prepared for
bad roads though - pot-holes are
numerous!

It is a long flight from England but the
effects of a 12 hour flight are less
severe as the time difference is only 3
or 4 hours, depending on the time of
year.

### Le Tousserok

Tousserok is delightfully isolated with a
lovely location on the east coast of the
island about 30 miles from Port Louis

and is ideal for honeymooners. All
rooms are air conditioned with sea
view.

### St Geran

This is one of the finest hotels in the
Indian Ocean. It is set on a peninsula
on the east coast of the island between
the ocean and a natural lagoon.

There is a golf course and tennis
courts.

### Flight Information

Flight Reductions:

Air Mauritius Friday and
Sunday flights - £60

British Airways Saturday
flight £40

Private Transfers -
Supplement of £22

### Value Plus

*   Between 16 April and 31 July
    book 2 weeks, 3rd week free on
    room only basis.

*   Honeymooners receive fruit,
    flowers, champagne, T-shirt,
    gondola ride and one special
    dinner.

- Masthead heading 2 font − Helvetica Narrow Bold Oblique 16 pt (Font).
- Body text font − Helvetica 12 pt (Font).
- Graphics horizontal line − .03″ wide; keep other defaults (Graphics).

2  After inserting all the above text and codes, and with the cursor at the end of the document, retrieve SKI.EX.

3  Define and turn on newspaper columns at the beginning of the text (Columns Tables).

4  Create a paired style − Palatino Bold Italic 14 pt (nothing entered after comment) − called Subheading (Style). Enter the font information as a description and save it as HOLIDAYS.STY.

5  The shaded background headings are achieved by entering text into a graphics box. Delete the first heading ('Learn to Ski Weeks at Risoul, Puy St Vincent and Les Orres'). Change the defaults for User boxes by selecting User box options and change the shading from 0 to 10% (Graphics). Insert a User box with the following definitions, keeping all other defaults (Graphics):

> Anchor type − Paragraph
> Horizontal position − Full

Select Edit and use the Style key to select the Subheading style. Type in the heading text, or alternatively use the Cancel key to restore the heading you deleted.

You can increase the height of the box to get more shading. If the text in the box needs centring vertically, insert an advance down code in front of the text.

6  At the beginning of the first paragraph insert another graphics box to hold the SKI1.PCX graphics file. First of all change the defaults for Figure boxes by selecting Figure box options and changing the border style to get the dropped shadow effect (Graphics). The default style is a single line for left, right, top and bottom sides. Change this to extra thick for right and bottom.

Insert a Figure graphics box with the following definitions, keeping all other defaults (Graphics):

> Filename − SKI1.PCX

Caption — Monetier. (Note that you may prefer to insert a hard return in front of the [Box Num] code for each caption to put more space between the box and the caption.)

Anchor type — Paragraph
Horizontal position — Full

7   Apply the Subheading style to subheading text (Style).
8   Change the tab settings for the small table under 'Cost of Accommodation' (Format).
9   Delete the heading 'Ski-ing for the Experienced' and force a new page.
10  *Page two.* Insert another user graphics box with the same options and definitions as the previous one (Graphics). The Subheading style is to be entered on the edit screen (Style) and the deleted heading text.
11  Apply the same style to 'Serre Chevalier' (Style).
12  Insert another Figure graphics box with the same definitions as the first one above (Graphics), except:

Filename — SKI2.PCX
Caption — The village of Serre Chevalier

13  Apply the Subheading style to the rest of the subheadings in this section (Style).
14  *Page three.* At the beginning of the next main heading — 'Winter in Mauritius!' — force a new page and delete the heading.
15  Place this text in another User graphics box (Graphics).
16  At the beginning of the next paragraph, insert another Figure graphics box, the third in the document (Graphics). However, the number in the caption is to be advanced to 4, so choose New Number from the Figure menu and insert 4, before you create the figure. The definitions are as for previous figures except for the following:

Filename — BKGRND-1.WPG
Caption — A typical Mauritius beach

17  Insert a Text graphics box (Graphics) after the paragraph ending '. . . tennis courts'. The definitions are:

Filename — INSET.EX
Horizontal position — Full

18  Under the heading 'Value Plus' the text is indented after the asterisk. With the current tab settings, the level of indent is too deep. Change the tab settings at this point so that the first tab is around .5″ from the column's left margin.

19  There is some blank space left at the bottom of column two on page 3. Fill this in with a small graphic. I used the Skern logo, size 1.5″ wide and centred. In the edit screen the graphic was scaled up and then moved (cropped) to exclude the text.

The finished result is shown in Figure 10.15. You should save it as HOLIDAYS.EX.

## 10.27  Further exercise: graphics and fonts

Try further improvements in the appearance of the Skern Lodge brochure and prospectus by changing fonts and inserting graphics. A selection of graphic files comes with the WordPerfect program (each one ending with the .WPG extension) which you can experiment with.

## 10.28  Tables of contents

WordPerfect allows you to generate tables of contents for your reports and other documents. Figure 10.16 shows an example of WordPerfect's default style for a table of contents, with three different levels of entry. Notice that WordPerfect indents the headings according to their level, and inserts against each the page number.

There are three stages involved in creating a table of contents:

1  Mark each item of text that's to be included in the table.
2  Define the location of the table and numbering style.
3  Generate the table.

These are described below.

```
┌─────────────────────────────────────────────────────────────┐
│  TABLE OF CONTENTS                                            │
│                                                              │
│  What you will achieve in this chapter . . . . . . . . . . . . . . . . . . . . . .    2   │
│                                                              │
│  Routines you will use in this chapter . . . . . . . . . . . . . . . . . . . . .    2   │
│                                                              │
│  Desktop Publishing . . . . . . . . . . . . . . . . . . . . . . . . . . . . . . .    2   │
│                                                              │
│  Fonts . . . . . . . . . . . . . . . . . . . . . . . . . . . . . . . . . . . . . .    3   │
│          The base font . . . . . . . . . . . . . . . . . . . . . . . . . . . .    3   │
│                                                              │
│  Graphics . . . . . . . . . . . . . . . . . . . . . . . . . . . . . . . . . . .    6   │
│          Graphics boxes . . . . . . . . . . . . . . . . . . . . . . . . . . .    6   │
│          Selecting the type of graphics box . . . . . . . . . . . . . . .    9   │
│          Defining a graphics box . . . . . . . . . . . . . . . . . . . . . .   12   │
│                  Filename . . . . . . . . . . . . . . . . . . . . . . . . . .   12   │
│                  Contents . . . . . . . . . . . . . . . . . . . . . . . . . .   12   │
│                  Caption . . . . . . . . . . . . . . . . . . . . . . . . . . .   13   │
│                                                              │
└─────────────────────────────────────────────────────────────┘
```

**Figure 10.16**  Sample table of contents

## Mark each item

Creating a table of contents is not a fully automatic feature, i.e. WordPerfect does not pick out the headings automatically from your text to create this table. You have to use the Block key to highlight each item of text that's to be an entry in the table, then mark it and indicate its level in the table. The steps for each entry are:

1  Block the text.
2  Press the Alt-F5 Mark Text key.
3  Choose ToC (table of contents).
4  Enter the level number for the table. For example, 1 would be the main level, 2 the first sub-level, etc. Level 1 entries appear at the left margin, level 2 at the first tab stop, etc.

## Define the location

This has to be done with the cursor on the page where you want the table of contents to appear, since a code is inserted in your text at this point. Since normally this would be on page 1, force a new page at the beginning of the document, and position the cursor on the new page. Then:

1  Press the Mark Text key and choose Define. The Mark Text Define menu then displays, shown in Figure 10.17.
2  Choose Define Table of Contents. You can now change the defaults for the numbering style from the Table of Contents Definition menu, shown in Figure 10.18.

*Generate the table*

Now you can actually generate the table. For this, press the Mark Text key again and choose Generate from the menu. This will display the Generate menu (Figure 10.19) from which you choose Generate. WordPerfect will then generate and display the table of contents.

Note that your cursor position when you carry out this operation is immaterial: as explained above, the table of contents will appear on whatever page you were at when you defined the numbering style.

## 10.29  Indexes

WordPerfect also allows you to create an index for your document. In this case, you select the words from your document you wish to include in the index. Note that WordPerfect will not index every mention of the word in your text, only those that you select. Figure 10.20 shows an example of an index. As you can see, WordPerfect automatically sorts the entries alphabetically, inserting the page numbers alongside. As with a table of contents, you can choose the page numbering style.

The steps for creating an index are almost the same as those for creating a table of contents, and are described in Section 24 of the Keystroke Guide. When you come to define the index, you choose the Define Index option from the Mark Text Definition menu, and this displays the menu shown in Figure 10.21. Note that the index in Figure 10.20 was created using all the defaults in this menu.

An alternative way of generating an index is to create what's called a *concordance file*, that is an ordinary WordPerfect document file containing a list of words you want indexed. Each word must be on a line by itself followed by a hard return. The final entry in the list must also be followed by a hard return. When you have created this file it's best to sort the entries in it, as this will speed up the generation of the index.

```
Mark Text: Define

     1 - Define Table of Contents

     2 - Define List

     3 - Define Index

     4 - Define Table of Authorities

     5 - Edit Table of Authorities Full Form








Selection: 0
```

**Figure 10.17**  The Mark Text Definition menu

```
Table of Contents Definition

     1 - Number of Levels          1

     2 - Display Last Level in     No
         Wrapped Format

     3 - Page Numbering - Level 1  Flush right with leader
                          Level 2
                          Level 3
                          Level 4
                          Level 5






Selection: 0
```

**Figure 10.18**  The Table of Contents Definition menu

```
Mark Text: Generate

    1 - Remove Redline Markings and Strikeout Text from Document

    2 - Compare Screen and Disk Documents and Add Redline and Strikeout

    3 - Expand Master Document

    4 - Condense Master Document

    5 - Generate Tables, Indexes, Cross-References, etc.




Selection: 0
```

**Figure 10.19**   The Mark Text Generation menu

Having created the concordance file, to generate the index you proceed as described above, except that you enter the name of the concordance file when you choose the Define Index option.

## 10.30   Exercise: creating an index

In this exercise you will create an index at the end of your HOLIDAYS.EX file. Figure 10.20 shows how the finished index might look.

If you need any help, the detailed steps are as follows.

1   Insert a hard page break at the end of the document. This will

**Index**

|                    | Page |
|--------------------|------|
| Chantemerle        | 3    |
| Guisane Valley     | 3    |
| Les Orres          | 2    |
| Monetier           | 2    |
| Puy St Vincent     | 2    |
| Risoul             | 2    |
| Serre Chevalier    | 3    |

**Figure 10.20**   Sample index

```
Index Definition

    1 - No Page Numbers

    2 - Page Numbers Follow Entries

    3 - (Page Numbers) Follow Entries

    4 - Flush Right Page Numbers

    5 - Flush Right Page Numbers with Leaders




Selection: 5
```

**Figure 10.21**   The Index Definition menu

create page 4, where the index is to appear. Turn off the
columns on this page.

2   Do an extended search (Home,F2) through the document,
    searching in turn for each occurrence of the resort names as
    shown in Figure 10.20. You need the extended search to find
    text which occurs in graphics boxes. As each one is found,
    mark it for inclusion in the index by proceeding as follows:

    a   Block it.
    b   Press Alt-F5 (Mark Text).
    c   Press 3 (Index).
    d   Press Enter to make the block the index entry.
    e   Press Enter again to cancel the index subheading prompt.

3   Choose the page numbering style for the index as follows.
    Move to the page where the index should appear – page 4.
    Place the cursor below the [Cols Off] code, and define the
    index as follows:

    a   Press Mark Text.
    b   Press 5 (Define).

    c   At the Concordance file prompt, press Enter (there is no concordance file).

    d   Choose the page numbering style you prefer; I selected 5 (flush right page numbers with leaders).

4   Finally, create (generate) the index as follows:

    a   Press Mark Text.

    b   Press 6 (Generate).

    c   Choose 5 (Generate). The following prompt will appear (this prompt always appears, even the first time you create a table, list or index):

           Existing tables, lists and indexes will be replaced. Continue? Yes (No)

    d   Type 'Y' for yes. The status line contains a message indicating that WordPerfect is passing through the document several times.

5   Eventually the index appears on the page where you defined it. Add in a heading 'Index' and the column heading 'Page' above the page numbers.

## 10.31 Exercise: creating a table of contents

In this exercise you will create a table of contents for the W&O.EX file on your disk, which is a two-page document of activities. The result is shown in Figure 10.22.

The detailed steps are as follows:

1   Retrieve W&O.EX, then save it as TOC.EX.

2   Mark text for inclusion in the table by using the Block key to select each paragraph heading in turn and using the Mark Text key to select ToC. At the Level prompt, type '1' and press Enter.

3   At the beginning of the document, force a hard page break. Place the cursor on the new, empty page, and select a suitable page numbering style as follows. Press the Mark Text key and choose Define. From the Mark Text Definition menu (Figure 10.17), choose Define Table of Contents. On the Table of Contents Definition menu (Figure 10.18) the page numbering style defaults to numbers at the right margin with dot leaders. Pressing 3 will display a menu of other available styles. Make your choice of style and exit.

```
SKERN LODGE ACTIVITIES

TABLE OF CONTENTS


                                                      Page
Orienteering  . . . . . . . . . . . . . . . . . . . .    1

Canoeing  . . . . . . . . . . . . . . . . . . . . . .    1

Cliff Rescue  . . . . . . . . . . . . . . . . . . . .    1

Abseiling . . . . . . . . . . . . . . . . . . . . . .    1

Raft Racing . . . . . . . . . . . . . . . . . . . . .    1

Water-skiing  . . . . . . . . . . . . . . . . . . . .    1

Snorkling . . . . . . . . . . . . . . . . . . . . . .    1

Windsurfing . . . . . . . . . . . . . . . . . . . . .    2

Archery . . . . . . . . . . . . . . . . . . . . . . .    2

Surfing . . . . . . . . . . . . . . . . . . . . . . .    2

Sailing . . . . . . . . . . . . . . . . . . . . . . .    2
```

**Figure 10.22** Table of contents for TOC.EX

4 Create the table of contents by using the Mark Text key again and selecting Generate. From the Generate menu (Figure 10.19), choose option 5, and confirm the replacement of other tables of contents, etc.

On page 1 you should see your table of contents. You can now add extras such as centring the page top to bottom, and you can type in any extra text for headings. Note that even though you have not inserted page numbering into the document, WordPerfect still numbers the items in the table of contents correctly.

If you want the pages numbered, and the numbering to start after the table of contents, insert page numbering at the top of page 2, and start the numbering at 1. You will then have to repeat step 4 above to get the numbers updated in the table of contents. Figure 10.22 shows the table of contents after the page numbers have been changed.

## 10.32   Exercise: creating a concordance file

1 Create a concordance file based on the TOC.EX file which you used for creating a table of contents. Type in all the items

Tuition
Map
Compass
Torridge
British Canoe Union
British Water Ski Federation
Swimming
Grand National Archery Society
Westward Ho!
Taw

**Figure 10.23**   The CONCORD.EX file

```
Index
```

```
                                                                Page
British Canoe Union . . . . . . . . . . . . . . . . . . . .    1
British Water Ski Federation  . . . . . . . . . . . . . . .    1
Compass . . . . . . . . . . . . . . . . . . . . . . . . . .    1
Grand National Archery Society  . . . . . . . . . . . . . .    2
Map . . . . . . . . . . . . . . . . . . . . . . . . . . . .    1
Swimming  . . . . . . . . . . . . . . . . . . . . . . . . .    1
Taw . . . . . . . . . . . . . . . . . . . . . . . . . . . .    2
Torridge  . . . . . . . . . . . . . . . . . . . . . . . 1,  2
Tuition . . . . . . . . . . . . . . . . . . . . . . . . 1,  2
Westward Ho!  . . . . . . . . . . . . . . . . . . . . . . .    2
```

**Figure 10.24**   The index for TOC.EX

you want indexed, each one on a separate line. Figure 10.23 shows my concordance file for this document. Note that Word-Perfect ignores capitals when it creates this file, so you do not have to think about matching the case of any items you type in. Save the file, calling it CONCORD.EX.

2   Retrieve TOC.EX and insert a hard page break at the end of the text. With the cursor on this new page, define the index as follows. Press the Mark Text key, choose Define, and then choose Define Index. When prompted for the concordance filename, type 'CONCORD.EX'. You can then choose the style of page numbering.

3   Finally generate the index. This will be displayed as in Figure 10.24 above.

# Keystroke Guide

## I  Advance

You can advance the printer up, down, left, or right a specific amount from the current position; you can also advance to a specified horizontal or vertical position on the page. To insert an Advance command, proceed as follows:

1  Press Shift-F8 (Format).
2  Press 4 (Other).
3  Press 1 (Advance). The Advance menu is displayed.

What happens next depends on your choice at this menu.

- If you choose Up, Down, Left, or Right, WordPerfect asks you for a distance in inches. Type this and press Enter.
- If you choose Line, WordPerfect displays the current vertical position of the cursor. You can then enter another vertical position.
- If you choose Position, WordPerfect displays the current horizontal position of the cursor. You can then enter another horizontal position.

After making your entry, press F7 to exit back to the document. WordPerfect inserts an [Adv] code at the cursor position. The horizontal or vertical position of any text following the code will not be visible on the document screen, only on the View Document screen.

## 2 Block

You can block text for emboldening, underlining, and change of font, as well as other operations.

To highlight a block of text, proceed as follows:

1  Place the cursor at the start of the block.
2  Press the Alt-F4/F12 Block key.
3  Move the cursor to the end of the block.
   If you prefer to use the mouse, drag over the text to highlight it.

With the block highlighted, you can carry out a block operation by pressing the appropriate key, listed below.

After the operation has been carried out, WordPerfect deselects the block. To reselect it, press the Block key then Ctrl-Home (Goto) twice.

Alternatively, place the cursor one space after the *end* of the block, and then after pressing the Block key move it to the beginning of the block.

### Delete

1  Press the Delete key. The message 'Delete Block? No (Yes)' appears.
2  Type 'Y' to delete the block, or 'N' (or any other character) to cancel the operation.

### Move, Copy, Append

1  Press Ctrl-F4 (Move).
2  Choose 1 (Block).
3  Choose 1 (Move), 2 (Copy), or 4 (Append).
4  Move the cursor to the point in the document where you want the block moved or copied, and press Enter.

If you choose Append, WordPerfect will prompt you for the name of the document to which the block should be appended. Type in the filename and press Enter. The block will be copied to the end of the document.

## Move, Copy, Delete, Append a tabulated column

Follow the above procedure except at step 2 you should select 2 (Tabulated Columns).

You can postpone moving or copying the block at step 4 by pressing F1 to escape from the operation. Later, when you wish to perform the move or copy, you:

1 Move the cursor to the desired location.
2 Press Ctrl-F4 (Move).
3 Press 4 (Retrieve).
4 Press 1 (Block).

Note that you must not carry out another move or copy operation before doing this.

## Centre and flush right

To centre or right-align several blocked lines of text:

1 Press Shift-F6 (Centre) or Alt-F6 (Flush Right).

## Switch case

To change block to upper or lower case:

1 Press Shift-F3 (Switch).
2 Press 1 (Upper case) or 2 (Lower case).

## Replace, spell check, or print

Press Alt-F2 for Replace, Ctrl-F2 for spell check, or Shift-F7 for print.

## Save

To save a block as a new file:

1 Press F10 (Save).
2 Type the filename and press Enter.

## Protect

To protect a block of text from being split by a page break:

1   Press Shift-F8 (Format).
2   Type 'Y' for Yes.
    WP inserts [Block Pro:On] and [Block Pro:Off] codes at the
    beginning and end of the block.

### Sort

To restrict the sorting to a blocked list, press Ctrl-F9 (Merge/
Sort).

### Table

To convert a block of tabular or parallel columns to a table:

1   Press Alt-F7 (Columns/Table).
2   Press 2 (Tables).
3   Press 1 (Create).
4   Choose either 1 (Tabular columns) or 2 (Parallel columns).

## 3   Bold

To embolden text as it is entered, press F6 (Bold), type the text,
and then press F6 or the right arrow key. The paired codes are
[BOLD][bold].

  To embolden existing text, block the text first with the Block
key and then press F6.

## 4   Cancel

The Cancel key is used to cancel both commands and edits:

● Press F1 to cancel a command prompt or menu. For
  example, if you have pressed a function key by mistake,
  F1 takes you back to the editing screen.
● Press F1 at the editing screen to cancel a deletion, i.e. to
  restore material that you have deleted. The text is restored at
  the cursor position. You can restore up to the last three
  deletions.

## 5  Centre page

For each page that you wish to centre vertically:

1  Place the cursor at the beginning of the page.
2  Using the Reveal Codes screen, check that the cursor is in front of any codes that may be at the start of the page.
3  Press 2 for Page Format.
4  Press 1 for Centre Page.
5  Type 'Y' for Yes.

The code for Centre Page is [Centre Pg].

## 6  Centre text

To centre text on the current line, press Shift-F6 (Centre).

## 7  Comment

To create a comment, proceed as follows:

1  Move the cursor to the required location of the comment.
2  Press Ctrl-F5 (Text In/Out).
3  Press 4 (Comment).
4  1 (Create). An empty comment box appears.
5  Type your required comment.
6  Press F7 to exit.

You will see your comment text displayed inside a box, and in the Reveal Codes screen a [Comment] code. The comment will not print and if you view the document, the comment box will not appear.
    To delete a comment, remove the [Comment] code.
    To edit a comment:

1  Move the cursor to the right of the comment.
2  Repeat steps 2 and 3 above.
4  Press 2 (Edit).
5  Edit the comment as required.
6  Press F7 to exit.

To convert a comment to ordinary text so that it will print, repeat steps 1 to 3 for editing a comment, then:

4   Press 3 (Convert to Text).

To turn off the display of comments on the editing screen, alter WordPerfect's Setup options. See Section 53.

## 8   Concordance

A concordance file can be created as an alternative to creating an index (described in Section 24). To create a concordance file, proceed as follows:

1   In a new document, type the list of entries that you want in the index, each one followed by a hard return. The final entry must also be followed by a hard return.
2   Save the document and return to the document you wish to index.
3   At the main document, follow steps 1 to 3 for defining an index (Section 24). When prompted, enter the concordance file name and press Enter.
4   Follow steps 5 and 6 for defining an index.

A [Def Mark:index,n;concordance filename] code is inserted in the document; 'n' is your chosen page numbering style.

WordPerfect sorts all entries alphabetically and displays them as headings (i.e. at the left margin).

## 9   Date

To insert the current date and/or time:

1   Press Shift-F5 (Date/Outline).
2   Press 1 for Date Text or 2 for Date Code.

If you choose Date Code, the code is [Date:3,1 4]. (The numbers specify the date format.)

To change the format of the date, follow step 1 above and then choose 3 (Date Format).

## 10 Delete

The Backspace and Del keys can be used to delete a few characters. Faster ways to delete more substantial amounts of text are:

- The word at the cursor — Ctrl-Backspace.
- From the cursor to the end of the word — Home, Del.
- From the cursor to the beginning of the word — Home, Backspace.
- From the cursor to the end of the line — Ctrl-End.
- From the cursor to the end of the page — Ctrl-Page Down.

To cancel a deletion, press F1 (Section 4).

## 11 Document summary

To create a document summary, proceed as follows:

1 Press Shift-F8 (Format).
2 Press 3 (Document).
3 Press 5 (Summary). The document summary will be displayed with the creation date and time already entered.
4 Press Shift-F10 (Retrieve) and type 'Y' to have WordPerfect complete some fields automatically.
5 Choose an item from the menu by pressing the corresponding number and enter the information for that item. Press Enter.
6 Press F7 to exit and return to the document.

To have WordPerfect prompt you to create a document summary whenever you save a new document for the first time, change WordPefect's Setup options. See Section 53 for details.

## 12 Exit

To exit WordPerfect without saving a document:

1 Press F7 (Exit). The 'Save document' prompt appears.
2 Type 'N' to exit without saving. The 'Exit WordPerfect?' prompt appears.
3 Type 'Y' to exit the program; type 'N' to remove the document, clear the screen and continue in WordPerfect.

To exit and save an unnamed document, follow 1 above, then:

2   Type 'Y'.
3   Type in the filename.
4   Press Enter. The 'Exit WordPerfect' prompt appears.
5   Type 'Y' to exit the program; or type 'N' to remove the document, clear the screen and continue in WordPerfect.

To exit and save a named document, again follow 1 above. If the document has not been changed since it was last saved, Word-Perfect will display '(Text was not modified)'. In that case you need not save again and can press N. If the document has been changed:

2   Type 'Y'. The 'Document to be saved' prompt will appear together with the filename.
3   Press Enter. The 'Replace with prompt' will appear.
4   Type 'Y' to overwrite the previous version, or 'N' to save under a new name. The 'Exit WordPerfect' prompt appears.
5   Type 'Y' to exit the program, or 'N' to clear the screen.

If you wish to remain in the file, press F1 (Cancel) when the 'Exit WordPerfect?' prompt appears.


## 13   Endnotes

To create, amend, or delete endnotes, follow the procedure outlined in Section 16 for creating, editing, and deleting footnotes.
   To see how many pages your endnotes take up, carry out the following endnote generation process. (However, it is not necessary to generate endnotes in order to print them.)

1   Press Alt-F5 (Mark Text).
2   Press 6 (Generate).
3   Press 5 (Generate Tables, Indexes, Automatic References, etc.).
4   Type 'Y' when asked if you want to continue.

View the document to see your endnotes. WordPerfect will place them at the end of the body text. If you add more body text at the end of the document, WordPerfect will insert it in front of any endnotes.

## 14   Flush right

To align the current line of text at the right margin, press Alt-F6 (Flush Right).

## 15   Fonts

You can change the design and appearance of text in a document by choosing a different font and point size. You can also change the default font and point size for all future documents.

### *Change the base font for the current document*
This can be applied to an existing document, or to a new document. To change the font for the current document, proceed as follows:

1   With the cursor at any point in the document, press Shift-F8 (Format).
2   Press 3 (Document). The Document menu will display, showing option 3 as the current base font.
3   Press 3 (Initial Base Font). A list of available fonts will display, with the currently selected font asterisked.
4   Move the cursor bar to the required font and press 1 (Select). WordPerfect prompts you with the current point size.
5   Type in the required point size and press Enter.
6   Press F7 (Exit) to return to the editing screen.

This operation does not insert a code into the document.

### *Change the font for all or part of a document*
Position the cursor at the beginning of the text where you want to use a different font or point size, and proceed as follows:

1   Press Ctrl-F8 (Font).
2   Press 4 (Base Font). A list of available fonts will display, as at step 3 above for changing the base font.
3   Repeat steps 4 to 6 above for changing the base font.

WordPerfect inserts a [Font] code in the document containing information about the design of font and point size. The font change applies in a forwards direction only and affects all text after the code.

## Change the default font

To change the base font for all future documents, proceed as follows:

1   Press Shift-F7 (Print).
2   Choose S (Select Printer).
3   With the cursor bar on your default printer, choose 3 (Edit). The Select Printer Edit menu will display.
4   Choose 5 (Initial Base Font). A list of available fonts will display.
5   Select the font and point size you require.
6   Press F7 to exit.

## 16   Footnotes

To create a footnote, proceed as follows:

1   Press Ctrl-F7 (Footnote).
2   Press 1 (Footnote).
3   Press 1 (Create). The footnote number appears.
4   Type the footnote text.
5   Press F7 to exit.

The footnote number in your text will appear on the screen with whatever attribute (colour) has been selected for superscript. The code inserted in the document at this point contains the footnote number and the text:

[Footnote:1;[Note Num]..footnote text..]

To see the footnote, view the document.
   To edit a footnote, follow steps 1 and 2 above, then:

3   Press 2 (Edit). 'Footnote number?' is displayed, with the number of the next footnote.

4   Press Enter to edit that footnote, or type in the number of the one you require.
5   Edit the footnote and then press F7 to exit.

To delete a footnote, place the cursor on the footnote number that is to be deleted, press the Delete key and confirm the deletion. WordPerfect will renumber any subsequent footnotes.

To change the style of your footnotes, follow steps 1 and 2 above and then:

3   Press 4 (Options).
4   Select from the Footnote Options menu the features you want to change.
5   Press F7 to exit.

WordPerfect inserts a [Ftn Opt] code in the document. Any changes have a forwards effect from the position of this code.

## 17   Graphics boxes

WordPerfect incorporates images in documents by enclosing them in graphics boxes. There are four different types of graphics box: Figure, Table, Text, User. Each type can contain a graphic or text or can remain empty. Each one has its own set of defaults and displays differently in terms of border, caption, and even background.

### Create a graphics box
To create a graphics box, proceed as follows:

1   Press Alt-F9 (Graphics). The following menu appears:

     1 Figure; 2 Table Box; 3 Text Box; 4 User Box; 5 Line; 6 Equation: 0

2   Choose from 1 to 4 according to the style of graphics box required. You then see the following menu, with the box style as a heading, and with identical options for all graphics box types:

     1 Create; 2 Edit; 3 New Number; 4 Options: 0

3   Choose 1 (Create). The Graphics Box Definition menu then displays, headed again by the box type. The choices are as follows:

1   *Filename*. Enter the name of the image of document that you wish to retrieve into the graphics box. Alternatively, press List (F5) and retrieve a file from the List Files screen. If the box is to remain empty, leave the filename blank.

2   *Contents*. This displays a menu of different types of information to be placed in the graphics box, and enables you to decide whether or not the graphics are to be kept on disk in a separate file or as part of the document. The choices are:

1 Graphic; 2 Graphic on disk; 3 Text; 4 Equation

If a graphics file has been retrieved into the box, WordPerfect inserts 'Graphic' as the contents. If a text file has been retrieved into the box, WordPerfect inserts 'Text' as the contents.

Option 1 results in the graphic being saved as part of the document. Option 2 results in the graphic being kept as a separate file; WordPerfect accesses this file when the document is used. If your graphic file is not in WordPerfect format and you choose Option 2, WordPerfect will ask if you wish to save the file in .WPG format, which speeds up the process of viewing or printing the document. If you enter Yes, WordPerfect copies the graphics file to .WPG format, resulting in two graphics files – one with the original format and the other in WPG format. If you enter No, your file stays in its current format.

Note that a graphic included in a style must be defined as Graphic on Disk.

3   *Caption*. Enter the caption text in the special editing screen. You may use a maximum of 256 characters. Numbering is entered automatically by a numbering code which you can delete. To reinsert the number, press Alt-F9.

4   *Anchor*. This allows you to anchor a graphics box to a paragraph, a page, or to a character. It will then stay with that paragraph, page or character if the text is subsequently reorganized. You choose from the following menu:

1 Paragraph; 2 Page; 3 Character: 0

If you wish to select a page anchor, make sure the cursor is at the top of a page. After choosing option 2 (Page), WordPerfect prompts 'Number of pages to skip:0'. Press Enter if the graphic should appear on the current page, or type in the number of pages to skip for the graphic to appear on a subsequent page. In practice, it is best that this type of graphics box is inserted at the beginning of the document so that subsequent editing is unlikely to move the box code from its original position. Placing a graphics box at the top of a later page in the document can mean that it eventually gets moved from that position, resulting in the graphic appearing on the wrong page.

5   *Vertical position*. You can determine your required vertical alignment of the box with this option. What happens next depends on the type of box anchor you have chosen. The three possibilities are as follows.

● *Paragraph*. The following prompt appears:

Offset from top of paragraph:

followed by a measurement which is the current distance of the cursor from the top of the paragraph. Enter a new value or press Enter to leave the value as it is.

● *Page*. The following menu appears:

1 Full Page; 2 Top; 3 Centre; 4 Bottom; 5 Set Position: 0.

These menu choices are as follows:

1   Will fill the whole page with the graphic.
2   Aligns it with the top margins.
3   Centres it between the top and bottom margins.
4   Aligns it with the bottom margin above any footers or other non-body text.
5   Produces the prompt 'Offset from top of page:' followed by a measurement which is the current cursor position. If you wish to specify an exact position, choose this and enter the required position.

● *Character*. This allows you to choose how the graphic aligns with text on the current line.

6   *Horizontal position*. This allows you to determine the exact

horizontal position of the graphics box in the paragraph or page. (In the case of a character-anchored box, this option is not used since the character location determines the horizontal position.) Again, what happens next depends on the type of box anchor you have selected.

If you have selected Paragraph, the following menu will appear:

Horizontal Position: 1 Left; 2 Right; 3 Centre; 4 Full: 0

These menu choices are as follows:

1   Aligns the graphics box with the left margin.
2   Aligns it with the right margin.
3   Centres it between the two margins.
4   Extends the box across the line from margin to margin.

If you have selected Page, the following menu will appear:

Horizontal Position: 1 Margins; 2 Columns; 3 Set Position: 0

These menu choices are:

1   *Margins* leads on to the same menu as in Paragraph horizontal position.
2   *Columns* enables you to align a box inside the column you specify; if you want a box between columns 1 and 2, enter '1-2'.
3   *Set Position* allows you to enter a precise measurement from the left margin.

If you have selected Character, the following menu will appear:

Character Box Alignment; 1 Top; 2 Bottom; 3 Centre; 4 Baseline: 0

This allows you to choose how you wish the graphics image to align relative to text on the line.

7   *Size*. If you have entered a filename for your graphic, WordPerfect reads the size of the graphic from the disk file and inserts automatically the measurements needed to display the graphic.

There are four options: Set Width/Auto Height, Set Height/ Auto Width, Set Both, and Auto Both.

- The first two allow you to specify a width or height, allowing WordPerfect to size the other dimension automatically, thus preserving the shape of the graphics image.
- *Set Both* allows you to enter manually both dimensions.
- *Auto Both* will restore the dimensions of the image when it was created originally, rather than when the graphics box was created.

8  *Wrap Text Around Box*. Choose between 'Yes' and 'No' to have text flowing around a box or printing across a box.
9  *Edit*. This option will display an edit screen for either a graphic or text. We deal with the possibilities below.

- *Graphics*. If the graphics box contains a graphic, you will see the image, together with menus at the bottom of the screen, shown in Figure KS.1. These allow you to rotate, or scale, or move the graphic, or display a mirror image of it.

  The main menu is the last line at the bottom of the screen. Its options take you through a sequence of operations to achieve a desired rotation, scaling, or move effect. Short-cut keystrokes are indicated in the line above the numbered menu.
  - *Move*. You can move an image horizontally or vertically within the (stationary) box. Enter positive or negative numbers to move the image to the right or left, and up or down. Alternatively, press the arrow keys. If you move the image past the border of the box, then the image is 'cropped'.
  - *Scale*. This means changing the image's size, i.e. making it smaller or bigger within the static graphics box. When you select Scale, you enter percentage values to scale the image horizontally and vertically. Alternaively, you could press PgUp or PgDn.
  - *Rotate*. You can rotate the image either by selecting 3

---

| Arrow keys Move; **PgUp/PgDn** Scale; +/- Rotate; **Ins** % Change; **Goto** Reset |
|---|
| **1** Move; **2** Scale; **3** Rotate; **4** Invert; **5** Black and White: 0      (10%) |

**Figure KS.1**  Graphics Edit menu

from the bottom menu and entering the number of degrees of rotation, or by pressing the + or − keys.

- *Invert*. This option changes each black dot in a bitmapped image to white and each white dot to black, giving an effect like a photographic negative. With line drawings, just the background colour is changed.
- *Black and white*. Select this to display and print a colour image in black and white.
- *Ins (% change)*. This changes the percentage amount displayed in the lower right corner of the screen to 1, 5, 10 or 25%, so determining the extent to which the image is affected by moving, scaling, and rotating.
- *Goto*. This cancels any changes made to the image.
- *Ins*. Another short-cut is provided by the Insert key − press this, and you can change the rate of rotation, scaling, or moving.

- *Text*. If the graphics box contains a text file, you will see the text. If the box is empty, the screen display will be blank; you can now type text and enhancement codes into the box, and edit text. Press Alt-F9 to rotate your boxed text.

Exit to your document, and a code is inserted in your document containing the type and number of the graphics box and the graphics filename. If you added a caption, there would also be a [Box Num] code and the caption text. If there is insufficient space on the current page for the graphics box, it will flow forwards to the next page.

The outline and graphics box number show on the normal editing screen, and you can view the graphic on the View Document screen.

## Deleting a graphics box
To delete a graphics box, find the graphics box code and delete it.

## Moving a graphics box
To move a graphics box, delete the graphics box code, move the cursor to the new position and use the Cancel key to restore it. If you move a paragraph containing a graphics box anchored to that paragraph, then the graphics box will move too.

*Editing a graphics box*

To edit a graphics box, there is no need to find the box in the document. Proceed as follows:

1  Press Alt-F9 (Graphics).
2  Choose the appropriate box type.
3  Choose 2 (Edit). The prompt 'Figure Number?' appears followed by a number.
4  Type the appropriate box number and press Enter. The Graphics Box Definition menu appears.
5  Make the necessary entries at this menu.
6  Press F7 (Exit) to return to the document.

*Changing the graphics box type*

To change the type of an existing graphics box follow steps 1 to 4 above for editing a graphics box. At step 5, press Alt-F9 (Graphics) and select the new graphics box type. Press F7 to exit back to the document.

*New Number*

By default, your graphics boxes will be consecutively numbered in the caption. If at any point in your document you wish to advance the new numbering, proceed as follows:

1  Press Alt-F9 (Graphics).
2  Select the graphics box type.
3  Choose 3 (New Number).
4  Type in the new figure number and press Enter.

A [New Fig Num:] code is inserted in the document, containing the new number.

*Changing the graphics box defaults*

You can change the default types of graphics boxes. These changes take effect from your current cursor position. Graphics boxes earlier in the document are not affected. To change these defaults, follow steps 1 and 2 above for New Number, and then proceed as follows:

1   Choose 4 (Options). A menu will display, containing the choices for the graphics box selected. The options for a Figure graphics box are shown in Figure KS.2.

1   *Border Style*. Choose this option and a menu of border styles which can be used for each of the four borders. For a dropped-shadow effect, choose Thick or Extra Thick for two adjacent borders, and Single for the other two.

2   *Outside Border Space*. Choose this to change the space allowed between the graphics box and the surrounding text.

3   *Inside Border Space*. Choose this to change the space allowed between the borders of the graphics box and the image within it.

4   *First Level Numbering Method*. You are allowed two levels of caption number (e.g. for a Figure box type, you could have Figure 1 for level 1, and Figure 1.1 for level 2). Choose this to change the numbering style used in captions. The choices are:

   1 Off; 2 Numbers; 3 Letters; 4 Roman Numerals

Although Off is included as an option, you cannot select it for the first level. You would have to delete the [Box Num] code

```
Options: Figure
     1 - Border Style
              Left                        Single
              Right                       Single
              Top                         Single
              Bottom                      Single
     2 - Outside Border Space
              Left                        0.167"
              Right                       0.167"
              Top                         0.167"
              Bottom                      0.167"
     3 - Inside Border Space
              Left                        0"
              Right                       0"
              Top                         0"
              Bottom                      0"
     4 - First Level Numbering Method    Numbers
     5 - Second Level Numbering Method   Off
     6 - Caption Number Style            [BOLD]Figure 1[bold]
     7 - Position of Caption             Below box, Outside borders
     8 - Minimum Offset from Paragraph   0"
     9 - Grey Shading (% of black)       0%

Selection: 0
```

**Figure KS.2**   The Figure Graphics Box Options menu

in the caption editing screen to turn it off. If you choose 3 or 4, the style for first-level numbering will be upper case.

5 *Second Level Numbering Method.* This is similar to item 4 above, except that letters and Roman numerals will be in lower case.

6 *Caption Number Style.* Choose this to change caption text and enhancements.

7 *Position of Caption.* You can choose between above or below the box, and inside or outside the borders.

8 *Minimum Offset from Paragraph.* Choose this to specify how far a paragraph-anchored box may be moved up into the paragraph to fit the graphics box onto the current page. If WordPerfect cannot fit in the box, it will be moved to the top of the next page.

9 *Grey Shading.* Choose this to enter a degree of shading as background to text or images.

Changing the graphics box defaults enters into the document an [Opt] code which shows the type of graphics box.

## 18 Graphics lines

The Alt-F9 Graphics key allows you to draw and edit horizontal and vertical graphic lines. These lines do not appear on the text editing screen. They can only be seen in View Document.

### Creating a horizontal graphics line

To create a horizontal line, proceed as follows:

1 Press Alt-F9 (Graphics).
2 Choose 5 (Line).
3 Choose 1 (Horizontal). The Graphics Horizontal Line menu will display; shown in Figure KS.3.

These menu options are as follows:

- *Horizontal Position.* Choose this to fix the starting and finishing points of the line. The following menu appears:

  1 Left; 2 Right; 3 Centre; 4 Full; 5 Set Position

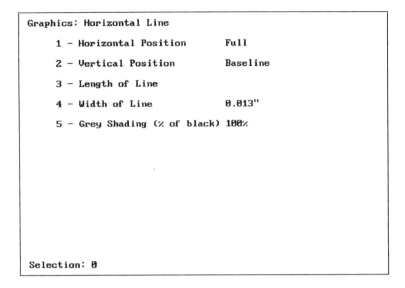

**Figure KS.3** Graphics Horizontal Line menu

Press 1 to start the line at the left margin, 2 to end it against the right margin, 3 to centre between left and right margins, and 4 to extend the line from left to right. Press 5 to start the line at some position relative to the left edge of the page.

- *Length of Line.* Choose this to enter a line length. If you selected 4 above, WordPerfect calculates and enters the line length for you.
- *Width of Line.* Choose this to change the width (thickness) up to a maximum of 54 inches. You can enter up to three decimal points.
- *Grey Shading.* Choose this to enter a percentage for the amount of shading required.

When you exit back to the document, WordPerfect inserts a [HLine] code containing information about its horizontal position, length, width and degree of grey shading.

### Creating a vertical graphics line
This allows you to insert vertical lines. Follow steps 1 to 2 for a horizontal line above, and then proceed as follows:

3 Choose 2 (Vertical). The Graphics Vertical Line menu will display. These menu options are as follows:

1 *Horizontal Position*. Choose this to position the line horizontally. The choices are:

1 Left; 2 Right; 3 Between Columns; 4 Set Position

Press 1 to place the line to the left of text at the left margin, or press 2 to place the line to the right of text at the right margin. Press 3 for lines between columns; specify a column number to position the line between that column and the one to its right. Press 4 to specify a distance from the left edge of the page.

2 *Vertical Position*. Choose this to position the line vertically. The possibilities are:

1 Full Page; 2 Top; 3 Centre; 4 Bottom; 5 Set Position

Press 1 for the line to extend from top to bottom margins, 2 to start the line at the top margin, 3 to centre the line between top and bottom margins, and 4 to start the line at the bottom margin. Press 5 to enter a distance from the top of the page for the line to begin.

3 *Length of Line*. Choose this to enter a value for the line length. Depending on your choice in earlier options, a line length may be calculated for you. Only use this option when you want to override the calculation.

4 *Width of Line*. As for horizontal lines.

5 *Grey Shading*. As for horizontal lines.

When you exit back to the editing screen, WordPerfect inserts a [VLine] code containing information on the horizontal position, line length, line thickness, and degree of grey shading.

## Editing a graphics line

In editing a graphics line, WordPerfect searches backwards for the first graphics line of that type (horizontal or vertical). If it cannot find one, it then searches forward. So if you have more than one graphics line of a particular type, position the cursor just after the code for that line before starting the editing process.

To edit a graphics line, follow steps 1 to 2 for inserting a graphics line, then proceed as follows:

3   Press 3 (Edit Horizontal Line), or 4 (Edit Vertical Line). The appropriate Graphics Line Definition menu displays for editing.

### Moving a graphics line

To move a graphics line, reveal the codes and delete the graphics line code. Then move the cursor to its new location, and use the Cancel key to restore the code.

### Deleting a graphics line

To delete a graphics line, reveal the codes and delete the graphics line code.

## 19   Hard space

To insert a space preventing a line break between two words, press Home,Spacebar.

## 20   Headers and footers

To create a header or footer, place the cursor at the beginning of your document and proceed as follows:

1   Press Shift-F8 (Format).
2   Press 2 (Page).
3   Press 3 (Header), or 4 (Footer).
4   Press 1 (Header A) or 2 (Header B); the same applies for Footer A or Footer B.
5   Press 2 (Every Page), or 3 (Odd Pages), or 4 (Even Pages).
6   Enter the text for the header or the footer.
7   Press F7 (Exit) twice.

This inserts a [Header] or [Footer] code in the document which contains information on any alignment or enhancement, plus the header or footer text.

To edit a header or footer, repeat steps 1 to 4 above, and then:

5  Press 5 (Edit).
6  Edit the header or footer text.
7  Press F7 (Exit) twice.

This edits the existing header or footer code.

## 21  Help

WordPerfect provides a comprehensive system of 'Help' screens, which you access by pressing F3. You can then press the first letter of the feature that you wish to find out about, or you can press the function key or cursor movement key that you want help with. If you press F3 while at a menu, you will get information about that menu's options.

The Help screens are the one place in WordPerfect which you can't get out of by pressing F1 or F7. You must instead press the spacebar or the Enter key.

## 22  Hyphenation

For automatic hyphenation:

1  Press Shift-F8 (Format).
2  Press 1 (Line Format).
3  Press 1 (Hyphenation).
4  Type 'Y' for Yes.

WordPerfect inserts the hyphenation code [Hyph On].

To end automatic hyphenation, repeat steps 1 to 3 above, and then type 'N' for N°. The code inserted is [Hyph Off].

For manual hyphenation:

- Hyphen character – press-.
- Soft hyphen – press Ctrl--.
- Hard hyphen – press Home,-.

## 23   Indents

If you wish to indent a whole paragraph you can use the F4 Indent key. This will indent the left margin up to the next [HRt] code, i.e. until you press the Enter key. The indent is at the next tab stop.

To indent a paragraph from the left, press F4 (→Indent). This inserts a [→Indent] code.

To indent a paragraph from left and right, press Shift-F4 (→Indent←). This inserts a [→Indent←] code.

## 24   Index

You can create an index in a document, consisting of words selected from that document. The entries are sorted alphabetically, and there are choices of style for page numbering. The steps are very similar to creating a table of contents:

1   Mark text.
2   Define the location of the table and the numbering style.
3   Generate the index.

### I   *Mark text for an index*
Proceed as follows:

1   Place the cursor anywhere on the word that is to be included in the index. If the entry is more than one word, press Alt-F4 to block the text.
2   Press Alt-F5 (Mark Text).
3   Press 3 (Index). 'Index Heading' will appear, followed by the selected word or phrase.
4   Press Enter to accept it. In the index this word or phrase will be displayed as a major heading at the left margin. The prompt 'Subheading' now appears.
5   Type in a subheading name if required. In the index this word or phrase will be displayed as a subheading at the first tab stop.
6   Press Enter.

The code [Index] is inserted in the document, containing the index heading text and, where appropriate, the index subheading text.

If you want a word in your text marked but included in the index under a different heading or subheading, follow steps 1 to 3 above, and then:

4  Type in the required heading and press Enter.
5  Type in the required subheading and press Enter.

## 2  Define the index

Start by placing the cursor at the end of the document, past all [Index] codes. Type in any heading text and hard returns to insert space before the index. Then proceed as follows:

1  Press Alt-F5 (Mark Text). The following menu appears:

   1 Cross Ref; 2 Subdoc; 3 Index; 4 ToA; 5 Define; 6 Generate:

2  Choose 5 (Define).
3  Choose 3 (Index). The following prompt will appear: 'Concordance filename: (Enter=None)'.
4  Press Enter for no concordance. The Index Definition menu displays (Figure 10.23), with options to change the page numbering style.
5  Choose the required style from this menu.
6  Press F7 (Exit).

A [Def Mark:Index] code is inserted in the document. If any [Index] codes exist after this definition code, they will not be included in the index.

## 3  Generate the index

To create the index, repeat the steps for generating a table of contents, see Section 64. An [End Def] code is inserted at the end of the index.

## Edit an index

Follow the steps for editing a table of contents, described in Section 64.

## 25  Initial codes

You can enter format codes in the Initial Codes screen instead of the document screen.

1  For the current document, use the Format Document menu (see below).
2  For all future documents, use the Setup Initial Settings menu (see Section 53 on Setup).

These codes are for such things as margins, justification, page numbering; in other words, most of the things found on the Format menus. For a complete list of features, see *Initial Codes* in the WordPerfect manual. Codes entered in this way do not appear on the Reveal Codes screen and are therefore more protected against deletion. It also means that documents are not cluttered with format codes.

### Initial codes in the current document

To place codes in the current document, proceed as follows:

1  Press Shift-F8 (Format).
2  Press 3 (Document).
3  Press 2 (Initial Codes). The Initial Codes screen appears, with the following two codes already in place:

[Lang:UK][Paper Sz/Type:8.27″ × 11.69″, Standard]

4  Use the Format key to add the format codes you require.
5  Press F7 (Exit).

When you save the file, these settings are saved with it. Codes entered in the normal way within the document itself override any conflicting initial codes.

## 26  Justification

Besides setting the left and right margins, the Line Format menu allows you to apply different justification to your text. The options are:

*Left* — justified at left margin.
*Centre* — text centred between margins.
*Right* — justified at right margin.
*Full* — justified left and right margins. This is the default justification.

Note that on the editing screen fully justified text appears as left-aligned. Use the View Document screen to see full justification.
To change justification:

1  Press Shift-F8 (Format).
2  Choose 1 for Line Format.
3  Press 3 for Justification. The following menu will appear at the bottom of the screen:

Justification: 1 Left; 2 Centre; 3 Right; 4 Full: 0

The code for left justification is [Just;Left].

To change the default justification, see Setup, Section 53.

## 27  Keyboard layout

This feature allows you to create and edit keyboard definitions. You can:

● Change the function key assignments so that, for example, Cancel (F1) is assigned to the Esc key.
● Define keys to perform as macros, thus allowing greater flexibility in creating macros.

Besides the original keyboard layout, WordPerfect provides five alternative keyboard files to choose from. These files all have a .WPK extension and are stored in the keyboard/macro directory. If you cannot find any, look in the Setup — Location of Files menu for the directory assigned to keyboard layout files. A list of the key assignments contained in these keyboard layouts is given in the keyboard appendix of the WordPerfect manual.
The merits of each of these alternative keyboards are briefly as follows:

1   *Alternat*. Change to this if you are more used to using the Esc key to cancel and the F1 key for accessing help; the F3 key is then assigned to the repeat feature.
2   *Enhanced*. This contains a mixture of enhancement, blocks, and cursor movement.
3   *Equation*. This would be very useful to anyone using the equation feature, allowing easy access to many mathematical symbols.
4   *Macros*. This contains quite a mixture of useful macros: for example, Alt-E will take you from any menu to the editing screen; Alt-M will insert a bookmark as text in a document, enabling you to search subsequently for that place in the document. Some of these macros use the Ctrl key.
5   *Shortcut*. This keyboard is a collection of macros for inserting enhancement, margins, tabs, etc. The Alt-E macro is a particularly powerful one which allows you to edit most Word-Perfect codes. For example, if you have inserted a tabs code which you wish to change, placing your cursor on that code and pressing Alt-E takes you directly to the tabs menu. After making changes and exiting, WordPerfect has replaced the original tabs code with the new one.

### Keyboard layouts and macros

Macros contained in keyboard layout files can be used only if the appropriate keyboard file has been selected first. You cannot delete or copy keyboard macros on the List Files screen, as they do not display in a directory.

Macros in keyboard layout files can take precedence over some ordinary macros (i.e. macros stored with a .WPM extension). If you have defined an Alt-macro, and execute it by pressing Alt and then a letter, WordPerfect checks first in the current keyboard layout. If a feature has been assigned to that macro name, Word-Perfect executes it. If not, WordPerfect searches through the macro files and executes that.

### Select a keyboard

To select a different keyboard layout, proceed as follows:

1   Press Shift-F1 (Setup).
2   Choose 5 (Keyboard Layout). The keyboard layout menu is displayed.

3   Move the cursor to the required keyboard file.
4   Choose 1 (Select). The Setup menu then displays your selected keyboard filename.
5   Press F7 (Exit).

The keyboard you select is stored in the WP{WP}.SET file and takes effect each time you start WordPerfect.

### Select the original keyboard
If you wish to return to the original keyboard, you have two choices.

- You can press Ctrl-6; this immediately disables the current keyboard and returns you to the original.
- You can repeat steps 1–2 above for selecting a keyboard, and choose 6 (Original) from the keyboard layout menu.

### Delete a keyboard
To delete a keyboard file, you have two choices:

1   Delete the file from the list of files. The procedure is:

a   Press F5 (List).
b   Move the cursor to the appropriate filename (it will have a .WPK extension).
c   Choose 2 (Delete), and confirm the deletion.

2   Delete the file from the keyboard layout menu. Repeat steps 1–3 for selecting a keyboard file, and then proceed as follows:

d   Choose 2 (Delete).
e   Press F7 (Exit).

### Copy a keyboard
This option allows you to copy an existing keyboard layout file to use as a model for a new one. Repeat steps 1–3 for selecting a keyboard file, and then proceed as follows:

4   Choose 5 (Copy).
5   Enter a name for the new keyboard file.
6   Press F7 (Exit).

The new keyboard file is added into the list of keyboard files, and given a .WPK extension.

## Create a keyboard
To create a new keyboard file, follow steps 1 and 2 for selecting a keyboard, and then proceed as follows:

3  Choose 4 (Create).
4  Enter a name for the new file.
5  Press F7 (Exit).

The new keyboard file is added into the list of keyboard files, and given a .WPK extension. Initially, it will have all the key assignments of the original keyboard.

## Edit a keyboard
To change a keyboard file, repeat steps 1–3 for selecting a keyboard, and then proceed as follows:

4  Choose 7 (Edit). A menu similar to that in Figure KS.4 is displayed, with a list of the macros contained in the current keyboard file.

```
Keyboard: Edit

Name: SHORTCUT

Key             Action              Description
Alt-U           {KEY MACRO 26}      Shadow
Alt-E           {KEY MACRO 15}      Edit a Code
Alt-R           {KEY MACRO 8}       Redline
Alt-T           {KEY MACRO 27}      Strikeout
Alt-I           {KEY MACRO 1}       Italics
Alt-O           {KEY MACRO 25}      Outline
Alt-P           {KEY MACRO 21}      Superscript
Alt-A           {KEY MACRO 32}      Add an Attribute
Alt-S           {KEY MACRO 6}       Small
Alt-D           {KEY MACRO 2}       Double Underline
Alt-F           {KEY MACRO 7}       Fine
Alt-G           {KEY MACRO 30}      Go Printer
Alt-L           {KEY MACRO 5}       Large
Alt-X           {KEY MACRO 3}       Extra Large
Alt-C           {KEY MACRO 33}      Page numbering
Alt-V           {KEY MACRO 4}       Very Large
Alt-B           {KEY MACRO 28}      Subscript

1 Action; 2 Dscrptn; 3 Original; 4 Create; 5 Move; Macro; 6 Save; 7 Retrieve:
```

**Figure KS.4**  Keyboard Edit menu

The menu options are as follows:

1 *Action*. This takes you directly to the Key Action screen for the macro at the current cursor position. This is similar to the macro editor screen, and displays the keystrokes for the macro. You can edit these or enter new keystrokes exactly as you would do for a macro file (described in Section 30).

2 *Descrptn*. This allows you to edit the current description of a keyboard macro.

3 *Original*. Use this option to change the key's function back to what it was on the original keyboard.

4 *Create*. This enables you to create a new definition for a key. You are prompted to press the key to which you want to assign the feature, and a description. You are then placed in the Key Action screen, and you follow the procedure outlined for the Action option above.

5 *Move*. This allows you to move the highlighted key assignment to another key. When prompted 'Key', press the key to which you wish to move the assignment.

There then follow two menu options relating specifically to macros.

6 *Save*. This allows you to save a key assignment as a .WPM file macro. Enter a name for the macro, and it will be added to your list of files in the macro directory.

7 *Retrieve*. If you have created a macro file using the Macro Define key, you may wish to include this in your keyboard layout file. For example, the selected keyboard layout may contain a macro for inserting double underlining, which you never use. If your macro and the keyboard macro have the same name, you will not be able to use *your* macro. The Retrieve option allows you to include your macro in the keyboard layout file, either replacing the double underlining macro, or under a new name.

When prompted 'Key', press the key to which the macro will be assigned. When prompted 'Macro', enter the name of the macro you are retrieving. Your macro details are now copied to the keyboard definition; any later changes to your macro will not affect this definition.

## Keyboard map

This gives you a picture of key assignments in a keyboard file. It also allows you to assign WordPerfect features and operations to keys. To use the map option, follow steps 1 to 3 for selecting a keyboard, and then proceed as follows:

4 Choose 8 (Map). The Keyboard map menu will display, similar to Figure KS.5.

The menu options are:

1 *Key*. This allows you to assign a feature or operation that exists on one key to the key on which the cursor is resting. For example, move the cursor to Alt-B and press F6 to assign emboldening to Alt-B. You should have the original keyboard selected before using this feature, in case you have, for example, assigned something else to F6 in the current keyboard.

2 *Macro*. This enables you to use the Key Action screen to create a macro for a key. Use it in the same way as using the Macro Editor screen (Section 32).

3 *Description*. You can enter a description for a key assignment.

4 *Original*. This will enable you to restore a key's function to what it was in the original keyboard.

5 *Compose*. This enables you to assign a WordPerfect special

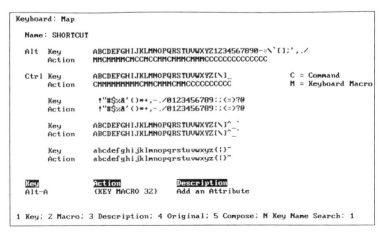

**Figure KS.5** Keyboard Map

character for a key. Type in the character set number and the character number, and then press Enter.

6  *N Key Name Search*. Use this to move quickly to the key you are looking for.

7  *Delete*. To delete a key assignment, move the cursor under that key then press Delete and confirm the deletion. The key returns to its function on the original keyboard.

## 28  Line spacing

You can select double line spacing, triple line spacing − in fact any line spacing you want − at the Line Format menu. The procedure is:

1  Press Shift-F8 (Format).
2  Choose 1 for Line Format.
3  Choose 6 for Line Spacing.
4  Type the number of lines you require spaced, including, if you wish, decimals.
5  Press Enter.
6  Press F7 (Exit) to return to the editing screen.

The code for double line spacing is [LnSpacing:2].

## 29  List files

This enables you to see the list of files on your hard or floppy disk. You can use this feature at any time, whether there is a document on the screen or when you are prompted to enter a filename. Press F5 and the message

Dir C:\WP51\TEXT\*.*

appears at the left of the status line (if this is your default directory). At the right of the status line is a message telling you to type = if you wish to make another directory your default for the current working session. For instance, to change to the WP51 directory:

1  Type =.
2  Type C:\WP51.
3  Press Enter.

If you don't want to change the default directory, simply press Enter to see the list of files, together with their size, date, and time of last saving. The heading contains the current date and time; the size of the current document in the memory, the amount of free disk space, the disk space taken by files in the list, and the number of files in the current directory.

Any directories appear at the top of the list, marked <DIR> at their right. If you have a large number of files, they will not all appear on the screen; an arrow head appears at the base of the central line separating the columns to indicate that there are more. Use the normal cursor movement keys (including Page Up, Page Down, Home and arrow keys) to scroll through the list of files.

To exit List, press F7 (Exit), or F1 (Cancel).

If, after pressing F5, you wish to see a subset of the listed files, use the DOS wildcard facility. For example, press F5 and then type 'CHAP*.*' to list all files beginning with CHAP.

At the foot of the list of files is the menu shown in Figure 1.7. The options it provides are:

1  *Retrieve.* This works in the same way as Shift-F10 (Retrieve). If a document is already retrieved, WordPerfect asks 'Retrieve into current document? No/Yes'. If you do not want to retrieve this document into the current one on the text screen, choose No.

2  *Delete.* This deletes files and empty directories. As explained at the end of this section, you can delete several files if you have *marked* them.

3  *Move/Rename.* This renames a file. Since you can use it to change any part of the pathname, it also allows you to move files. Like Delete, this feature can be used to move a set of marked files.

4  *Print.* This sends a file directly to your printer. You can enter a range of pages to print, or print all pages. Again, you can mark several files for printing.

5  *Short/Long Display.* This provides two ways of viewing the document list, short and long display. The first shows the DOS filenames in two columns, the second shows long document names and document descriptions. When Long is active, the list display operates more slowly.

6  *Look.* This allows you to look at files without retrieving them. The usual Search keys are available while using Look (see Chapter 5).

7 *Other Directory*. This allows you to change to another directory by entering its name. It then becomes default directory for the current session. If the directory does not exist, WordPerfect will create it.

8 *Copy*. This enables you to copy the current file (or a number of marked files) to another drive or directory. Alternatively, you can copy the file to the current directory under a different filename.

9 *Find*. This allows you to search all files in the list for word patterns. When you select this you are taken to a submenu from which you can choose to search the entire text of the files, or restrict the search to the first page, or to the document summary, or to the filenames. This search can take a minute or two for long lists. You can reduce the number of files searched by:

a Using the DOS wildcard feature.

b Marking files to search using the * facility.

c Using the Conditions option in the submenu. This allows you to reduce the number of files by using both wildcards and entering a range of dates.

*N Name Search*. This takes you into Name Search mode and removes the menu from the screen. Then, as you start to type the name of the file, the highlight bar moves instantly to the first match it finds. To exit the Name Search mode and restore the menu, press Enter or the arrow keys.

To delete, print, move or copy several files:

1 Mark those files by moving the highlight bar to them and pressing *. If you mark a file in error, unmark it by highlighting it again and pressing *. Mark/unmark all files by pressing the Alt-F5 Mark Text key.

2 Choose the command you wish to apply to the marked files.

## 30 Macros

A macro is a collection of keystrokes which can be executed with only a few keystrokes, usually Alt plus another key. A macro can be permanent or temporary. Before you can use a macro, you must first create (or *define*) it.

## Create a permanent macro

There are two ways of creating a macro, either from the normal editing screen, or from the macro editor. To create a macro from the normal editing screen, proceed as follows:

1   Press Ctrl-F10 (Macro Define). You are prompted 'Define macro:'.
2   Enter the name of the macro:

   a   hold down the Alt key and type a single letter,
   b   type 1 to 8 letters to give your macro a descriptive name or

   You are prompted 'Description:'.
3   Enter a brief description (you are allowed up to 39 characters), and press Enter. You now have 'Macro Def' flashing on the normal editing screen, indicating that all your keystrokes will be recorded.
4   Type the keystrokes to be recorded.
5   Press Ctrl-F10 (Macro Define) to finishing defining the macro. The macro file is saved to the default directory with a .WPM extension.

If you cannot find macro files, look in the Setup − Location of Files menu for the directory assigned to macros.

## Create a temporary macro

To create a temporary macro, proceed as follows:

1   Press Ctrl-F10 (Macro Define) as above.
2   Press Enter without entering a name. You now have 'Macro Def' flashing on the normal editing screen.

   Repeat steps 4 and 5 above. The macro is saved to the default macro file WP{WP}.WPM in the default directory. It will be replaced when you create another temporary macro.

## The macro editor

To create a macro from the macro editor, proceed as follows:

1   Press Home, Ctrl-F10 (Macro Define).
2   Enter the name of your macro as above for defining a macro.

3 Enter a description as above. You are now in the macro editor, see Figure KS.6.

4 Create the macro by inserting the required keystrokes. The notes below explain how to insert commands and keystrokes.

5 Press F7 (Exit) when finished to end the definition and save the macro.

When inserting and editing commands and keystrokes, you should observe the following rules:

• *Inserting text*. Simply type the required text in the appropriate location. Use the Enter and cursor movement keys as you would on the normal editing screen.

• *Inserting function key commands*. Press the appropriate function key. The exceptions are Macro Define (Ctrl-F10), Cancel (F1), Help (F3), and Exit (F7). These must be inserted in *command insert mode*, by pressing Ctrl-V first, as explained below.

• *Inserting program commands*. Select from the macro command box by pressing Ctrl-PgUp.

• *Deleting text and commands*. Use Backspace or Delete.

• *Inserting editing and cursor keys*. The editing and cursor movement keys default to being editing keys. To use them as command keys, enter command insert mode first by pressing Ctrl-V or Ctrl-F10. Ctrl-V places you in command insert

```
Macro: Action

    File              MYMACRO.WPM

    Description       sample macro

    ┌────────────────────────────────────────────┐
    │{DISPLAY OFF}                                 │
    │                                              │
    │                                              │
    │                                              │
    │                                              │
    │                                              │
    │                                              │
    └────────────────────────────────────────────┘

Ctrl-PgUp for macro commands; Press Exit when done
```

**Figure KS.6**  Macro Editor

mode for the next keystroke. Pressing Ctrl-F10 places you in command insert mode for all future keystrokes until you press Ctrl-F10 again.

## Execute a macro

This depends on how you named it when it was defined.

- If you named the macro using Alt plus another key, you can run it by holding down the Alt key and typing the other key.
- If you gave it a descriptive name by typing in 1 to 8 letters, proceed as follows:

  1  Press Alt-F10 (Macro). You are prompted 'Macro:'.
  2  Type the macro name (you need not type in the .WPM extension).
  3  Press Enter.

- If you named it with the Enter key (as a temporary macro), press Alt-F10 and then Enter key.

## Copy a macro

To copy a macro from one drive or directory to another, proceed as follows:

1  Press F5 (List) and Enter.
2  With the cursor on the macro file, choose 8 (Copy).
3  Type in the new drive or directory and press Enter.

## Move or rename a macro

To move a macro from one drive or directory to another, or to rename the macro, repeat the instructions for copying a macro and proceed as follows:

1  Press F5 (List) and Enter.
2  With the cursor on the macro file, choose 3 (Move/Rename).
3  Type in the new name, drive or directory and press Enter.

## Delete a macro

To delete a macro, proceed as follows:

1 Press F5 (List) and Enter.
2 With the cursor on the macro file, choose 2 (Delete), and confirm the deletion.


## Edit a macro
You can do this either in the macro editor or the ordinary text editing screen.


## In the macro editor

1 Press Home, Ctrl-F10 (Macro Define). You are prompted 'Define Macro'.
2 Type the name of the macro and press Enter. The existing description then appears at the 'Description:' prompt.
3 Edit the description, or press Enter to retain the description. You are then taken to the macro editor where you can edit the keystrokes in the editing window.
4 Press F7 (Exit) to finish editing and exit, saving the macro.


## On the text editing screen

1 Press Ctrl-F10 (Macro Define). You are prompted 'Define Macro'.
2 Type the name of the macro and press Enter. The following prompt appears:

MYMACRO.WPM Already Exists: 1 Replace; 2 Edit; 3 Description: 0

If you choose 'Replace' you then have to confirm the replacement. You are then prompted to enter a description, and are returned to the normal editing screen where you can define the new macro.

If you choose 'Edit', you are then taken to the macro editor where you can change the keystrokes in the editing window.

If you choose 'Description' you are prompted for a new description, and then taken to the macro editor.

## 31   Maths

The Maths feature allows you to perform calculations on tabbed columns. These calculations can be simple subtotals, totals, or grand totals; or they can be more complex calculations involving formulas.

Whichever type of maths you wish to use, the basic procedure is as follows:

1   Set tabs for the columns, bearing in mind that the Maths feature will convert normal tab settings to decimal tabs.
2   Enter the column headings.
3   Define the maths columns if necessary (see Maths Define below).
4   Turn Maths on.
5   Enter text, figures, and operators (see Maths On below).
6   Calculate.
7   Turn Maths off.

### Maths On

To use the simple Maths feature, i.e. to add up columns of figures, proceed as follows:

1   Press Alt-F7 (Columns/Table).
2   Choose Maths On. A [Maths On] code is inserted in the document, and 'Maths' appears in the status line. Any tab settings are automatically changed to decimal tabs.
3   Type one of the following operators where an addition is required:

> \+ for a subtotal
> = for a total
> \* for a grand total

### Maths Off

At the end of your maths text, turn the Maths feature off as follows:

1   Press Alt-F7.

2 Choose Maths Off. A [Maths Off] code is inserted in the document.

Tab settings are returned to their previous style.

## Calculate

To perform calculations, proceed as follows:

1 With 'Maths' displayed in the status line, press Alt-F7 and choose Maths, Calculate. The operator symbols will still appear on the editing screen, but will not print out.

Besides the operators listed above, there are three more, i.e. t, T, and N. They are used as follows:

t: To add a positive number to a total. Place the cursor in a blank line above the = operator, then type a 't' followed by the number.

T: To add a positive number to a grand total. Proceed as for a total, but instead of typing 't', type 'T'.

N: To add a negative number to either a total or grand total. Use the operator 'N' in a similar way to 'T'.

## Maths definition

Use this feature where you want to carry out horizontal totalling, or to perform calculations such as addition, subtraction, multiplication, or division across columns. To insert a Maths definition, proceed as follows:

1 Place the cursor *after* any existing [Tab Set] code and *before* any existing [Maths On] code.

2 Press Alt-F7 (Column/Table).

3 Choose 3 — Define The Maths Definition menu shown in Figure KS.7 will appear.
   This menu allows you to define Maths for up to 24 columns — A to X — where A is the first tabbed column. The column at the left margin is not counted in a Maths definition. The definition consists of a column type, negative number symbol, and decimal place numbers. You can enter formulas in a maximum of four columns.

```
Maths Definition           Use arrow keys to position cursor

Columns                    A B C D E F G H I J K L M N O P Q R S T U V W X

Type                       2 2 2 2 2 2 2 2 2 2 2 2 2 2 2 2 2 2 2 2 2 2 2 2

Negative Numbers           ( ( ( ( ( ( ( ( ( ( ( ( ( ( ( ( ( ( ( ( ( ( ( (

Number of Places to        2 2 2 2 2 2 2 2 2 2 2 2 2 2 2 2 2 2 2 2 2 2 2 2
  the Right (0-4)

Calculation    1
  Formulas     2
               3
               4

Type of Column:
    0 = Calculation   1 = Text      2 = Numeric    3 = Total

Negative Numbers
    ( = Parentheses (50.00)          - = Minus Sign  -50.00


Press Exit when done
```

**Figure KS.7**   Maths Definition menu


The entries on the Maths Definition menu are as follows:

- *Type.* The default type is numeric, the other types being:

  0 for a column where you enter a formula.
  1 for a column containing text, not numbers.
  2 for a column where you need to enter an operator such as +, = or *.
  3 for a column which totals from the column to the left.

  You change a column type by moving the cursor across to the appropriate column letter using the right arrow key. If you change it to a calculation column, the cursor moves down to the Calculation Formulas field, and you type in the appropriate formula. Use the column letters (A–X) to refer to the columns you require.

- *Negative Numbers.* WordPerfect defaults to the use of parentheses for displaying these numbers. You can change this to the minus sign by entering the - symbol.

- *Number of Places to the Right.* WordPerfect defaults to two decimal places. You can choose from 0 to 4. If your figures are not decimals, you should change the default to 0.

4   After making the appropriate changes to the Definition menu, press Exit once. If you have not already turned maths on, choose Maths On from the Maths menu. If there is already a

[Maths On] code, simply press Exit a second time.
A [Maths Def] code is inserted in the document.

When tabbing across to a column containing a Maths formula, a ! symbol will appear in that column. Like the other operators, this will not print out. WordPerfect will display the result after you perform a calculation.

## 32  Merge

Merging involves incorporating variable data — such as names and addresses — with standard text held in a main document, or primary file. The variable data may come from a document — called the *secondary file* — or from the keyboard.

These documents contain merge commands which appear on the text editing screen in curly brackets — e.g. {END FIELD}. These commands display in the Reveal Codes screen as normal codes, i.e. in square brackets. The code equivalent of the {END FIELD} command is [Mrg:END FIELD].

### Create a secondary file
To create a secondary file, proceed as follows:

1  Type the first item of variable data for the first record.
2  Press the F9 End Field key. This inserts the {END FIELD} command at the end of this data and moves the cursor down to the start of the next line. It also inserts the [Mrg:END FIELD] code into the document.
3  Repeat this process for the other items of data in the first record. The cursor will end up positioned at the start of the line below your last field.
4  Press the Shift-F9 Merge Codes key. The Codes menu appears.
5  Press 2 or E to choose the {END RECORD} command ([Mrg:END RECORD] in the Reveal Codes screen). Word-Perfect inserts this on the line below the record, and then a page break below this. It then moves the cursor to the next line (at the start of the next page) ready for you to enter the next record.
6  Continue entering the data until your set of records is complete, then save the file.

Note the following:

- In a record where a field contains more than one line of data, type the first line, then press Enter, then the next line.
- In a record where a field is empty, simply insert the {END FIELD} command by itself.
- If you inadvertently insert, in a non-merge document, an {END FIELD} command, you can delete it in the normal way. However, the 'Field:' number still remains in the status line. To remove it, press Home, Home, up arrow.

### Create a primary file

To create a primary file, enter the text of the document. Where variables are to be inserted, proceed as follows:

1  Press Shift-F9 (Merge Codes).
2  Press 1 or F. The prompt 'Enter field:' appears at the foot of the screen.
3  Type the number of the field you wish to insert, and press Enter.

WordPerfect inserts the {FIELD} command in your document, followed by the field number and a tilde. For example, field 1 (the first field) would appear as '{FIELD}1~'. A [Mrg:FIELD] code is inserted at the same position.

- If any records in the secondary document have blank fields, add question marks after the appropriate field numbers in the primary document if you wish to prevent blank spaces being inserted. See Figure 7.7.

### Merge to the screen

Having saved and exited both primary and secondary files, proceed as follows:

1  Press Ctrl-F9 (Merge/Sort).
2  Choose 1 (Merge). The prompt 'Primary file' appears.
3  Type the name of your primary file. Use the F5 key and retrieve the file from the list if you cannot remember its name.

4   Press Enter. The prompt 'Secondary file' appears.
5   Type the name of your secondary file. Again retrieve from List Files if you cannot remember the filename.
6   Press Enter.

WordPerfect then creates a merge document consisting of the primary file merged with the secondary file. The screen displays the end of this file, showing the last record's merge. This document can be printed in the normal way.

## Cancel a merge

After following the steps for merging to the screen, a message '*Merging*' appears in the status line. If you wish to cancel the merge, press F1 (Cancel).

## Merge directly to the printer

To send a merge directly to the printer, proceed as follows:

1   Retrieve the primary file.
2   Place the cursor on the line below the last line of text.
3   Press Shift-F9 (Merge Codes).
4   Press 6 (More). The merge commands box appears, with a name search option: press the first letter of the command you want.
5   Choose {PRINT}. This inserts the {PRINT} command in the document, and the [Mrg:PRINT] code in the Reveal Codes screen.
6   Press Shift-F9 (Merge Codes). The Merge Codes menu is displayed.
7   Press 4 (Page Off). The {PAGE OFF} command is inserted in the document, and the [Mrg: PAGE OFF] code is inserted in the Reveal Codes screen.

Then repeat the steps above for merging to the screen, and the result of the merge will be sent direct to the printer.
   Note that:

• Instead of pressing Shift-F9, 6, to display the merge commands box, you can press Shift-F9 twice.

• Instead of inserting merge codes using the function keys, you can use the keyboard as follows:

|  |  |  |
|---|---|---|
| End Field | − Ctrl-R | displays as $^\wedge$R |
| End Record | − Ctrl-E | displays as $^\wedge$E |
| Field | − Ctrl-F | displays as $^\wedge$F |
| Print | − Ctrl-T | displays as $^\wedge$T |

## Format the merged document
WordPerfect gives you the following options for inserting formatting commands in the finished merge document.

• If you have merged to the screen, you can insert formatting codes at the beginning of the merge document.
• If you are merging to the printer, place the formatting codes in Initial Codes for the primary file (see Section 25). Inserting them here rather than within the primary file speeds up the merge.

## Commands display
You can turn off the merge commands display so that you don't see them on the editing screen. See Section 53 on Setup.

## Name the fields
To name the fields in a secondary file so that you can refer to them by name rather than number, proceed as follows:

1  Place the cursor at the beginning of the secondary file.
2  Press Shift-F9 (Merge Codes).
3  Press 6 (More).
4  From the merge commands box, choose Field Names. 'Enter Field 1:' appears in the status line.
5  Type the field name of your choice and press Enter.
6  Continue typing in field names until you have completed a record.
7  Press F7 (Exit).

The field names will appear at the top of the secondary document, as shown in Figure 7.6. You can refer to the fields either by name or by number in the primary file.

*Print the secondary document*
To print the data in a secondary document, suppressing the page breaks between records, proceed as follows:

1 Retrieve the secondary document.
2 Press Shift-F9 (Merge Codes).
3 Press 4 (Page Off). This inserts a {PAGE OFF} command in the document and a [Mrg: PAGE OFF] code in the Codes screen.
4 Press F7 to exit, saving the file under a different name.

Now create a new primary file consisting only of field numbers or names, as shown in Figure KS.8. (This figure shows field numbers, plus optional field labels − 'School', 'Address', etc. Field labels help to identify clearly the data in different fields.)
 Save and exit the file, then complete the merge either to the screen or to the printer.

*Merge to mailing labels*
To print to mailing labels:

1 Create a secondary file, containing the names and addresses. Figure KS.9 shows an example of a single record in such a secondary file.
2 Create a primary file, inserting field numbers where you want the name and address data to print on a label.

Figure KS.10 shows a primary file which would be suitable for printing address labels from the secondary file shown in Figure KS.9.

3 Merge to the screen, as explained under 'Create a primary file'.

```
{FIELD}1~ {FIELD}2~ {FIELD}3~
School: {FIELD}4~
Address: {FIELD}5~
{FIELD}6~
{FIELD}7~ {FIELD}8~
Type of School: {FIELD}9~
```

**Figure KS.8** Primary file for printing data

```
Miss{END FIELD}
Mary{END FIELD}
Roberts{END FIELD}
Prestwood Secondary School{END FIELD}
Wendover Way{END FIELD}
Littlewood{END FIELD}
Surrey{END FIELD}
SE4 4MR{END FIELD}
Secondary School{END FIELD}
{END RECORD}
====================================
```

**Figure KS.9**   A single record in a secondary file

```
{FIELD}1~ {FIELD}2~ {FIELD}3~
{FIELD}4~
{FIELD}5~
{FIELD}6~
{FIELD}7~ {FIELD}8~
```

**Figure KS.10**   Primary file for printing address labels

4   Choose a label form, as follows:

   a   Move the cursor to the top of the merged document.
   b   Press Shift-F8 (Format).
   c   Press 7 (Paper Size/Type). The Paper Size/Type list appears.
   d   Move the cursor to the labels definition in the list.
   e   Press 1 (Select).
   f   Press F7 to exit.
   g   View the document to see the addresses repeating down the page.
   h   Save the file and exit.

   This inserts a [Paper Sz/Type] code in the document.

5   You can now send the merge to the printer. If you merge *direct* to the printer, you first have to insert the Labels Form code in the Initial Codes for the primary file. Retrieve the primary file, and proceed as follows:

   a   Press Shift-F8 (Format).
   b   Press 3 (Document).

c   Press 2 (Initial Codes). The current initial codes will display as follows:

[Lang:UK][Paper Sz/Type:8.27″ × 11.69″,Standard]

Repeat steps a to f above for inserting a [Paper Sz/Type] code at this screen.

d   Press F7 — Exit.

e   Save the file and exit.

Now complete the merge with the Ctrl-F9 Merge/Sort key.

To create a labels form, see Section 42.

### Keyboard merge

To enter variable data from the keyboard into a merge document, create a primary file by typing in the standard text. Where you want variables to be inserted, proceed as follows:

1   Press Shift-F9 (Merge Codes).

2   Press 3 (Input). The prompt 'Enter message:' appears.

3   Type the message you want to be prompted with at merge time.

4   Press Enter. This inserts an {INPUT} command in the document, followed by the message and a tilde. A [Mrg:INPUT] code is also inserted in the document.

5   Save the file and exit.

Figure 7.9 shows an example of a keyboard merge primary file. To complete the merge, proceed as follows:

1   Press Ctrl-F9 (Merge/Sort).

2   Press 1 (Merge). The prompt 'Primary file:' appears.

3   Type the primary filename.

4   Press Enter. The prompt 'Secondary file:' appears.

5   There is no secondary file, so press Enter. The screen displays the primary file text as far as the first {INPUT} command and displays the prompt message in the status line.

6   Type the variable data.

7   Press F9 to move forward to the next {INPUT} command.

Repeat steps 6 and 7 until all the variables have been entered.

You should press the Enter key where more than one line is required in a variable.

## Insert an audible prompt

If you wish to be prompted audibly by a beep to enter variables, add a further merge command in the primary file wherever an {INPUT} command occurs. Retrieve the keyboard merge primary file, and proceed as follows:

1  Move the cursor after the first {INPUT} command.
2  Press Shift-F9 (Merge Codes).
3  Press 6 (More). The merge commands box appears.
4  Choose {BELL}. A {BELL} command is inserted in the document, and a [Mrg:BELL] code is inserted in the Codes screen.

Repeat these steps for all the {INPUT} commands.

## 33   Mouse

The mouse provides a quick and easy way to move around your document, block text, and access WordPerfect's menus. The mouse pointer is displayed as a reverse-video box. Terms used to describe mouse operations are:

- 'point' − move the pointer to the required location.
- 'click' − click the left mouse button once.
- 'double-click' − click the button twice in quick succession.
- 'drag' − hold down the button while moving the mouse.

   To move the cursor: Point to the required location and click the left button.
   To scroll the screen up or down, press the right button and drag up or down.

## To select features and options

Click the right button to display the menu bar (see Figure 1.2); click the right button again to remove the bar. To select an option, point to it and click left. Double-clicking the left button has the same effect as pressing the left button and then Enter. To exit a menu and return to the editing screen, click the right button.

*To block text*
Drag over the text.

*To change mouse defaults*
See Setup, Section 53.

## 34  Move, copy, delete, append

To move, copy, delete, or append a sentence, paragraph or page, place the cursor anywhere within the required block and then:

1   Press Ctrl-F4 (Move).
2   Press 1 (Sentence), 2 (Paragraph), or 3 (Page).
3   Press 1 (Move), 2 (Copy), 3 (Delete), or 4 (Append). If you select 1 or 2, you then have to respond to the prompt by moving the cursor to a new position and pressing Enter to retrieve the block. If you select 3, the text is deleted. If you select 4, WordPerfect asks you to enter the name of the file to which the text is to be appended.

## 35  Move around a document

You will find that you cannot move the cursor unless there is text and/or codes on the screen. This explains the sideways movement of the cursor when you move up or down a document: left to the left margin at a blank line, right to your previous horizontal position otherwise.

The various cursor movements keys are:

One word left — Ctrl-left arrow
One word right — Ctrl-right arrow
Beginning of line — Home, left arrow
End of line — Home, right arrow or End
Beginning of next paragraph — Ctrl-up arrow

Beginning of previous paragraph — Ctrl-down arrow
Top of screen — Home, up arrow
Bottom of screen — Home, down arrow
Top of document — Home, Home, up arrow
Bottom of document — Home, Home, down arrow
Top of document in front of codes — Home, Home, Home, up arrow
Beginning of line in front of codes — Home, Home, Home, left arrow
Top of previous page — Page Up
Top of next page — Page Down
Goto — Ctrl-Home

## 36  Newspaper columns

To start newspaper column format, position your cursor where the columns should begin, and define the columns as follows:

1 Press Alt-F7 (Columns/Table).
2 Choose 1 (Columns). The Column Definition menu appears, containing the following options:

   1 *Type.* The choices are Newspaper, Parallel, and Parallel with Block Protect, with the Newspaper type already entered as the default. For information on parallel columns, see Section 43.
   2 *Number of Columns.* Enter the number of columns required here; the default is 2.
   3 *Distance between Columns.* Enter the required space between columns; the default is 0.5″.
   4 *Margins.* WordPerfect has entered defaults for the left and right margins of each column. You can change these if you wish, pressing Enter after each one.

3 Press F7 (Exit) to accept the default choices offered on this menu, otherwise press the number of the menu option you want to change, type your own choices and press Enter.
4 Choose 1 to turn columns on.

If you are applying column format to existing text, press Ctrl-F3 and select Rewrite to rearrange the text. After step 3, Word-Perfect inserts in your document a [Col Def] code which also contains the margins of the columns in your document. After step 4, a [Col On] code is inserted.

## Change the margins of columns

Because the [Col Def] code contains the current column margins, you would have to redefine the columns if you subsequently change document orientation or margins. To do this, position the cursor on the existing [Col Def] code, and repeat steps 1 to 3 for defining columns. If the columns effect is already turned on, miss out step 4. A new [Col Def] code containing the new margins is inserted in the document, and you can now use the Delete key to remove the old code.

   If you wish to turn columns off at a later point in your document:

1   Move the cursor to that point.
2   Press Alt-F7 (Columns/Table).
3   Choose 1 (Columns).
4   Choose 2 (Off).

A [Col Off] code is inserted at this point in your document.
   Note the following:

- In column mode, 'Col 1' is inserted in the status line.
- When you reach the end of the page, the cursor moves automatically to the next column; 'Col 2' appears in the status line.
- To move the cursor from column to column, press Ctrl-Home (Goto) followed by the left or right arrow key.
- To force text from one column to the next, press Ctrl-Enter.

## 37   Outline

This feature automatically numbers paragraphs and sub-paragraphs down to eight levels. To turn on and use outlining, proceed as follows:

1   Press Shift-F5 (Date/Outline).
2   Press 4 (Outline).
3   Press 1 (On). The word 'Outline' appears at the left of the

status line, and an [Outline On] code is inserted in the document.

4   Press Enter. WordPerfect inserts the first level of number – 'I.' – at the left margin, and a [Par Num:Auto] code in the document.

5   Press F4 (Indent) to indent the left margin of your paragraph, and type your paragraph.

6   Press Enter to start a new paragraph. WordPerfect treats this as a first level paragraph, numbering it 'II.'.

7   Press Tab if you want to change it to a lower-level sub-paragraph. Further Tab presses reduce the level. Shift-Tab reverses this, so increasing the level.

8   Repeat steps 4 to 7 for each paragraph that you wish to type.

When you have finished, press Shift-F5, 4, 2 (Off) to turn off outlining. This inserts an [Outline Off] code in the document.

To enter an unnumbered paragraph, reveal the codes and delete the [Par Num:Auto] code. If you delete one of these codes in error, you can reinsert it as follows:

1   Press Shift-F5 (Date/Outline).

2   Press 5 (Paragraph Numbering). You will be prompted 'Para-graph Level (Press Enter for Automatic):'.

3   Press Enter.

Alternatively, you can try to undelete the code with the Cancel key.

To insert an extra outline paragraph within existing outline paragraphs, place the cursor at the end of the previous paragraph, and press Enter. A new number is inserted, and subsequent numbers are updated.

To move an existing outline paragraph to a different level, place the cursor after the [Par Num:Auto] code and press Tab to move to a lower level, or Shift-Tab to move to a higher level.

## Move, copy and delete outline families

An outline 'family' is the numbered paragraph on the line where the cursor is currently placed, plus any numbered paragraphs of subordinate levels below it. To move, copy, or delete a family, place the cursor on the first line of the family and proceed as follows:

1  Press Shift-F5 (Date Outline).
2  Press 3 (Move Family), 4 (Copy Family), or 5 (Delete Family).

- If you select Move, the family is highlighted and you are prompted to use the arrow keys to relocate the family. Press Enter when the family is in the right place.
- If you select Copy, a copy of the family is highlighted, and you can again use the arrow keys to position the new copy and then press Enter.
- If you select Delete, you have to confirm the deletion by pressing Y for Yes. The deleted family is stored in a temporary file which can be retrieved with the Cancel key.

Note that a family must end with two hard returns for a successful move or copy to a different location.

*Change the paragraph numbering style*
There are four pre-defined numbering styles available. (You can also define your own style, as explained later in this section.) To use an already defined numbering style in the current document, proceed as follows:

1  Press Shift-F5 (Date/Outline).
2  Press 6 (Define). The current paragraph definition displays on the Paragraph Number Definition menu.
3  Select 2, 3, 4, or 5. Your choice displays alongside the heading 'Current Definition' on the menu.
4  Press Exit.
5  Press 1 (On).

WordPerfect inserts a [Par Num Def:] code in the document.

To change the default outline numbering style for all documents, you can insert a paragraph number definition code in Initial Codes, as explained in Section 25.

If the outline text already exists, you can change the numbering style by placing the cursor on the [Outline On] code and repeating steps 1 to 3 above for changing paragraph numbering style.

The other options in the Paragraph Number Definition menu are as follows:

1  *Starting Paragraph Number.* This defaults to 1, but it allows you to advance the starting number to any number you want.

Enter the number as an Arabic numeral regardless of the style
you are using.

 This possibly is useful if you turn Outline off and on in a
document. In this situation, WordPerfect starts numbering
from 1 again. To resume the numbering sequence, place the
cursor on the second [Outline On] code, repeat steps 1 and 2
above, and then:

3  Press 1 (Starting Paragraph Number).
4  Type in the starting number and press Enter.
5  Exit back to the document.

2  *Attach Previous Level.* This indicates whether WordPerfect
will incorporate the numbers of higher-level paragraphs in the
labels it gives lower levels. For example, the legal numbering
style is set to attach the previous level of numbering, giving a
number at level 3 of, e.g. 1.1.1.; the other three styles do not
attach the previous level of numbering. The settings for these
four pre-defined styles cannot be changed. The only way for
you to change the attach setting is to create a user-defined
numbering format, described below.
3  *User-Defined.* This allows you to define your own numbering
style. When you select this option, the User-Defined menu
displays at the bottom of the screen, as shown in Figure 9.11,
allowing you to insert the required letters and numbers. If you do
not want any number or letter at a level, delete the displayed
number from this menu and leave it blank. Use the Tab or Enter
key to move from level to level.

 After entering the numbers or letters, you must type 'Y' for Yes
or 'N' for No in the Attach Previous Level heading.

 Finally, proceed with steps 4 and 5 for changing paragraph
number style.
4  *Enter Inserts Paragraph Number.* This defines the way the
Enter key functions when Outline is on. 'Yes' means that
Enter will insert a paragraph number. 'No' means that it will
insert a hard return and nothing else. If you set this option to
'No', you must manually insert a paragraph number as follows:

1  Press Shift-F5 (Date/Outline).
2  Press 5 (Para Num).
3  Press Enter.

5  *Automatically Adjust to Current Level.* This tells WordPerfect the level an automatic paragraph number should have when it is inserted. If it is set to 'Yes', WordPerfect inserts the next number of the current level. For example, if your last number was '1.1.1.', pressing Enter will insert '1.1.2.'.

   If you change the setting to 'No', then pressing Enter will always insert the next level 1 number at the left margin.

6  *Outline Style Name.* This option takes you into the Outline Styles menu to create or select an outline style, as explained in Section 38.

## 38  Outline style

The standard outline format is restricted to numbers, letters, and punctuation. An outline style can include codes to add enhancements and alignment. It can also allow you to save a user-defined style to use in other documents.

### Create an outline style

1  Press Shift-F5 (Date/Outline).
2  Choose 6 (Define).
3  Choose 9 (Outline Style Name). The Outline Styles menu will display.
4  Choose 2 (Create). The Outline Styles Edit menu is displayed, as shown in Figure 9.14.
5  Choose 1 (Name), and type a name for the outline style (up to 12 characters including spaces).
6  Choose 2 (Description) and type a description for the outline style (up to 54 characters).
7  Choose the other options – Type, Enter and Codes – as required. They are similar to those for creating a style in the Styles menu (see Section 59 on Styles):

   • *Type* tells WordPerfect whether the style is paired or open.
   • *Enter* defines the operation of the Enter key for a particular style. It is only relevant for paired styles.
   • *Codes* enables you to enter the codes for a style.

8  Press F7 (Exit) after entering the necessary information until

you return to the Outline Styles menu, where your outline
style should be listed.

An outline style created in this way is saved with the document.
It is also added to your Styles menu list for that document. You
can edit an outline style from the Styles menu, but you cannot
turn on an outline style from this menu.

### Save outline styles
At the Outline Styles menu you can save an outline style to a
separate file for use in other documents. Follow steps 1 to 3
above for creating an outline style, and then proceed as follows:

4   Press 5 (Save).
5   Enter a name for the style file. It will be saved to the style
    directory. If no directory exists, it will be saved to the default
    directory.

### Select an outline style
Follow steps 1 to 3 for creating an outline style, and then proceed
as follows:

4   Move the cursor to the style you wish to select, and press 1
    (Select). The Paragraph Number Definition menu displays,
    with your selected outline style name entered.
5   Press F7 (Exit) to exit to the Date/Outline menu.
6   Press F7 (Exit) if you wish to exit to the document without
    turning Outline on. Otherwise, to exit with Outline turned on,
    press 4 (Outline), then 1 (On).

### Edit an outline style
Follow steps 1−3 for creating an outline style, then proceed as
follows:

4   Press 3 (Edit).
5   Make the necessary changes to the style, and press F7 (Exit).
    If the outline style is saved to a file, save these changes with
    the Save option.

You can also edit an outline style from the Styles menu.

## Retrieve outline styles

To retrieve a previously saved list of outline styles, follow steps
1–3 for creating an outline style, then proceed as follows:

4   Press 6 (Retrieve).
5   Enter the name of the style file. If any names in the current
list match those in the incoming styles, WordPerfect will prompt
'Style(s) Already Exist, Replace?'. If you type 'N' for No,
WordPerfect only retrieves the styles whose names do not
match current style names. If you type 'Y' for Yes, WordPerfect
retrieves all of the styles, replacing current styles with the new
files of the same name.

You can also retrieve an outline style file at the Styles menu.

## Delete outline styles

Follow steps 1–3 for creating an outline style, and then proceed
as follows:

4   Press 4 (Delete). You are prompted by the following menu:

   Delete Styles: 1 Leaving codes; 2 Including codes;
   3 Definition only: 0

- Choosing 1 will remove the outline style name from the
  list, and all style codes of that name in the document;
  however, the codes contained in the outline style are
  retained.
- Choosing 2 will delete the outline style name from the list,
  the outline style codes in the document, and the codes
  within the style.
- Choosing 3 will delete the outline style name from the list.
  Any outline styles of the same name in the document will
  remain intact. This is useful when you have a long list of
  style names and wish to find out which ones you are
  actually using in a document. After deleting the names
  from the list, return to the document and press Home,
  Home, ↓. Return to the outline styles list, and Word-
  Perfect will have reinserted those styles being used in the
  current document.

You can also delete outline styles from the Styles menu.

## 39 Page breaks

Place the cursor where the new page should start, and press Ctrl-Enter. A [HPg] code is inserted.

## 40 Page margins

Set the left and right margins at the Line Format screen. To do this, place the cursor at the beginning of the document, then:

1 Press Shift-F8 (Format).
2 Choose 1 to select Line Format.
3 Choose 7 to select Margins.
4 Type the measurements you require for the left and right margins.
5 Press F7 (Exit) to return to the editing screen.

The code inserted in your document for left and right margins of 2″ is [L/R Mar:2″,2″].

   Set the top and bottom margins at the Page Format screen. To do this, place the cursor at the beginning of the document, then:

1 Press Shift-F8 (Format).
2 Choose 2 to select Page Format.
3 Choose 5 to select Margins.
4 Type the measurements you require for the top and bottom margins.
5 Press F7 (Exit) to return to the editing screen.

The code inserted in your document for top and bottom margins of 2″ is [T/B Mar:2″,2″].

   To change default margins, see Setup (Section 53).

## 41 Page numbering

With the cursor at the top of your document, proceed as follows:

1 Press Shift-F (Format).
2 Press 2 (Page).

3 Press 6 (Page Numbering). The Format Page Numbering menu displays, with some defaults already in place. The various options contained in the menu are as follows:

1 *New Page Number.* Choose this to start numbering at something other than 1, or to change from Arabic to Roman numerals. Place the cursor at the top of a page within a document to change the numbering from that point onwards.
2 *Page Number Style.* The default page numbering style is the page number. To change the style, e.g. to include some text, type in the new style, typing Ctrl-B where the page number should occur; this appears as '^B'.
3 *Insert Page Number.* This choice allows you to insert the current page number within body text. To use this option, place the cursor in the document wherever you want to refer to the current page number, and then follow steps 1−4 for page numbering.
4 *Page Number Position.* Choosing this option displays the Page Numbering Position menu, see Figure 4.6, with numbers identifying the different positions available for displaying page numbering. After making your choice from this menu, press F7 to exit back to the Format Page Numbering menu.

4 Make your selection from the menus as desired, and press F7 to exit.

WordPerfect inserts in the document a [Pg Numbering] code showing where on the page you have positioned the page number. If you change the style, a [Pg Num Style] code is also inserted, indicating the style.

## 42 Page size and orientation

The default page size and orientation is standard A4 portrait (8.27″ wide × 11.69″ deep). To change this for the current document, position the cursor at the beginning of the document and then:

1 Press Shift-F8 (Format).
2 Choose 2 to select Page Format. The current paper size and type will be shown at option 7.

3 Choose 7 to display a list of alternatives from which you may select the one you want.
4 Press F7 to exit back to the editing screen.

A [Paper Sz/Typ] code will be inserted in your document, and if you view the document you will see the change of size or orientation. This code has a forwards effect. This means that if there are further pages in the document, each one will be the paper definition selected. If this is not what you want, you have to insert a different paper definition code at the top of the next page to print it in normal size or orientation.

## Orientation
You can select landscape orientation by following steps 1–4 above. If, at step 3, landscape orientation is not listed, proceed to the next section 'Add a new paper definition'.

## Add a new paper definition
Repeat steps 1–3 above, and then proceed as follows:

4 With the cursor on the standard type − 8.27″ × 11.69″ portrait − press 3 (Copy). (You could select 2 (Add), but if you are adding landscape orientation, there are only two items to be changed so it is probably quicker to copy.) You will see a copy of the standard type added into the list.
5 With the cursor on one of the standard paper definitions, press 5 (Edit). You will then see the menu displayed in Figure KS.11.
6 Change items 1 and 3 to the appropriate size and font type and exit. Back at the list of paper sizes, you will see your new paper definition.
7 Place the cursor on the required definition and choose Select.
8 Press F7 (Exit).

## Add a label definition
To add a label form to your list of paper definitions, follow steps 1–3 for changing page size and orientation. The Format Paper Size/Type menu displays. From this menu, proceed as follows:

```
Format: Edit Paper Definition

        Filename                 APLASPLU.PRS

   1 - Paper Size                8.27" x 11.69"

   2 - Paper Type                Standard

   3 - Font Type                 Portrait

   4 - Prompt to Load            No

   5 - Location                  Continuous

   6 - Double Sided Printing     No

   7 - Binding Edge              Left

   8 - Labels                    No

   9 - Text Adjustment - Top     0"
                         Side    0"

Selection: 0
```

**Figure KS.11**  Edit menu for Paper Definition

4  Press 2 (Add). The Paper Type menu displays.
5  Choose 4 (Labels). The Format Edit Paper Definition menu displays (see Figure KS.11).
6  Choose 1 (Paper Size) to change the page size if necessary.
7  Choose 3 (Font Type) to change the orientation if necessary.
8  Choose 8 (Labels) and type 'Y' for Yes. The Format Labels menu displays (see Figure KS.12).

Some brief details on the options contained in this menu are given below. Any measurements can be entered as fractions if you prefer − WordPerfect will convert them to decimals.

1  *Label Size.* Enter the width and height of an individual label.
2  *Number of Labels.* Enter the number of columns and rows per page.
3  *Top Left Corner.* Enter the distances between the label and the top of the page and the left of the page.
4  *Distance between Labels.* Enter the distance between labels horizontally (Column) and vertically (Row).

```
Format: Labels

    1 - Label Size
                    Width           2.56"
                    Height          0.984"

    2 - Number of Labels
                    Columns         3
                    Rows            10

    3 - Top Left Corner
                    Top             0.393"
                    Left            0.197"

    4 - Distance Between Labels
                    Column          0.098"
                    Row             0"

    5 - Label Margins
                    Left            0.103"
                    Right           0.103"
                    Top             0"
                    Bottom          0"

Selection: 0
```

**Figure KS.12**   Format Labels menu

> 5   *Label Margins.* Enter the margins you want on an individual label − Left, Right, Top, Bottom.

9   Make changes as necessary to this menu, based on your label dimensions.

10   Press F7 (Exit). You are taken to the Paper Size/Type menu, which will show the labels form added to the list of paper definitions.

## 43   Parallel columns

The procedure for applying either kind of parallel column (ordinary parallel and parallel with block protect) is to follow steps 1 and 2 for defining newspaper columns (Section 36) and then:

3   Choose 1 − Type.
4   Choose from the menu that appears the column type you want.

Continue with steps 3 and 4 in Section 36 (Newspaper Columns). You now have codes similar to those for newspaper columns in your document, plus a [Block Pro On] code if you selected the parallel with block protect type of column.

If you are using the parallel column without block protect, each horizontal block of text begins with a [Col On] code and ends with a [Col Off] code. If you are using parallel column with block protect, each horizontal block of text begins with a [Block Pro:On][Col On] code and ends with a [Block Pro:Off][Col Off] code.

The following notes apply to both types of parallel column:

● When you begin typing in column mode, 'Col 1' is inserted in the status line.
● When you end each item, press Ctrl-Enter to move to the next column and start the next item. The relevant column number is displayed in the status line.
● Press the Ctrl-Home Goto key followed by the left or right arrow key to move from column to column.
● When deleting a horizontal block of text, make sure you also delete the [Col] codes (and the [Block Pro] codes if applicable) at the beginning and end.

If you wish to apply parallel columns to existing text, after defining the columns and switching them on, you will have to replace [HRt] codes at the end of each paragraph with Ctrl-Enter whenever you want to start a new column.

## Change margins of columns

If the document margins or orientation are changed after defining the columns, follow the steps for changing margins of newspaper columns.

## 44 Paragraph numbering

This can be used instead of Outline if you wish to mix numbered and unnumbered paragraphs. The Enter and Tab keys function as normal, and to insert paragraph numbers, proceed as follows:

1 Move the cursor to the position at which the paragraph number is to appear.
2 Press Shift-F5 (Date/Outline).

3   Press 5 (Para Num). The following will appear onscreen:

   Paragraph Level (Press Enter for Automatic):

4   Do one of the following:

   ●   Press Enter to insert the appropriate number for the current
       cursor position. This inserts a [Par Num:Auto] code in the
       document, and the numbering level can be subsequently
       changed. Or
   ●   Type in a number (1 to 8) to insert a number at that level.
       This inserts a [Par Num:n] code with the appropriate level
       number, and becomes a fixed number.

To use a style other than the default numbering style, follow the
steps for 'Change paragraph numbering style' indicated above
under Outline.

### Change levels

You can change the level of an automatic paragraph number by
placing the cursor on the number and pressing Tab or Shift-Tab.
A fixed number cannot be changed.

## 45   Print

To print the file you are currently working on:

1   Press Shift-F7.
2   Select 1 for Full Text, or 2 for current Page, or 5 to print
    Multiple Pages.

To print a file that is stored on disk, you have two choices:

1   a   Press Shift-F7 (Print).
    b   Select 3 (Document on disk).
    c   Type the document's name.
    d   Indicate which pages are to be printed or press Enter for
        all.
2   a   Press F5 (List).
    b   Press Enter.

c   Move the highlight bar to the file you wish to print.
d   Press 4 (Print).
e   Press Enter to print all pages, or type in the required range of selected pages.

If you wish to see how the document will look prior to printing, press Shift-F7,6. Use the PgUp and PgDn keys to move forwards and backwards through the document. Press F1 to return to the print menu, F7 to return to the editing screen.

## 46   Repeat key

Esc is used by WordPerfect to repeat an action a number of times; press F3, Esc to see the full list of uses. The default repeat number is 8; change this by pressing Esc, typing the new number, and pressing Enter. To change the number for the current working session only, press Esc, then the new number and then the key to be repeated.

## 47   Replace

This feature can be used to search for text and/or codes and either delete them or replace them with other text and/or codes.
   To replace one string by another, proceed as follows:

1   Press Alt-F2 (Replace).
2   At the 'w/Confirm? No (Yes)' message that appears on the status line, type 'Y' if you want the opportunity to confirm or reject each individual replacement; or press 'N' (or any other key) if you want to accept the default of no confirmation (i.e. automatic replacement throughout the document).
3   Press the up arrow key if you want to search backward from the current cursor position (otherwise WordPerfect will search forward).
4   Type the search string. If you wish to search for a code, press the appropriate function key.
5   Press F2.
6   Type the replacement string. (Or press the appropriate function key for a code.)
7   Press F2.

To extend the replacement to include headers, footers, footnotes, endnotes, graphics box captions, and text boxes, press Home, Alt-F2.

To search for text and/or codes and delete them, follow the instructions 1−7 above, but type nothing at all at step 6.

## 48 Retrieve a document

Use the Retrieve command if you know the filename:

1 Press Shift-F10.
2 Type the filename.
3 Press Enter. The document appears on the editing screen, and the filename appears in the status line.

If you don't know the filename, use List Files (Section 29).

## 49 Reveal codes

Press Alt-F3 or F11 to split the screen in two and display, in the lower half, your document's text *and* codes. Codes are emboldened and enclosed in square brackets to distinguish them from text. To close the Reveal Codes screen, press Alt-F3 or F11 a second time.

## 50 Size and appearance

These are both available on the Ctrl-F8 Font key. This gives you the choice of a Size menu or an Appearance menu. To change the size of text as it is entered:

1 Press Ctrl-F8 (Font).
2 Press 1 (Size).
3 Select the size from the menu.
4 Type in the text.
5 Press the right arrow key to return to ordinary text.

The paired codes inserted in your document will depend on the size selected.

To change the appearance, proceed as for size, but select the Appearance menu instead of the Size menu.

To change the size or appearance of existing text, use the Block key (Alt-F3) to highlight the text and then proceed as above.

## 51 Save

F10 allows you to save and continue working on your document. The first time you use this on an unnamed document, proceed as follows:

1  Press F10.
2  Type in the name.
3  Press Enter.

To save a named file, proceed as follows:

1  Press F10. The current filename appears.
2  Press Enter. The 'Replace' prompt appears.
3  Type 'Y' to replace the previous version of the file.

## 52 Search

To search *forward* through your document from the cursor position, you:

1  Press F2 (→Search).
2  Enter the search string (i.e. the word/s and/or code/s).
3  Press F2 again to carry out the search.

WordPerfect finds the first occurrence of the string and positions the cursor on it. To find the next occurrence, you:

4  Press F2,F2 again.

To search *backward* through the document from the cursor position, you press Shift-F2 (←Search) at step 1.

Alternatively, if you've already started a forward search with F2, you can switch to a backward search by pressing the up arrow key.

To extend the search to include headers, footers, footnotes, endnotes, graphics box captions, and text boxes, press Home, F2 or Shift-F2.

## 53   Setup

To change any WordPerfect defaults press Shift-F1 (Setup). The menu in Figure KS.13 is displayed.

The choices it provides are:

*1   Mouse.* Choose this to change mouse responsiveness and other mouse functions. The Setup Mouse menu displays. From this menu, proceed as follows to change a right-handed mouse to a left-handed mouse:

1   Press 6 (Left-Handed Mouse).
2   Type 'Y' for Yes.

*2   Display.* Choose this to control the way information displays on the screen.

```
Setup

     1 - Mouse

     2 - Display

     3 - Environment

     4 - Initial Settings

     5 - Keyboard Layout

     6 - Location of Files




Selection: 0
```

**Figure KS.13**   Setup menu

The Setup Display menu is then displayed, see Figure KS.14.
From this menu you can select the following:
*Comments box display.* Proceed as follows:

1  Press 6 (Edit-Screen Options), see Figure KS.15.
2  Press 2 (Comments Display). Type 'N' to have the comments
   display suppressed.

*Screen Display.* To change your screen display, proceed as follows:

1  Press 1 (Colours/Fonts/Attributes). WordPerfect then displays
   the options available for your monitor. If you have a colour
   system, option 1 (Screen Colours) displays a menu for choosing
   the screen colours of the various attributes.
2  Press Shift-F3 (Switch) to change display of Doc 2 screen.

   To display the menu bar as a default, proceed as follows:

1  Press 4 (Menu Options).
2  Press 7 (Menu Bar Separator Line), and type 'Y' for Yes. This
   inserts a line separating the menu bar from the document
   text.
3  Press 8 (Menu Bar Remains Visible), and type 'Y' for Yes.

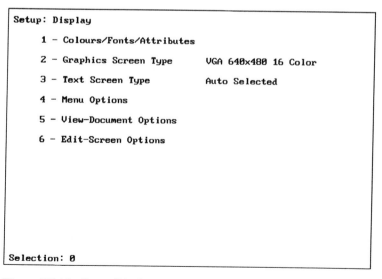

```
Setup: Display

       1 - Colours/Fonts/Attributes

       2 - Graphics Screen Type      VGA 640x480 16 Color

       3 - Text Screen Type          Auto Selected

       4 - Menu Options

       5 - View-Document Options

       6 - Edit-Screen Options




Selection: 0
```

**Figure KS.14**  Setup Display menu

```
Setup: Edit-Screen Options

    1 - Automatically Format and Rewrite    Yes

    2 - Comments Display                     Yes

    3 - Filename on the Status Line          Yes

    4 - Hard Return Display Character

    5 - Merge Codes Display                  Yes

    6 - Reveal Codes Window Size             10

    7 - Side-by-side Columns Display         Yes




Selection: 0
```

**Figure KS.15**   Setup Edit-Screen Options menu

*Merge commands display.* To turn off (or on) the display of these commands in primary and secondary files, proceed as follows:

1   Press 6 (Edit Screen options).
2   Press 5 (Merge Codes display).
3   Type 'N' to turn off the display of merge commands in all merge documents. Or, if they are already turned off, type 'Y' to turn on the display.

*3   Environment.* The settings contained in this menu affect your working environment in WordPerfect. To use this menu press 3 (Environment). The Environment menu (see Figure KS.16) appears, from which you can select the options shown below.
*Document summary.* To have WordPerfect prompt you automatically to create a document summary when you save a file for the first time, proceed as follows:

1   Press 4 (Document Management/Summary).
2   Press 1 (Create Summary on Save/Exit?) Type 'Y' to be

```
Setup: Environment

    1 - Backup Options

    2 - Beep Options

    3 - Cursor Speed                      50 cps

    4 - Document Management/Summary

    5 - Fast Save (unformatted)           Yes

    6 - Hyphenation                       External Dictionary/Rules

    7 - Prompt for Hyphenation            When Required

    8 - Units of Measure

    9 - Alternate Keyboard                No
        (F1 - Help, Esc - Cancel, F3 - Repeat)




Selection: 0
```

**Figure KS.16**   Environment menu

prompted automatically for a document summary. Use the F3 Help key for information on the other menu choices.

*Backup options.* To change the timed backup and document backup options:

1   Press 1 (Timed Document Backup), or press 2 (Original Document Backup).

*4 Initial Settings.* To change the default settings for all future documents, press 4 (Initial Settings). You can then choose from the following:
*Initial codes.* To change the initial codes present for each document:

1   Press 5 (Initial Codes). The default initial codes present are:

[Lang:UK][Paper Sz/Typ:8.27″ × 11.69″, Standard]

2   Use the appropriate function keys to enter additional codes.

These settings are stored in the WP{WP}.SET file and will be used for all future documents. Any formatting codes placed in an individual document will override the initial settings.

*Decimal Align Character.* To change the decimal align character:

1  Press 5 (Initial Codes).
2  Use the Other Format menu (Shift-F8) to change the decimal align character from full stop to another keyboard character.

5  *Keyboard Layout.* This allows you to select a different keyboard layout. Press 5 (Keyboard Layout) to display a list of keyboard layouts. For more information, see Section 27.
6  *Location of Files.* This indicates the directory where Word-Perfect should search for certain files. To enter any settings here, press 6 (Location of Files).

## 54  Sort

You can have WordPerfect sort lines, paragraphs, secondary merge files, or rows in a table. You can sort the entire document, or use the Block key to select sections of a document for sorting. The original unsorted document is called the *input* file, and the resulting sorted document is called the *output* file.

### Line sort
The input file can consist of a single column or many columns. There must be a single [Tab] code between each column. The sort procedure is as follows:

1  Press Ctrl-F9 (Merge/Sort).
2  Press 2 (Sort). WordPerfect then asks 'Input file to sort: (Screen)' – in other words, which file do you want to sort?
3  Press Enter, indicating that the file is already onscreen. (If it wasn't onscreen, you would have to enter its filename at this point.) WordPerfect then asks 'Output file for sort: (Screen)'.
4  Press Enter to have the sorted list shown onscreen. (If you wanted it saved to disk, you would have to enter a filename at this point.) The Sort menu in Figure 7.11 will now display.
5  Enter the keys and other criteria you wish to use for sorting. These are explained below.
6  Press 1 (Perform Action) to begin sorting.

The Sort menu contains the following options:

1   *Perform Action.* This begins the sorting operation.
2   *View.* This allows you to scroll through the input file.
3   *Keys.* This allows you to change your type of sort from alphanumeric (text or a mixture of text and numbers) to numeric (numbers only). It also allows you to set your sort priorities. You can set up to nine priorities, i.e. nine keys. To insert a key definition, enter your sorting requirements under the following headings:

*Type* − 'a' for alphanumeric (text or a mixture of numbers and text); 'n' for numbers only.
*Field* − the number of the field to be sorted.
*Word* − the word number in the field. For example, '1' for the first word in the field, and '-1' for the last word in the field.

The values for key1 are initially set at 'a 1 1' indicating the following:

- your *sort* type is alphanumeric,
- the *field* to be sorted is the first field (i.e. column),
- the first *word* in the field is to be used as a basis for sorting.

You can sort your records by using up to nine keys (i.e. you can have up to nine priorities of sort). If, for example, you are sorting surnames alphabetically, and you find that you have several people called Jones, you might also wish to have forenames sorted. You would use key1 for the main sort on surname, and key2 for the subsidiary sort on forename. To insert further key values, press the right arrow to move the cursor to that key. WordPerfect inserts automatically the 'a 1 1' default; however, you can overtype this with your own choice.

To delete a key definition, move the cursor to the appropriate key number, press the Delete key, and then the left arrow key.
4   *Select.* As well as sorting lists, you can select specific records for sorting, using the menu of symbols which appears when you choose Select. For further information see 'Select and Sort' below.
5   *Action.* If you have entered a Select statement, you can choose whether to select and sort those records, or to select without sorting.
6   *Order.* This changes the default sort order from ascending to descending.
7   *Type.* You can choose from line, paragraph, or secondary

merge document. If you are sorting a table, WordPerfect selects automatically the table sort.

## Paragraph sort

Paragraphs of any length can be sorted as long as they end with two or more hard returns. To execute a paragraph sort, follow steps 1 to 4 for line sorting, and then:

5 Choose 7 (Type). The Type menu will appear.
6 Choose 3 (Paragraph). The Sort menu display will now appear as in Figure 7.14, with an extra subheading – 'Line' – in the key display.
7 Enter the keys and other sorting criteria.
8 Press 1 (Perform Action).

## Merge data sort

To sort your data records (held in a secondary file), proceed with steps 1–4 for line sorting, and then:

5 Choose 7 (Type).
6 Choose 1 (Merge). The Sort menu display will now appear as in Figure 7.16, with a key display similar to that for paragraph sorting.

Repeat steps 7 and 8 above for paragraph sorting.

## Table column sort

Move the cursor to a table cell, then press the Merge/Sort key. You are taken directly to the Sort menu with the table type already selected (see Figure 7.15). Proceed as follows:

1 Press Ctrl-F9 (Merge/Sort).
2 Enter the keys and any other sorting criteria.
3 Press 1 (Perform Action).

## Block sort

To restrict the sort to a section of a document:

1  With the cursor at the beginning of the section to sort, press Alt-F4/F12 (Block).
2  Use the arrow keys to highlight the section.
3  Press Ctrl-F9 (Merge/Sort). You are taken directly to the Sort menu.
4  Enter the keys and any other sorting criteria.
5  Press 1 (Perform Action).

### Date sort

The day, month, and year can be treated as separate words for sorting purposes if you separate them with forward slashes or hard hyphens, e.g. 27/06/94 or 27-06-94. They could then be entered as different words under different key numbers. You can insert a hard hyphen by pressing the Home key, and then typing the hyphen character.

### Select and sort

To select records which meet certain criteria, you enter these criteria in the Sort menu. Follow the steps for displaying the Sort menu and defining the keys you wish to use when you sort and select text. Make sure that you have defined a key for the field from which you wish to select data. Then proceed as follows:

1  Press 4 (Select). The Select menu will appear, and will look something like Figure 7.18, with a list of select symbols.
2  Type the key number you have defined for the selected data. Then use the appropriate symbol and the data you are selecting; you can use only one word here.
3  Press F7 (Exit).
4  Press 1 (Perform Action).

You can also do a *global* select to extract all records containing a key word. Type 'keyg=', followed by the word. This will then select all records containing the word in any field.

## 55   Special characters

The Compose key allows you to include in your documents characters which are not found on your keyboard. A list of all these characters is in the WordPerfect manual appendix, Word-Perfect Characters.

Not all the characters can be displayed on the normal editing screen; they are sometimes represented as a box. To see the characters as they will print, look at the View Document screen.

### Insert a special character

To insert a special character, proceed as follows:

1   Press Ctrl-V or Ctrl-2 (Compose). Pressing Ctrl-V displays a prompt 'Key:', and displays the keys you press thereafter; pressing Ctrl-2 does not give a prompt and does not display the keys you press. They both perform the same function.
2   Type the number of the appropriate character set, followed by a comma, followed by the number of the character.
3   Press Enter.

You will see the character or a box on the normal editing screen. In the Codes screen you will see a code representing that character.

The Help screens on Compose provide information on the WordPerfect and IBM character sets.

## 56   Spell check

If you run WordPerfect from floppy disks, then before using the spell check you should save your document and then insert the speller disk in Drive A.

The spell check procedure is:

1   Position the cursor on the word or page you wish to check. If you are checking the entire document, it doesn't matter where the cursor is.
2   Press Ctrl-F2 (Spell).
3   Select 1 (Word), 2 (Page), or 3 (Document) to check the spelling of the current word, page or document, using the default common English words file.
     Select 4 (New Sup.Dictionary) to prompt WordPerfect to use another file for the spell check.
     Select 5 (Look Up) to check an alternative spelling of a word.

Select 6 (Count) to count the number of words in the document without checking the spelling.

If a word is not found in the spell check file, it is highlighted and a list of similar words may be displayed on the screen. You can select a replacement by pressing the reference letter alongside the word of your choice.

Alternatively, you can select from the menu as follows:

1  *Skip Once* ignores the current word but will highlight it if it occurs again in the document.

2  *Skip* ignores the word throughout the document.

3  *Add* adds the word to a supplementary dictionary which the speller will use as a secondary dictionary. WordPerfect calls this file WP{WP}UK.SUP. It is created automatically the first time you add a word and then added to on future occasions.

4  *Edit* allows you to correct the word yourself.

5  *Look Up* lets you look up a word without first typing it in your document. You can type in a complete word or a word pattern. If you choose pattern, you can type in a rough approximation of how the word should be spelt, using the asterisk to replace an unknown number of letters or the question mark to replace one unknown letter. WordPerfect then displays any words which match your pattern.

6  *Ignore Numbers* ignores numbers which form part of words during the spell check.

If there are double words in the document, i.e. identical consecutive words, the two words are highlighted together with a menu:

Double word: 1 2 Skip; 3 Delete 2nd; 4 Edit; 5 Disable Double Word Checking

Press 1 or 2 to ignore the word for the rest of the check; press 3 to delete the second word; press 4 to alter the text yourself; press 5 to ignore all further double word occurrences.

## 57  Split screen

To allow both Doc 1 and Doc 2 to be displayed simultaneously, you can split the screen (or create a window) as follows:

1   Press Ctrl-F3 (Screen).
2   Select 1 (Window). WordPerfect prompts 'Number of lines in this window: 24'.
3   Type in the number of lines to be displayed in the current window, or press the up arrow key to reduce the current window.
4   Press Enter.

To close a window, restoring the full screen, proceed as follows:

1   Press Ctrl-F3 (Screen).
2   Select 1 (Window). WordPerfect prompts you with the number of lines in the current window.
3   Type '24', or press the up or down arrow key until the prompt displays the number of lines as 24.
4   Press Enter.

## 58   Spreadsheets and WordPerfect

The spreadsheet import and spreadsheet link features allow you to extract information from a spreadsheet file and include it in a WordPerfect file. 'Link' causes updating of the imported information when changes are made to the original file. 'Import', on the other hand, brings in the information but does not provide automatic updating.

### Retrieve the whole spreadsheet as a table
To retrieve an entire spreadsheet in table format, proceed as follows:

1   Press Shift-F10 (Retrieve).
2   Type the filename, using the full pathname if the file is not in the WordPerfect default directory. (You can also use the F5 List key to retrieve from a list of files.)
3   Press Enter.

### Import or link a spreadsheet
This feature allows the following:

- Importing part of a spreadsheet into a WordPerfect document.
- Importing the whole spreadsheet as text in tabular form.
- Importing the whole spreadsheet as a table.
- Creating a link to the original file for future updating.

To use this feature, place the cursor where the spreadsheet file is to be imported and proceed as follows:

1  Press Ctrl-F5 (Text In/Out).
2  Press 5 (Spreadsheet). The Import menu is displayed.
3  Press 1 (Filename).
4  Type the name of the file, using the full pathname if the file is not in the default WordPerfect directory. WordPerfect enters the whole range in the Range option of the menu.
   Alternatively, press F5 (List) and retrieve from a list of files.
5  Press 2 (Range) and type in the range if you want a part of the spreadsheet, using a colon, full stop or two full stops between the start and end cells.
   Alternatively, press F5 (List) to display the range defined in the spreadsheet file. Move the cursor to one of these ranges and press Enter.
6  Press 3 (Type).
7  Choose Table or Text to import as a table or as tabular columns.
8  Press 4 (Perform Import or Link).

Creating a link inserts [Link] codes at the beginning and end of the imported spreadsheet. These display on the text editing screen as comment boxes.

### Link options
To set these options, proceed as follows:

1  Press Ctrl-F5 (Text In/Out).
2  Choose 5 (Spreadsheet).
3  Choose 3 (Link Options). The Link Options menu is displayed, shown in Figure KS.17.

### Delete a link
Delete either of the [Link] or [Link End] codes.

```
Link Options:

    1 - Update on Retrieve        No

    2 - Show Link Codes           Yes

    3 - Update All Links




Selection: 0
```

**Figure KS.17**   Link Options menu

## *Edit a link*
To edit a link, place the cursor after the link you wish to edit,
repeat steps 1 and 2 above, and then proceed as follows:

3  Press 3 (Edit Link). WordPerfect displays the Link Options
   menu.
4  Make any necessary changes.
5  Press 4 (Perform Link).

## 59  Styles

Styles allow you to store collections of formatting, alignment, and
enhancement codes, which can then be applied to text. They can
also contain text. Like many other format codes, they can be
applied to text as you insert it, or to existing text.

There are two kinds of style: open and paired. An open style
contains codes to be applied to the whole document, such as
margins and justification. A paired style contains codes to be
applied to just a block of text, such as emboldening or italics.

## Create an open style
To create an open style, proceed as follows:

1 Press Alt-F8 (Style). This displays the style list.
2 Press 3 (Create). This displays the Styles Editing menu shown in Figure 9.3.
3 Press 1 (Name) to enter a suitable name (up to 11 characters).
4 Press 3 (Description) and enter a description (up to 54 characters).
5 Press 2 (Type) and choose Open.
6 Press 4 (Codes). This displays the Style Reveal Codes screen. Use the normal function keys to enter the required formatting codes. You can also type ordinary text on this screen if you wish.
7 Press Exit twice to return to the style list, which now has the name of your new style added to it.


## Create a paired style
To create a paired style, repeat steps 1—4 for an open style and then proceed as follows:

5 Press 4 (Codes). This displays the Style Reveal Codes screen as shown in Figure 9.7. The comment box represents the text to which you want to apply the style; any Style On codes are inserted before the comment, any Style Off codes are inserted after the comment. Note, however, that if you insert an enhancement or font code, WordPerfect will include automatically the appropriate Off code for you.
6 Repeat step 7 above for an open style.

In creating a paired style, you have the option of changing the function of the Enter key by selecting 5 (Enter) from the Styles Edit menu (see Figure 9.2). The following menu then displays at the bottom of the screen:

Enter: 1 Hrt; 2 Off; 3 Off/On: 0

• Option 1 is the default, leaving the Enter key to do what it normally does — insert a hard return.
• Option 2 makes Enter turn off a paired style. The first time

you use it, the cursor moves past the Style Off code; thereafter it returns to its normal function of inserting hard returns.

• Option 3 makes Enter turn off a paired style, and then turn it on again. It therefore moves the cursor past the Style Off code and then inserts a pair of Style On and Style Off codes. If you move the cursor past a Style Off code with an arrow key, Enter will function as normal.

### Create styles from existing text

You can create a style from existing codes. First use the Block key to select the appropriate codes, then proceed as follows:

1 Press Alt-F8 (Style).
2 Press 3 (Create).
3 Enter a name and description. The blocked codes should display in the Style Codes screen.

If the block included any text, this will be ignored, as will any codes which exist after the text.

### Apply an open style

1 Press Alt-F8 (Style).
2 Move the cursor bar to the appropriate style name in the list.
3 Press (On).

You will be returned to the text editing screen, with an [Open Style] code inserted in the document; this code will contain the style name.

### Apply a paired style

To apply a paired style to text as you type it in, repeat steps 1−3 for applying an open style. However, instead of inserting a single style code, you will insert a pair of style codes (Style On and Style Off), and any text inserted between the two will be styled accordingly.

To apply a paired style to existing text, block the text first with the Block key, and then repeat steps 1−3 for applying an open style.

When the cursor is on any of these style codes, the code will expand to reveal the contents of the style code.

If you exit the style list with F7, no styles will be selected for use.

## Save styles

Any styles created in a document are saved to the document when it is saved. To use a style list in other documents, proceed as follows:

1 Press Alt-F8 (Style).
2 Press 6 (Save). Type a filename for your style list; it is suggested that you give style files a filename with the .STY extension for easy identification. WordPerfect will save the file to the directory selected for style files.

Changes which are subsequently made to a style file in a document must be saved to the style file at the Style menu if you wish to use them in other documents.

## Delete styles

To remove a style from some text, reveal the codes and delete the appropriate style code.

To remove a style from a style list, proceed as follows:

1 Press Alt-F8 (Style).
2 Place the cursor bar on the appropriate style name and press 5 (Del), etc. You are prompted by the following menu:

> Delete Styles: 1 Leaving codes; 2 Including codes; 3 Definition only: 0

- Choosing 1 will remove the style name from the list, and all style codes of that name in the document; however, the codes contained in the style are retained.
- Choosing 2 will delete the style name from the list, the style codes in the document, and the codes within the style.
- Choosing 3 will delete the style name from the list. Any styles of the same name in the document will remain intact. This is useful when you have a long list of style names and wish to find out which ones you are actually using in a document. After deleting the names from the list, return to the document and press Home,Home,↓ . Return to the style list, and

WordPerfect will have reinserted those styles being used in the current document.

### Edit styles
To change the contents of a style, proceed as follows:

1  Press Alt-F8 (Style).
2  Select 4 (Edit). You can then alter the name, description or codes for a style.
3  Press Exit to return to the document.

Note the following:

*  If at step 2 you change the style name, WordPerfect will ask if you wish to rename the styles in the document. If you type 'Y' for Yes, the previous style name is changed to the new style name in the current document. If you type 'N' for No, the style names in the document remain unchanged, and Word-Perfect will recreate the style on the Styles menu with the style's original name. This is a good way of creating a new style based on an old one. The original style is not lost because WordPerfect will recreate it when WordPerfect encounters it in a document.
*  Changing the contents of a style will update automatically the style in the current document when you exit the Styles menu. To save the edited style for use in other documents, use the Save option in the Styles menu.
*  To update an edited style in another document, retrieve the document, and proceed as follows:

   1  Press Alt-F8 (Style).
   2  Press 7 (Retrieve). Enter the style filename, and confirm the replacement of existing styles with the incoming styles.
   3  Press Exit. The styles in the current document will be auto-matically updated throughout.

### Retrieve styles
To retrieve a list of styles saved as a file on disk, proceed as follows:

1  Press Alt-F8 (Style).

2  Press 7 (Retrieve), and enter the style filename. If any style
names match those in the current list, WordPerfect will
prompt 'Style(s) Already Exist, Replace?'. If you type 'N' for
No, WordPerfect will retrieve only those styles whose names
do not match the current style names. If you type 'Y' for Yes,
WordPerfect retrieves all of the styles, replacing current styles
with the incoming ones.

*Set the default style file*
To make a style list the default style file, proceed as for saving a
style above, giving the list a name. Then:

1  Press Shift-F1 (Setup).
2  Press 6 (Location of Files).
3  Press 5 (Style Files).
4  Press Enter and type the style filename, giving the full path.
5  Press Exit.

The next time you use the Style key in a document where no
styles exist, WordPerfect will retrieve the default style list.

*Update*
The Update option in the Styles menu allows you to retrieve the
default style file to the screen, as follows:

1  Press Alt-F8 (Style).
2  Press 8 (Update). If existing styles in the current list have
names which match those in your default style list, WordPerfect
will automatically overwrite them.

*Include graphics in styles*
If you wish to include a graphics image in a style, you must use
the Contents option in the Graphics Box Definition menu and set
the contents to Graphic on Disk (see Section 17).

## 60  Switch documents

WordPerfect allows you to work on two documents at the same
time. It refers to these as Doc 1 and Doc 2, and each can be used

to create a new document or to retrieve an existing document.

You can switch between the two document screens by pressing Shift-F3.

## 61  Tab Align

The Tab Align feature is used with numerical data. It moves the cursor to the next tab setting and aligns the text at a full stop. The characters typed before the full stop (the default alignment character) are pushed to the left, while those after it are inserted normally. To use this feature, press Ctrl-F6 (Tab Align). 'Align char =.' appears in the status line and a [DEC TAB] code is inserted in the document.

Any text that you type then right-aligns at the next tab setting until you type a full stop; it will thereafter left-align.

To change the alignment character to any other keyboard character, proceed as follows:

1  Press Shift-F8 (Format).
2  Press 4 (Other).
3  Press 3 for Decimal/Align Character.
4  Type in the new character.
5  Press Enter twice, and Exit.

A [Decml/Algn Char::,,] code is inserted in the document, where : is the alignment character and the , is the thousands separator.

To change the default alignment character, see Setup (Section 53).

## 62  Tab settings

This feature is used to set positions for typing columns of text or numbers in a table. WordPerfect's default tab positions are set every .5" across the line, and these positions can be seen by pressing Alt-F3 (Reveal Codes) and looking at the triangles in the bar separating the two parts of the screen. Pressing the Tab key moves the cursor to the next tab, and inserts a [Tab] code in the document.

To change the tab positions, proceed as follows:

1   Press Shift-F8 (Format).
2   Choose 1 for Line Format.
3   Choose 8 for Tab Set.
4   Move the cursor along the ruler that appears at the bottom of the screen, deleting existing tabs (by pressing DEL) and entering your own by typing the tab code (L, C, R, D, or .) for the different types of tab. You can move from tab to tab by pressing the up and down arrow keys. You can also move directly to a specific tab position by typing its number, then pressing Enter.
5   Press F7 (Exit) twice to return to the editing screen.

To delete all tabs to the right of the cursor, press Ctrl-End.
   To set evenly spaced left tabs, you:

1   Type the position of the first tab.
2   Type a comma, then the spacing between each tab.
3   Press Enter.

A set of tabs will then be automatically inserted on the ruler at the required positions. For example, typing '1.3,2' and pressing Enter will insert tabs at 1.3, 3.3, 5.3, and so on up to the right margin of the page. These will be in addition to any existing tabs, if these were not deleted first.
   The code that is inserted in your document when you set the above tabs is [Tab Set:1.3″, every 2″].
   To change default tab settings, see Section 53 on Setup.

## 63   Table

This feature allows you to display data in columns and rows without first setting any tab stops.

### *Create a table*

1   Press Alt-F7 (Column/Table).
2   Choose 1 (Create).
3   Enter the number of columns you want in your table (you are allowed a maximum of 32).
4   Enter the number of rows you want (maximum 32,765).

The table is displayed onscreen, with the Table Edit menu below. In the status line is an extra entry displaying the current cell address.

5   Press F7 to exit the Table Edit menu.

In the Codes screen a [Tbl Def:] code and a [Tbl Off] code are inserted at the beginning and end of the table; there are [Row] codes instead of [HRt] codes, and [Cell] codes instead of [Tab] codes.

## Move around a table
Figure KS.18 describes the keystrokes for moving the cursor around a table.

## Edit a table
If you have an enhanced keyboard, you can add or delete a row with Ctrl-Insert or Ctrl-Delete respectively. The added row is inserted at the cursor position; the deleted row is the one in which the cursor is currently located. Otherwise you have to use the Table Edit menu, which is also used for all other editing of the table format.

## Table Edit menu
This is shown in Figure KS.19, and contains the choices shown below.

● *Column widths*. Move the cursor to any location in the column and press Ctrl-← or Ctrl-→ to decrease or increase its size. To set an exact width, select Format, 2, 1, and enter the width.
● *Insert, delete and size*. ('Size' specifies the number of columns and rows in the table.) These three options allow you to add and delete rows and columns, either within a table, or at the right or bottom of a table.

## Within a table

1   If you are adding a row or rows, place the cursor just below

| Location | Regular Keyboard | Enhanced Keyboard |
|---|---|---|
| One cell right | Tab or Goto (Ctrl-Home), → | Alt→ |
| One cell left | Shift-Tab or Goto (Ctrl-Home), ← | Alt← |
| One cell up | ↑ if cursor is at top of cell | Alt↑ |
| One cell down | ↓ if cursor is at bottom of cell | Alt↓ |
| Beginning of text in cell | Goto (Ctrl-Home), ↑ | |
| End of text in cell | Goto (Ctrl-Home), ↓ | |
| Far left of row | Goto (Ctrl-Home), ← | Alt-(Home, ←) |
| Far right of row | Goto (Ctrl-Home) → | Alt-(Home, →) |
| Top of column | Goto (Ctrl-Home), Home, ↑ | Alt-(Home, ↑) |
| Bottom of column | Goto (Ctrl-Home), Home, ↓ | Alt-(Home, ↓) |
| First cell in table | Goto (Ctrl-Home), Home, Home, ↑ | Alt-(Home, Home, ↓) |
| Last cell in table | Goto (Ctrl-Home), Home, Home, ↓ | Alt-(Home, Home, ↓) |

**Figure KS.18**   Moving the cursor around a table

the point where the new row(s) are to be inserted. If you are adding a column or columns, place the cursor just after the point where the new column(s) are to be inserted. If you are deleting rows or columns, move the cursor into the first row or column to be deleted.

2   Press Insert or Delete.

Table Edit:  Press Exit when done         Cell A1 Doc 1 Pg 1 Ln 1.14" Pos 1.12"

Ctrl-Arrows Column Widths; Ins Insert; Del Delete; Move Move/Copy;
1 Size; 2 Format; 3 Lines; 4 Header; 5 Maths; 6 Options; 7 Join; 8 Split: 0

**Figure KS.19**   Table Edit menu

3 Type 1 for rows or 2 for columns.
4 Enter the number of rows or columns to be added or deleted.

## At the right or bottom of a table

1 From the Table Edit menu, choose 1 (Size).
2 Type 1 (Rows) or 2 (Columns). The current number of rows or columns is displayed.
3 Type in the new total and press Enter.

   If you delete rows or columns, they can be undeleted later from the Table Edit menu. Move the cursor to the original location of the rows or columns and press Cancel (F1). You will be prompted 'Undelete column (or row)? No (Yes)'. Type 'Y' for Yes.

## *Move/Copy*

You can use the Ctrl-F4 Move key to move or copy a block, row or column in a table. To use the Move key, display the Table Edit menu and proceed as follows:

1 Place the cursor in the row or column to be moved or copied. If you are moving or copying a block of cells, rows or columns, use the Alt-F4 Block key to highlight them. You need block only one cell in each row or column.
2 Press the Move key. The following menu appears:

   Move: 1 Block; 2 Row; 3 Column; 4 Retrieve: 0

3 Choose from options 1, 2, or 3 as appropriate. Option 4 (Retrieve) allows you to retrieve again a section which you have previously moved or copied. If you choose option 1 and no block is defined, the current cell only is affected. The following menu then appears:

   1 Move; 2 Copy; 3 Delete: 0

4 Choose Move or Copy. It is quicker to use the Delete key (Del) when in table edit mode for deleting rows or columns.
5 Move the cursor to the position where the rows or columns are to be retrieved.
6 Press Enter to retrieve the block.

*Format*

Choose this option to change the format of cells or columns and also change row height. The menu in Figure KS.20 is displayed.

The current cell's format is displayed at the left – vertical alignment, justification, and attributes; the current column's format is displayed on the right – width, justification, and attributes. The format options displayed on this menu are as follows:

1  *Cell*. When you choose this, the Cell menu appears:

> Cell: 1 Type; 2 Attributes; 3 Justify; 4 Vertical Alignment; 5 Lock: 0

The options in this menu are:

1  *Type*. WordPerfect assumes that all table entries are numbers so that they can be included in calculations. However, if a cell entry is to be excluded from a calculation (for example a telephone number), choose 2 (Text) from the Type menu.

2  *Attributes*. When you choose this, the Attributes menu appears:

> 1 Size; 2 Appearance; 3 Normal; 4 Reset: 0

The Size and Appearance options are those found on the Font key (Ctrl-F8). 'Normal' changes all attributes in the cell back to the normal base font. 'Reset' changes cells to the attributes of the current column.

3  *Justify*. When you choose this, the Justify menu appears:

> 1 Left; 2 Centre; 3 Right; 4 Full; 5 Decimal Align; 6 Reset: 0

This allows you to choose between left, centre, right, full and decimal alignment. The Reset option will change the justification of the current cell(s) back to the column's justification.

4  *Vertical Alignment*. When you choose this, the Vertical Alignment menu appears:

> 1 Top; 2 Bottom; 3 Centre: 0

```
Cell:  Top; Left; Normal              Col: 1.71"; Left; Normal
Format: 1 Cell; 2 Column; 3 Row Height: 0
```

**Figure KS.20**   Table Format menu

WordPerfect defaults to aligning text with the top of the cell, leaving .1″ between the top of the text and the top line. Here, you can choose to have the text aligned in the centre or at the bottom of the cell.

5   *Lock*. When you choose this, the Lock menu appears:

   1 On; 2 Off: 0

You can use this option to lock a cell or block of cells to prevent text being entered into them or to prevent text being changed after it has been entered.

2   *Column*. When you choose this, the Column menu appears:

   Column: 1 Width; 2 Attributes; 3 Justify; 4 Number Digits: 0

This is similar to the menu for a cell, apart from 'width' and 'number of digits'.

- Choosing Width allows you to change the width of the current column by entering a value.
- Choosing Number Digits allows you to change the number of decimal places used in a calculation. WordPerfect defaults to 2.

3   *Row Height*. When you choose this, the Row Height menu appears:

   Row Height--Single line: 1 Fixed; 2 Auto; Multi-line: 3 Fixed; 4 Auto: 3

These options determine whether the line height should be adjusted to fit a single line or multiple lines. 'Single line: Fixed' and 'Auto' allow only one line of text for each cell in the row; the 'Auto' sets the row height according to the largest font used in the row. 'Multi-line: Fixed' and 'Auto' allow multiple lines to wrap within the fixed height for the row; 'Auto' again sets the height according to the largest font used in the row.

## Lines

Back at the Table Edit menu, this option allows you to change the style of border lines and also to add shading to cells. Choose this, and the Lines menu appears:

>Lines: 1 Left; 2 Right; 3 Top; 4 Bottom; 5 Inside; 6 Outside; 7 All; 8 Shade: 0

The default line style for a table is a double line around the outside, and single lines between columns and rows.

To change the line style or to add shading, place the cursor in the appropriate cell. If you wish to change a number of cells, use the Alt-F4 Block key first to highlight these cells. If you then choose 8 (Shade) from the Lines menu, the choices in the Shade menu are 1 (On) or 2 (Off). If you choose options 1 to 7 from the Lines menu, the following menu will appear:

>1 None; 2 Single; 3 Double; 4 Dashed; 5 Dotted; 6 Thick; 7 Extra Thick: 0

Choose the style you want from this menu.

## Header

When a table is longer than one page, this Table Edit menu option allows you to specify which row/s can be used as a header. To specify a header row, choose 4 (Header). You are then prompted to enter the number of rows. If you type '2', Word-Perfect will use the first two rows of your table.

## Maths

This is similar to the regular Maths feature, with the following menu:

>Maths: 1 Calculate; 2 Formula; 3 Copy Formula; 4 + 5 = 6 *: 0

Option 1 is used when you have edited some numbers and want to recalculate. Options 4, 5 and 6 are the operators described in the section on Maths: use '+' for a sub total, '=' for a total, and '*' for a grand total. Option 2 allows you to enter a formula into the current cell, and option 3 allows you to copy that formula to other cells. When the cursor is located in a cell containing a formula or a maths operator, this information will display in the status line.

## Options

These options are shown in Figure KS.21, and they affect the whole table.

*Option 1* allows you to change the amount of space within cells between the text and the lines.
*Option 2* allows you to change the display of negative results from a minus sign to parentheses.
*Option 3* allows you the following choices:

> Table Position: 1 Left; 2 Right; 3 Centre; 4 Full; 5 Set Position: 0

Choosing Full will expand the table so that if fills the space between the left and right margins. Choosing Set Position allows

```
Table Options

    1 - Spacing Between Text and Lines
            Left                    0.083"
            Right                   0.083"
            Top                     0.1"
            Bottom                  0"

    2 - Display Negative Results    1
            1 = with minus signs
            2 = with parentheses

    3 - Position of Table           Left

    4 - Grey Shading (% of black)   10%




Selection: 0
```

**Figure KS.21**  Table Options menu

you to specify a position measured from the left edge of the page.

*Option 4* allows you to set the degree of shading for shaded cells.

## Join/split cells

These Table Edit menu options allow you to join or split the current cell(s). To join a number of cells, proceed as follows:

1   Use the Alt-F4 Block key to select the cells.
2   Choose Join.
3   Type 'Y' to confirm.

To split a cell, place the cursor in it and proceed as follows:

1   Choose Split.
2   Type '1' to split it into rows or '2' to split it into columns.
3   Enter the number of rows or columns.

## Remove a table

To remove a table but not the text contained in it, remove the [Tbl Def] code at the start of the table; WordPerfect then converts the [Cell] codes to [Tab] codes and the [Row] codes to [HRt] codes. To remove the text but keep the table, use Alt-F4 to mark the text as a block and then delete it.

## Convert existing text to a table

To convert existing tabulated or parallel columns to table format, proceed as follows:

1   Use the Block key to highlight the columns.
2   Press the Column/Table key, Alt-F7.
3   Press 1 (Create).
4   Press 1 (Tabular Column) or 2 (Parallel Column).

## 64   Table of contents

WordPerfect can generate a table of contents for a document. Up to five levels of numbering can be used, with various styles of numbering. The table of contents entries appear in the order in which they occur in the document.

There are three stages to creating a table of contents:

1   Mark text.
2   Define the location of the table and the numbering style.
3   Generate the table.

These are explained below.

1   *Mark the text.* To include text in a table of contents, proceed as follows:

a   Use Alt-F4 (Block) to select the word or phrase.
b   Press Alt-F5 (Mark Text). The following menu displays:

        1 ToC; 2 List; 3 Index; 4 ToA:

c   Choose 1 − ToC.
d   Enter the table level number at which the text should be shown (1 to 5).

A pair of codes is inserted at the beginning and end of the marked text − [Mark;ToC,] [End Mark:ToC,], each one showing the level number. Repeat these steps for the whole document.

2   *Define the table of contents.* This means defining the location of the table of contents and the numbering style for each level of heading. First, move the cursor to the place where you want the table of contents to appear, and type your heading text followed by some hard returns. Then proceed as follows:

a   Press Alt-F5 (Mark Text). The following menu appears:

        1 Cross Ref; 2 Subdoc; 3 Index; 4 ToA; 5 Define; 6 Generate:

b   Choose 5 (Define). The Mark Text Define menu appears (see Figure 10.17).
c   Choose 1 (Define Table of Contents). The Table of Contents Definition menu appears (Figure 10.18 and explained below).
d   Make any necessary changes to the menu here, and press F7 (Exit).

A [Def Mark: ToC] code is inserted in the document.

The choices in the Table of Contents Definition menu are as follows:

- *Number of Levels.* Enter the number of levels to be included in the table.
- *Display Last Level in Wrapped Format.* Choose 'Yes' if you want the headings following one another a single paragraph of information. The page numbers are included in parentheses after each heading.
- *Page Numbering.* The default style is flush right with leader dots. To change this style, choose this and you can change to one of the following:
  - No page numbering.
  - Page numbers following the entries and separated by a space.
  - Page numbers in parentheses following the entries and separated by a space.
  - Flush right page numbers.

3   *Generate the table of contents.* The cursor position is unimportant when you perform this operation. To create the table of contents, proceed as follows:

a   Press Alt-F5 (Mark Text).
b   Choose 6 (Generate). The Mark Text Generate menu displays (Figure 10.19).
c   Choose 5 (Generate Tables, Indexes, Cross-References, etc.). A prompt appears asking if you wish to replace any existing tables, lists and indexes.
d   Type 'Y' for Yes to proceed, or 'N' for No to return to your document without generating.

Generation begins and a counter at the bottom of the screen shows the progress of the generation. Eventually the list will appear on the screen, and an [End Def] code will be inserted at the end of the list.

## Edit a table of contents

After generating a table of contents, you may need to repeat the process. For example, if page numbering changes; or if extra entries have been added; or if entries have been removed; or if you wish to change the style of numbering. To do so, repeat the steps above for generating a table of contents.

To remove an entry, delete its [Mark:ToC] code before regenerating.

## 65  Thesaurus

To use the thesaurus for looking up synonyms, proceed as follows:

1  Move the cursor to the word.
2  Press Alt-F1 (Thesaurus). A list of words appears, each word preceded by a letter.
3  Press 1 (Replace Word). The prompt 'Press letter for word' will appear.
4  Press the letter that corresponds to the word you require.

If the word is not in the thesaurus, 'Word not found' will appear, followed by the prompt 'Word:', inviting you to type in an alternative.

The other options in the thesaurus menu are as follows:

● 2 *View Doc*. Press this to scroll through your document.
● 3 *Look Up Word*. Press this to enter another word to look up.
● 4 *Clear Column*. Press this to remove the currently marked column from the thesaurus display.

Use the arrow keys to move the reference menu of letters from one word list to another.

## 66  Underline

To underline text as it is entered, press F8 (Underline), type the text, and then press F8 or the right arrow key. The paired codes inserted in your document are [UND][und].

To underline existing text, block the text first with the Alt-F4 Block key and then press F8.

## 67 Widow/orphan protection

Place the cursor at the beginning of the document, then proceed as follows:

1 Press Shift-F8 (Format).
2 Press 1 (Line).
3 Press 9, and then type 'Y'.

The code [W/O On] is inserted in your document.

# Index